HEGEL'S DIALECTIC

SOVIETICA

PUBLICATIONS AND MONOGRAPHS

OF THE INSTITUTE OF EAST-EUROPEAN STUDIES AT THE

UNIVERSITY OF FRIBOURG/SWITZERLAND

Edited by

PROF. DR J. M. BOCHEŃSKI

VOLUME 33

ANDRIES SARLEMIJN

HEGEL'S DIALECTIC

D. REIDEL PUBLISHING COMPANY

DORDRECHT-HOLLAND / BOSTON-U.S.A.

HEGELSCHE DIALEKTIK

First published in 1971 by Walter de Gruyter, Berlin/New York

Translated from the German by Peter Kirschenmann

Library of Congress Catalog Card Number 74-80522

ISBN 90 277 0481 3

Published by D. Reidel Publishing Company
P.O. Box 17, Dordrecht, Holland

Sold and distributed in the U.S.A., Canada, and Mexico
by D. Reidel Publishing Company, Inc.
306 Dartmouth Street, Boston,
Mass. 02116, U.S.A.

TABLE OF CONTENTS

PART II / DIALECTIC AND METAPHYSICS

CHAPTER 1 / 'METAPHYSICS' – A PHILOSOPHICAL DISCIPLINE   103

CHAPTER 2 / METAPHYSICAL METHOD IN GENERAL   112

PREFACE TO THE ENGLISH EDITION

This book was written in 1968, and defended as a doctoral dissertation before the Philosophical Faculty at the University of Fribourg (Switzerland) in 1969. It treats of the systematic views of Hegel which led him to give to the principle of non-contradiction, the principle of double negation, and the principle of excluded middle, meanings which are difficult to understand. The reader will look in vain for the philosophical position of the author. A few words about the intentions which motivated the author to study and clarify Hegel's thought are therefore not out of place.

In the early sixties, when occupying myself with the history of Marxist philosophy, I discovered that the representatives of the logical-positivist tradition were not alone in employing a principle of demarcation; that those of the dialectical Marxist tradition were also using such a principle ('self-movement') as a foundation of a scientific philosophy and as a means to delimit unscientific ideas. I aimed at a clear conception of this principle in order to be able to judge whether, and to what extent, it accords with the foundations of the analytical method. In this endeavor I encountered two problems: (1) What is to be understood by 'analytical method' cannot be ascertained unequivocally. (2) The representatives of the dialectical or Marxist tradition, on the one hand, do not sufficiently clarify what is meant by 'principle of self-movement' and by 'dialectical contradiction' in a Hegelian context and, on the other hand, presuppose the results of Hegel's *Logic* in the elucidation and logical justification of their position.

I decided not to solve all of the problems pertinent to these issues, but to write instead an 'analytical' treatise on Hegel's *Logic* with the purpose of clarifying the issues. 'Analytical' is here taken to mean three things: (1) a discussion based on a precise interpretation of texts; (2) a particular consideration of theses which deviate from the analytical position (an analysis of what is given that is based on the principles of formal logic); (3) a renunciation of 'modernizing' Hegel's dialectic (so as not to confront the reader with two philosophical systems — that of Hegel and that of the interpreter). Since contemporary discussions show how little is clarified when the Hegelian terms 'God' and 'the absolute' are replaced with 'matter' in Marxism-Leninism, or with 'the whole' in Neo-Marxism, I have not attempted to abstract from the 'metaphysical' aspects of Hegel's dialectic and *Logic*. On the other hand, I had to forgo any detailed treatment of the best-known critics of Hegelianism (Moore, Russell, Carnap, Popper, Topitsch), as their criticisms rest on philosophical positions or on misunderstandings which can only be evaluated or corrected in a very extended discussion.

My sincere thanks go to Prof. Dr J. Bocheński whose method for historical research I followed, Prof. Dr T. Blakeley who promoted the English edition, and Prof. Dr P. Kirschenmann who solved the difficult task of translating in an excellent manner.

May the historical insights here communicated be useful to the reader for an objective and critical assessment of contemporary dialectic.

January 1974

TRANSLATOR'S NOTE

I have decided *not* to adopt the practice common in Hegel literature of using capitals for at least some of Hegel's categories and terms (Existence, Concept, Idea, the Ideal, the True and the Good, the Absolute, the Understanding, Reason, and the like). I have for the most part followed the author, who systematically employs his own means of emphasis. He uses quotation marks to indicate Hegel's terms and lengthier expressions (although not exclusively for that purpose). In text analyses that immediately follow quoted texts, terms and phrases taken from the text are in italics. (For further clarification of the author's means of emphasis, see his remarks Concerning Notes and Abbreviations). Moreover, since Hegel's categories and the terms employed by him in an unusual sense are discussed in detail in the book, their technical meaning is hardly in danger of going unnoticed. I have deemed it helpful, however, to append the German original in parentheses to certain terms in a few places.

In translating quoted texts, I have consulted and made use of the following translations:

G. W. F. Hegel, *The Phenomenology of Mind,* transl. by J. B. Baillie, Harper & Row, New York, 1967; *Hegel: Texts and Commentary*, transl. and ed. by W. Kaufmann, Doubleday, Garden City, 1966; *Hegel's Science of Logic,* transl. by A. V. Miller, Allen & Unwin, London, 1969; *The Logic of Hegel*, transl. from *The Encyclopaedia of the Philosophical Sciences* by W. Wallace, 2nd ed., Oxford, Clarendon, 1892; G. W. F. Hegel, *Lectures on the Philosophy of Religion, Together with a Work on the Proofs of the Existence of God,* transl. by E. B. Speirs and J. Burdon Sanderson, 3 vols. Humanities Press, New York, 1962; *Hegel's Lectures on the History of Philosophy*, transl. by E. S. Haldane and F. H. Simson, 3 vols., Routledge & Kegan Paul, London, 1955; *The Dialogues of Plato,* transl. by B. Jowett, Encyclopaedia Britannica, Chicago, 1952; I. Kant, *The Critique of Pure Reason*, transl. by J. M. D. Meiklejohn, J. M. Dent & Sons Ltd, London, 1934; I. Kant, *Metaphysical Foundations of Natural Science,* transl. by J. Ellington, Bobbs-Merrill, Indianapolis, 1970.

I wish to thank my wife, Ann Kirschenmann, for valuable corrections, stylistic help, and for doing her share of the typing.

PETER KIRSCHENMANN

INTRODUCTION

In introductions, "that which in former ages
occupied the mature minds of men [is supposed to have] sunk to the level of information, exercises, and even games, of boyhood".

Hegel, *Phenomenology of Spirit*

1. SUBJECT MATTER

This book is concerned with the essential features of Hegel's dialectical
method. It may be considered an introduction to the system of thought
developed by the older Hegel, for this method pervades his entire system and
coincides with *the* form which is attributed to absolute spirit: For Hegel,
everything which is *(alles Seiende)* exists as a moment in a cycle pulsating
with the force of contradiction.

Each of the parts of philosophy is a philosophical whole, a circle closed in itself. In each
one, however, the philosophical idea is found in a particular determinateness or medium.
The single circle, because it is in itself a totality, bursts through the limits of its medium
and establishes another sphere. Thus, the whole will form a circle of circles, each being
a necessary moment.[1]

The interwoven ('sublated') circular figures form the absolute idea, the representation of the absolute spirit.

The cycle theory is an invention of the young Hegel. Already in his
Jenenser Logik und Realphilosophie (1805/6) he repeatedly speaks of the
circle and explains in detail how the present, past and future unite in the
cycle of time.[2] Later, he attributes even greater importance to the theory of
universal rotation; in his main works it is elevated to become the only method
and the central theme of his system. It is exhibited in each single consideration, which is thus tied to the preceding and subsequent ones so that each
argumentation becomes an inseparable part of a minutely elaborated system
of thought. The dialectical form, while governing the entire system, does not
find explicit expression on every page of his works, however much this would
have helped in reading his writings. Yet Hegel conforms to the fashion of

his day which judged the profoundness of a thinker by his complicated way of expression.[3] A good example in point is the preface to the *Phenomenology*, which becomes understandable only after much training in dialectical thinking. Aside from these stylistic considerations, the widely ramified problems to be solved by the cyclical method also forced Hegel to use uncommon expressions like 'return-into-itself', 'intro-reflection' *(Reflexion-in-sich)*, 'self-determination', 'self-movement', 'retrograding justification' *(rückwärtsgehende Begründung)*, 'absolute counter-thrust' *(Gegenstoss)*, 'absolute negation', 'negation of negation', bending-into *(Umbeugung)*, 'self-preservation', 'being-related-to-itself', 'the self-contradictory that resolves itself', etc. These diverse expressions highlight specific aspects of the same basic idea. Each says in its own way that, in virtue of the contradiction, all elements of total actuality are mere moments of an all-encompassing cycle and, accordingly, that dialectical inquiry will always return to the same point. This basic idea is the object of our analysis.

2. RELEVANCE

The importance of this investigation does not stand in need of detailed explanation. Have not Hegel's doctrine of contradiction and his idealism evoked passionate enthusiasm and rejection alike among the greatest minds? Hegel's decisive influence on the subsequent course of Western thought has been generally recognized. Even with little philosophical training one knows that Hegel is considered the predecessor of Soviet philosophy and of Marxist philosophy in general. As Karl Marx stated, every German thinker since Hegel borrowed one element from his gigantic system and then opposed it to the original and to elements emphasized by other Post-Hegelians.[4] This situation has changed little since then. Soviet philosophy, Marxist and non-Marxist existentialism, Nikolas Lossky's intuitionism, Nicolai Hartmann's philosophy of problem stocks, so-called 'God is dead' theories, Socio-Critical Theory, etc., are but forms of the same tendency to admire Hegel and, at the same time, feel utterly superior to him. A. Kojève goes as far as labelling all philosophers of the last century as either Left-Wing or Right-Wing Hegelians. In order to pass an adequate judgment on these 'isms' the historian cannot dispense with studying Hegel's system, since it has anticipated in synthetic unity the contents of all subsequent philosophical speculations.

By means of the cycle theory Hegel establishes the inseparable unity of the absolute subject and its object. In Jean-Paul Sartre's Marxist existentialism, this unity is transferred to an anthropocentric level.[5] In the cosmocentric

Hegelianism of Soviet philosophy, on the other hand, the dialectical contradiction explains the universal connectedness of all phenomena and processes. This thesis, too, has been integrated into the cycle theory by Hegel. Even T. W. Adorno's socio-critical 'negative dialectic' cannot be explicated but in terms of Hegel's figures of thought. The 'unrolling of problems', Nicolai Hartmann's central notion, remains obscure without insight into Hegel's method and, without it, may never even have been thought of. The difference in intuitionism between knowing (*Kennen*) and cognizing (*Erkennen*) also derives from Hegel's speculation on immediacy and mediation—both being categories of the cyclical movement.[6]

3. THE FATE OF HEGEL INTERPRETATIONS

In view of the importance of the doctrine of cyclical movement it may come as a surprise that, two hundred years after the birth of its originator, it must still be chosen as the topic of a treatise. Should it not have received exhaustive treatment long ago? The failure to synthesize the essential constituents of the dialectic has had a disastrous effect on the *interpretation* of Hegel's thought. Invariably, one would discredit one of the elements of the dialectic so that his method *as such* became more questionable than intelligible. Every 'dialectical process' implies a complexity; for Hegel, such a process means a circular movement based on contradiction. Ontologically, this movement is attributed to the all-embracing subject; methodologically, it is taken as the way of thinking which conveys insight into the nature of the absolute. The prerequisites of the dialectical method, then, are threefold: (a) the circular movement, (b) the contradiction and its resolution, and (c) Hegel's idealism. Lacking their unity, these elements will lose their meaning and are defenselessly delivered to criticism. Separated from the theory of contradiction, circular movement and idealism remain unintelligible for dialectical materialists; formal logicians can see but absurdities in the theory of contradiction taken in isolation.

3.1 *Dialectical Materialists*

Ludwig Feuerbach who is known as a precursor of dialectical materialism was enthused by the immanentist tendencies in Hegel's ontology. However, his evaluation of the dialectic was negative because of its idealist implications.[7] Karl Marx blamed him for this position; Marx insisted on retaining the revolutionary aspect of the method, dialectical contradiction, bringing only Hegel's ontological idealism into disrepute. Friedrich Engels, Franz

Mehring, Josef Dietzgen, Georgij Plekhanov and Vladimir Il'ič Lenin were convinced that they could give a new foundation to materialism in terms of the theory of contradiction, but they paid little attention to the unity between Hegel's idealism and theory of contradiction. It is true that, in his *Philosophical Notebooks,* Lenin attempted to demarcate materialist from idealist dialectic and to rid the doctrine of circular movement of its subjective idealistic presuppositions;[8] yet this opposition turned out to be problematic for him as well, and the boundary between materialism and idealism became blurred.[9] At times, he even writes that Hegel's method and thought appeared to him to be materialistic.[10]

Hegel himself endeavored to show by means of his method that everything is sublated into an absolute subject, the absolute spirit. For this reason, Gustav Wetter thinks it impossible to justify a materialism by the same method.[11] Nonetheless, the Soviets stick to their 'materialist transformation'[12] of Hegel's dialectic, without recognizing that this transformation implies a qualitative change and that the transformed method requires a new explication and justification. Taken as dogma, the judgment of the 'classics' concerning the 'materialism' of Hegel's method renders an objective study of the relationship between Hegel's method and idealism unthinkable in the Soviet Union. It is only R. O. Gropp who implicitly concedes the idealism of Hegel's method. In a paper published in the journal *Problems of Philosophy* he indicates that one may easily fall into idealism when following Hegel's method too slavishly.[13] Characteristic of the Soviet interpretation of Hegel is S. A. Éfirov's book *From Hegel ... to Gennaro.* According to him, Hegel's method allows only two consistent interpretations: it can be interpreted either dialectical-materialistically, as do the Soviets, or in an idealist-solipsistic way, as done by Gennaro.[14] As is known, Hegel believes another position to be consistent.

The Soviets will provide the climate for a more adequate interpretation of Hegel only when they acknowledge that they have taken over *only one* element of Hegel's entire method, namely, the dialectical contradiction.

3.2. *Dialectical Idealism*

Immanuel Fichte and Christian Weisse share with the dialectical materialists their admiration for Hegel's method; but they choose the opposite direction and attempt to surpass Hegel's idealism. Weisse discovers a contradiction between the genius of the method and the bleak 'barrenness' of its results.[15] It bothers him that in Hegel individuality is sublated into universality and that any transcendence is denied. He rejects the hypostatization of concepts in principle and calls for the free creative act of a transcendent being.[16] Fichte finds Hegel's basic error in the assumption of a *determinately existing (daseienden)* contradiction. Contradictions can solely exist in the sphere of subjective-dialectical thought; in the actual world, however, love which overcomes all oppositions is to be exclusively accepted as the source of all development.[17]

Trendelenburg and Haring have already criticized such attempts to sever Hegel's method from its idealism.[18] It is indeed a curious fact that one should want to follow Hegel's way of investigation ('method') and reject his results. Since Hegel identifies his method with the form of his system — he expressly rejects a separate methodology — his dialectic and his idealism are inseparably tied to each other. If one follows the way *(methodos)* taken by him one cannot reject his idealism without departing from this way, i.e. without renouncing at least one element or one aspect of Hegel's method.

3.3. *Criticism by Formal Logicians*

In his *Logical Investigations* (1840) and in a series of papers, *The Logical Question in Hegel's System* (1842/43), Adolf Trendelenburg attempts to show that the dialectical method is untenable. In this attempt he relies on psychology and formal logic. Hegel's dialectic presupposes pure thought. Trendelenburg denies the possibility of such a mode of thought because all thoughts rely in some way on imagination.[19] In Friedrich Überweg's work *The System of Logic and History of Logical Doctrines* (1857), Trendelenburg's criticism has received enthusiastic acclaim.[20]

In his treatise *On the Dialectical Method: Historical-Critical Investigations* (1868), Eduard von Hartmann wishes to substantiate that Hegel's methodology precludes not only intelligible thinking, but any thinking — thus, also dialectical thinking.[21] The conclusion of the work *On the Principle of Contradiction and the Meaning of Negation* (1881) by the Danish author J. J. Borelius coincides with Eduard von Hartmann's position. According to this author, Hegel has misunderstood the principle of contradiction.[22] In the essay *Hegel as Logician* (1968), Magdalena Aebi follows in the steps of the authors mentioned.

Although these authors neglect a positive explication of Hegel's dialectic — E. von Hartmann devotes only three pages to it — they occupy an important place in the history of Hegel interpretations, for they show by their criticism that several points of the system call for more detailed discussion.

3.4. *Old-Hegelians and Later Interpreters*

When Hegel died in Berlin on November 14, 1831, his system had reached the climax of its glory. With the support of the minister of education, von Altenstein, it had been elevated to the Prussian state philosophy.[23] Since 1827 the *Yearbooks for Scientific Criticism (Jahrbücher für wissenschaftliche Kritik)* had promulgated Hegel's thought. Immediately after his death several of his friends – including Ph. Marheineke, J. P. Schulze, E. Gans, L. v. Henning, H. Hotho, C. L. Michelet, and F. Forster – collaborated to edit a complete edition of his works. Furthermore, Georg Gabler – Hegel's successor at the university in Berlin – the theologian Karl Daub in Heidelberg as well as Johann Erdmann and Johann Karl Rosenkranz, both professors of philosophy in Halle, defended and promulgated Hegelianism in their works.

However, the situation changed quickly. The system was discredited from a scientific point of view by formal logicians, from a political viewpoint by the July revolution, and from a religious viewpoint by the advent of the Left Hegelians – Bauer, Ruge, Strauss, and Feuerbach. Eichhorn, successor to von Altenstein, called the aging Schelling to Berlin. The influence of the latter and Otto Liebmann's motto "There must be a return to Kant!" undermined for quite some time Hegel's impact on German philosophy.[24]

In order to protect Hegelianism from these dangers, Count Cieszkowski and Michelet founded the Philosophical Society on January 4, 1843, in Berlin. As a substitute for the *Yearbooks* which no longer appeared after 1847, Michelet started the journal *Thought (Der Gedanke)* in 1861. The Society celebrated Hegel's 100th anniversary – with a delay of one year because of the Franco-Prussian War – with the unveiling of a Hegel memorial. Of the money collected for this purpose a certain amount was left over which enabled the Society to offer a prize for the best exposition of Hegel's dialectic. Eighteen months later, no essay had yet been submitted; the prize was augmented and the deadline postponed by two years. By 1885 three contributions had been received, two of which were refutations of Hegel's system. However, the Philosophical Society deemed none of these treatises worthy of the offered prize. These facts evidence the waning interest in Hegel's philosophy in Germany at the time.

Michelet, who with Lasson and Friedrich had formed the prize committee, did not want his judgment to be identified with that of the Society. He renounced his membership and published on his own the treatise by Haring (1888). It is still regarded today as an important contribution of the Old-Hegelian School. One third of this publication of about 60 pages is devoted to an exposition of Hegel's method, and more than half of this deals with

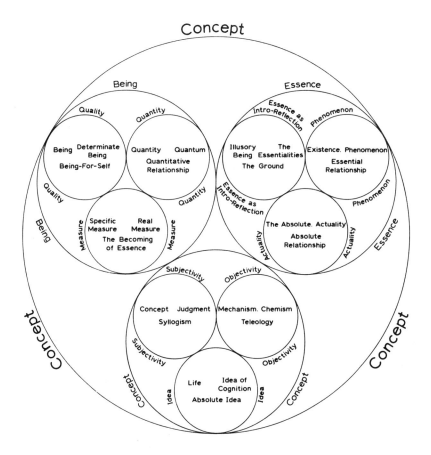

the absolute concept. Otherwise, the author discusses the relationship of thesis, antithesis, and synthesis. His rendition of Hegel's cycle theory amounts to no more than a description of half a page of the following schema.[25]

Unlike Michelet, who considers a clearer exposition of Hegel's method as impossible, we believe that Haring's treatise leaves several questions unanswered; these have remained unsolved even in contemporary interpretations of Hegel.

(a) The first inadequacy no doubt consists in the incomplete explanation of Hegel's idealism. While he begins with an explication of the concept,

Haring does not clarify how, by means of Hegel's method, one can discover the absolute concept in the given reality. In E. Coreth (1952) and W. Albrecht (1958) this problem does not find an unambiguous solution either. They do not sufficiently take into account the criticism expressed by Trendelenburg (1840-43) and Nicolai Hartmann (1935) who said that Hegel's method presupposes the idealism it is meant to establish. Albrecht's objection that Hartmann made use of a distinction between real and conceptual dialectic that is foreign to Hegel's system is not very convincing, since Albrecht in turn does not distinguish between the starting-point of the method and its goal, and leaves thus undiscussed the justification of conceptual dialectic and Hegel's idealism.[26]

(b) Haring claims that dialectical contradiction is due to the unity of thesis and antithesis.[27] In this way he by-passes the question of the relationship between dialectical and formal contradiction. In contemporary expositions by H. A. Ogiermann (1948), J. Hyppolite (1953) and R. Garaudy (1962), this question is not answered either. E. Coreth and Fr. Grégoire (1946) defend two opposing views with respect to this question. A solution to this problem would no doubt advance Hegel scholarship considerably.

(c) Haring's schema is an inadequate rendering of Hegel's cycle theory. For Hegel the subdivisions of logical moments are not merely a program for the development of dialectical thought, or a table of contents; they also refer, more importantly, to a movement which takes place in objective being. How is it possible that – as Haring's schema shows – the movement of the absolute idea takes place outside being? It indeed is unlikely that Hegel conceived of the circle of true infinity (an element in the circle of being) as being outside the circle of absolute life (a moment in the circle of the idea). Haring fails to look for a connection between the doctrine of circular movement and the problem of dialectical contradiction. Coreth, too, speaks of both problems without connecting them and providing a synthesis.

It is generally known that for Hegel the movement is due to the contradiction. Should not, therefore, the circular *movement* be seen in connection with the contradiction? And could not these elements explain each other? It was probably because of these inadequacies that Haring's paper was rejected by the Hegel committee.

While the Philosophical Society fought over the awarding of the prize, Anton Bullinger published on his own his paper *Hegel's Doctrine of Contradiction, Defended Against Misunderstandings* (1884); it was, however, ineffective in diminishing these 'misunderstandings' – i.e. the attacks by Trendelenburg and Überweg. Hegelianism was displaced by Neo-Kantianism, and interest in Hegel seemed to have vanished for good. The fight for or against the 'German Aristotle' moved abroad.

Eugen Schmitt (1888) from Hungary accused Michelet of having falsified Hegel's doctrine of contradiction under the pressure of the formal-logical critique. Adolf Phalèn (1912) charged the other Old-Hegelians with the same adulteration. He himself attempted to connect the theory of contradiction and the cycle method.[28] However, the correctness of his interpretation was put into doubt by R. Kroner (1924) and J. Kruithof (1959) because he reduced Hegel's ontology to the epistemological problem.[29] In Russia, Ivan Il'in's book appeared in 1916; in its German translation of 1946, it is still of great influence today. By means of his cycle schema Il'in attempts to establish the identity of being and thought; but again, the cycle theory remains separated from the problems of dialectical contradiction.

The Dutch writer and philosopher G. J. P. J. Bolland first followed Eduard von Hartmann's critique, but broke with it in 1902, and even became the father of Dutch Hegelianism. Subsequently, H. J. Betz (1905) and J. Clay (1919) tried to refute Bolland — together with Hegel. Since then, interest in Hegel's philosophy has all but vanished in Holland.[30]

The prelude to English interpretations of Hegel was provided by J. Hutchison Stirling with his book *The Secret of Hegel* (1865); it has been said of him that he may well have discovered the secret, but did not tell it.[31] Hegel scholarship flourished in England for a short time, namely from 1880 to 1910. Among its representatives E. Caird, E. McGilvary, J. B. Baillie, W. T. Harris and J. McTaggart, the last-mentioned with his book about the *Logic* is doubtless the most important. His interpretation, however, was soon criticized by McGilvary (1898), and more recently by Kruithof.[32] Among contemporary authors, W. T. Stace (1923) and G. R. G. Mure (1950) are of some influence.

In Italy, A. Vera (1859), A. Rosmini (1883), G. Maggiore (1924), E. de Negri (1934), L. Pelloux (1938), A. Devizzi (1939) and F. Chiereghin (1966) have been engaged in explicating Hegel's dialectic. They all have in common a predilection for the speculative aspect of Hegel's system. As to the contradiction problem, they generally represent diverging and at times confused positions. B. Croce (1901) and G. Gentile (1913) failed to consider this problem; they were concerned with elaborating a personal and new form of dialectic rather than explicating Hegel's.

Interest in Hegel flourished a second time in Germany when G. Lasson, J. Hoffmeister and H. Glockner edited the complete works, and H. Nohl the *Early Writings*. The Publications of R. Kroner (1924), B. Heimann (1927),

H. Marcuse (1933), G. Günther (1933), N. Hartmann (1929), W. Sesemann (1935), A. Dürr (1938) and H. Glockner (1936) are still discussed today. Yet the problem of Hegel's dialectic did not receive a final solution in this period either. Glockner was more concerned with his personal Hegelianism than with explicating Hegel; Günther directed his attention only to the epistemological aspect of the dialectic; Marcuse focussed on the historical aspect; Kroner dispensed with an exhaustive analysis of Hegel's method; while Dürr — under N. Hartmann's influence — avoided trying to discover some unity in the dialectic. N. Hartmann's own exposition as well as Sesemann's remained obscure because they mixed explication with critique. Their objections are directed particularly against the dialectic of the *Logic*, which they oppose to the dialectic of the *Phenomenology*.[33]

We find the same situation in the French interpretations of Hegel, which originated with J. Wahl (1929) and A. Kojève (1947). Through his lectures (1939-40) Kojève introduced Sartre, Merleau-Ponty, Fessard, Hyppolite and Queneau to the problems of the *Phenomenology*. Yet in France, too, critique displaced the desire to understand the system. Consciousness — in contradiction to Hegel's view — remained 'unhappy', the opposition between human and absolute consciousness insurmountable, the transition from *Phenomenology* to *Logic* unacceptable.[34] Sharp protests against this procedure of the French school came from Hyppolite (1933) and Garaudy (1962). But they were not able to avoid dualism in their interpretations either; because of their adherence to Marx they disparage the system and admire only the method.[35]

Thus, it has proved disastrous for the task of explicating Hegel that the unity of dialectic was overlooked, neglected, left out of consideration, or intentionally rejected.

In Hegel's system the method does not permit dualism. Moreover, the opposition between the dialectic of *Phenomenology* and that of *Logic* is overcome in the system. The contradiction of reality, the first negation, is the point of departure of *Phenomenology*, whereas *Logic* starts with the contradiction of abstract ideality — the second negation. In both 'sciences' dialectical research is ultimately concerned with double negation and does not rest with simple negation. The opposition of methods lies solely in the point of departure. If *Logic* is regarded as consisting of undialectical problems — as done, e.g., by N. Hartmann and Soviet philosophers — Hegel's dialectic will remain obscure because a notion of dialectic foreign to Hegel is employed in its interpretation. Explication is to be separated, or at least distinguished, from critique transcending the system — or else the interpretation will become blurred. It is cheap to accuse Hegel of inconsistency by demanding that he follows the laws of a methodology foreign to him.[36]

The discussion of the nature of dialectic is closely tied to the question of Hegel's solution of the ontological problem of immanence. However, there also are diverging views with respect to this question. According to Hoffmeister and Lasson, Hegel defends Christianity, while Grégoire considers him a pantheist and precursor of Marx' and Feuerbach's materialism; Garaudy, too, takes Marxist atheism to be the 'rational core' of Hegel's system. Hegel — as we believe — followed his method consistently and denied and negated the transcendent God, but was no less consistent in his denial and negation of the material world. This double and inseparable negation results in the Hegelian 'spirit' in whom 'God' and 'world' are 'sublated' as moments. He who overlooks the 'moment feature' *(Momentanität)* in the negation of transcendence will only discover atheism in Hegel's system. If one is impressed by the negative significance that Hegel imparts to the finite, one will easily regard him as the greatest apologist of Christianity. Here, too, Hegel scholars stand in danger of giving a one-sided interpretation of Hegel's subtle position which rests on the law of double negation.

4. DIVISIONS

Dialectic. The demonstration that what is objectively given contains contradictions and is to dissolve of necessity forms the point of departure of Hegel's system; it leads to the question of why the 'absurd' world of experience exists at all. This problem finds its solution in the negativity of abstract ideality. The method of the whole system develops from the unity of negative and positive dialectic; the material, formal, and final objects of the system will have to be analyzed separately.

Dialectic and Metaphysics. A comprehensive understanding of a subject-matter includes the knowledge of what it is not. This is why we shall examine the relationship of dialectic and metaphysics. Hegel claims that his method can only be justified in terms of a metaphysics, namely, *The Science of Logic*, and further that it essentially differs from the metaphysical method employed by the rationalists and in part even by Kant. On the one hand, then, Hegel's dialectic bears a necessary relation to metaphysics and, on the other hand, it is essentially opposed to it. This gives rise to an ambiguity of 'metaphysics' which will be examined in Part II: first the necessary unity of dialectic and metaphysics, and then its opposition to metaphysics in general, and to Spinoza's metaphysics in particular

Dialectical Metaphysics. After the discussion of the differences and com-

mon features of metaphysics and dialectic we shall point out the dialectical solution of some of the problems of previous metaphysics. Part III
could also be entitled 'The Dialectical Schema and Its Application'. As does
every part of Hegel's system, our treatise will conclude with considerations
concerning the problems of teleology.

PART I

DIALECTIC

CHAPTER 1

DIALECTIC OF THE REAL

1.1. UNITY AND MAIN THEME OF THE DIALECTIC

As long as the question of the unity of Hegel's method is disputed, it blocks insight into the nature of the dialectic and, therefore, must be answered first. There are two opposing interpretations regarding the question of whether Hegel used a uniform method or whether he merely assumed a dialectical attitude which in different analyses led to different methodological rules of of the game.

(a) Leaving aside the "more empirical forms of the dialectic in other works of Hegel", Coreth examines the method of the *Logic* alone. He comes to the conclusion that the core of the dialectic can be expressed in terms of a law that is objectively valid, formally univocally determined, and philosophically determinable. He regards the unity of analysis and synthesis as the essence of Hegel's methodology.[1] In favor of Coreth's position, one can point to the fact that Hegel himself reduces his method to one logical principle,[2] and considers the *Logic* alone as its adequate presentation and justification.[3] Nonetheless, the results of Coreth's study are not entirely satisfactory. The mere requirement of unity of analysis and synthesis is not at all a sufficiently clear characterization and demarcation of Hegel's dialectic, for there presumably is hardly any philosophical system which would renounce this unity. In addition, Coreth fails to explain in which sense the *logical* dialectic is most basic and to what extent the other methods differ from it.

(b) In contrast to Coreth, N. Hartmann stresses that the dialectic is not a logical 'scalpel', and that Hegel lacks any 'methodological awareness'.[4] According to him, Hegel's dialectic strives for the 'grasping of the inner nature of the absolute', everything else being 'matters of detail'.[5] In any case, he has thus assumed and conceded a unifying characteristic of the dialectic.

The requirement to consider everything as a moment in the development of the absolute, and to ascertain its significance for the absolute whole, characterizes Hegel's methodology.

[The absolute idea] is the sole subject matter and content of philosophy. ... it is the business of philosophy to cognize it in its various shapes.[6]

The absolute then is the only object of Hegel's philosophy. Yet the method is borrowed from the object. One might draw the conclusion that, for him, there is only one object and only one method. But then the system would contain only one science, which is not the case. This paradox is solved as follows. Just as the one absolute reveals itself in *various* 'shapes' *(Gestaltungen)*, so does the one method contain *various* ways of investigation corresponding to these 'shapes'. The 'work of detail' required by the richness of the absolute subject is focussed on one object.

The method is the *'way'* to the solution of the problem of philosophy, namely, to the answer to the question about the nature of the absolute. 'Method' is taken by Hegel in its Greek meaning, and rendered as 'way' *(Weg)* or 'course' *(Gang).*[7] In order to become familiar with this way, one has to walk along it. The discussion of philosophical method is itself a philosophical problem. Therefore, the method cannot be explained and justified *before,* but only *during* the philosophical investigation.[8] According to what Hegel himself says, *Logic* alone can give an adequate account of the dialectic. But it does not provide an unproblematic insight into the nature of the method. This science starts at once with the analysis of pure *ideal* being. If this starting-point has not received any justification in Hegel's system then the *Logic*, the essential foundation of the method, is void.

How does the dialectician discover the absolute in reality? Which theory in Hegel's system illuminates best the ascent to the absolute subject? Can this be achieved by the theory of contradiction? It is true that this theory is highly revolutionary and could explain the ascent, since it is through the negativity or contradictoriness of the real that dialectical thought *rises* to the ideal. However, it is not immediately evident why 'the contradictory' *(das Widerspruchsvolle)* — to be translated as 'the meaningless' — should have to exist. For this reason, the dialectical theory of contradiction cannot without difficulties explain the ascent. Besides, it is not improbable that Hegel arrived at these revolutionary assumptions through more basic and older problems.

We premise the additional hypothesis that *Hegel's* methodology is only suitable to bring the immanentist-idealist solution of the problem of values and universals to bear upon all other problem areas of philosophy. Our account will show this in detail. As known, Hegel's system is focussed on idealism. For a correct understanding of the dialectical method, three kinds of idealism must sharply be distinguished. According to *subjective idealism,* the real only exists in human thought. Hegel rejects this position as a matter of principle. Objective or absolute idealism contends that everything exists in an all-comprehensive and absolute thinking. This differs from ontological idealism — also called "extreme realism with respect to the problem of universals" — according to which universals as such are objectively given and possess a priority over contingent, objectively given being. This form is the point of departure of the dialectic; it inevitably includes an element negating the world of experience.

Is our attempt to understand dialectical method by means of Hegel's solution of the problem of values and universals not bound to fail from the beginning? We noted above that this method primarily leads to knowledge of the absolute. If the problem of the absolute were to have nothing in common with the problem of values and universals, our attempt could never furnish any insight into Hegel's unified method. However, the two questions are identical; for only the absolute subject is the truly concrete and good.[9] His original solution of the question of values and universals is for Hegel a general means for demonstrating that every determination *(Bestimmung)* and tendency of reality as given is but a moment in the thinking and striving of the absolute subject and, therefore, is to be attributed to this subject as being the only concrete and good. Hegel's dialectic, then, starts from ontological idealism in order to establish objective idealism.

We have shown that (a) the dialectical method is the way which leads to knowledge of the absolute, (b) the unity of this method is founded in the nature of the absolute, and (c) for Hegel *only* the absolute is concrete, so that the ascent from things to the absolute can most easily be explained by means of his solution of the problem of values and universals.

1.2. NEGATIVE DIALECTIC

Negative dialectic, i.e., dialectic with which one starts and does not yet reach positive results, is directed against the view that contingent things and existent institutions are themselves the subject of their being; what is truly self-subsistent in them is what is comprehensible, universal, ideal.[10] This does not mean doubting the objectivity of our knowledge. In epistemology, Hegel is an unambiguous representative of realism; he has only expressions of scorn for his predecessors — Berkeley, Locke, Kant and Fichte.[11] However, Hegel insists on both the objectivity of sense images and that of universal determinations; he goes on to ask which should be said to be prior. On the basis of the following arguments he comes out in favor of the universal.

(a) *Equal status of sensory and abstract knowledge.* There is for Hegel no reason to suppose that universals are worse copies than sense images. Both representations of being, the sensory and the abstract, impose themselves with mechanical necessity.[12] Scientific representation of being, while abstract, is still not arbitrary since it rises above all accidentality.[13] Sense experience, however, is tied to the particularity of human individuals and depends on what accidentally presents itself to *this* individual subject − in *this* place and at *this* time. Therefore, scientific knowledge contains a representation of objective being which is equal to, if not better than the sensory.[14]

(b) *All being is scientifically knowable.* In the justification of this position on the question of values and universals, Hegel also relies on the view that the world of experience contains nothing which could not be grasped by conceptual thought. Scientific knowledge is capable of providing a completely adequate representation of the structure of being. This presupposes that the entire content of being is universal, i.e. ideal.[15] For a better understanding of this argument it should be noted that what is involved here is an ontological and ethical statement which rests upon an analysis of the process of knowing. The development of science enables us to comprehend the nature of actuality better and better. From this fact, Hegel concludes *for epistemology:* the entire content of the world of senses can be explained scientifically; and *for ontology:* the sensual world is in itself completely intelligible and determined by *universals.* It is in itself ideal, for non-ideality would restrict its intelligibility.[16]

Hegel's ontological idealism is primarily directed against mysticism which assumes that there is something unknowable in objective actuality.[17] For him, there is nothing unintelligible and nothing ineffable.[18] Everything that is can also be thought and formulated, although not in one word or one sentence. This position does not compel one to assume a limit, either in the development of the sciences or in the development of objective being. Intelligibility of being merely implies its ideality.[19] A moderate realist, however, rejects this implication; for him the individual is inexhaustible and ineffable and remains thus essentially in opposition to ideality and value judgment. This objection against Hegel was already raised by Feuerbach.[20]

(b) *The nullity of the sensual.* All of the *Phenomenology* is a fight against naive consciousness which takes what is given by the senses as 'true' *(das Wahre)*[21]; Hegel shows that the sensual is 'vanishing',[22] changeable and contradictory being, whereas the ideal is independent and subsistent being. Universal concepts, laws, and ideals appear in various ways always and everywhere in reality; they are what is permanent in the objective whole.

Does this mean that things and structures do not exist at all? Do the laws not owe their effectiveness to the very existence of the world of things? Is not a thing or an institution the subject of its determinations or its basic ideals? For Hegel, the world of things and institutions only possesses the appearance of being because the *thesis* that things are independent subjects contains a contradiction: A thing is self-subsistent (*selbständig*, independent) only *to the extent* that it differs from other things; independence then presupposes a difference. Yet difference implies relatedness, too; independence is thus relatedness, i.e. dependence, and is *therefore contradictory*![23]

In order to avoid contradiction, one frequently distinguishes between substance, its accidents and its relations, and claims that a thing or an institution is, on the one hand, determined *for itself* and, on the other hand, *with respect to other things*. Hegel regards this distinction as 'sophistry' which merely covers up, but does not solve, the contradiction: for the new opposition again implies a relation.[24] Any attempt to characterize independence more precisely and distinguish it from dependence must accept a new relation, i.e. a new dependence, together with the assumption of this opposition. Every independence then means at the same time dependence. Through this contradiction, the alleged independence of sensual things and of the institutional world is reduced to an 'illogical' illusion which should indeed 'vanish'. At this point we are faced with the question, typical of negative dialectic, of how this contradictory dependence can arise in the first place.

In his analysis of 'phenomena' *(Erscheinungen)*, Hegel also criticizes the view which takes what is objectively given to be self-subsistent.[25] Here the term 'phenomenon', as in the language of the natural and social sciences, stands for 'process'.[26] For the understanding *(den Verstand)*, which according to Hegel's epistemology is concerned with the world of phenomena and things, phenomenon is but an accidental unity of a general, if determinate, force and general, if determinate, laws. What is permanent and independent, then, is not the phenomenon itself – since it is only a momentary synthesis – but the universal laws and forces which manifest themselves in many phenomena at the same time.

In practical life, too, one unknowingly presupposes the priority of the universal,[27] for everyone believes in the irresistible success of an *absolutely* rational action. When man knows all real and realizable concepts, laws and structures, and makes his activity accord with this knowledge, he will act *freely*. Such activity cannot come into conflict with any necessity, because it is in harmony with everything that is necessary, possible, or real. According to this conception of freedom, the irrational and unintelligible is considered a factor not to be taken seriously. Implicitly, then, it is assumed that only the rational is 'active'(*wirkend*, effective), objective, and realizable.

What is rational is actual,
and what is actual is rational. [28]

Does this theory of rational actuality inevitably imply ontological idealism? Comparing this theory with moderate realism will facilitate answering the question. For moderate realists, the absolute being is unconditionally free; nonetheless, they insist on the distinction between ideal and real being, between absolute and finite being. The following argumentation by Hegel, however, calls for the dissolution of this distinction. If reality as given were to contain something irrational and basically unintelligible, then such an element could offer resistance to absolutely rational activity, and then our striving to increase practical *knowledge* would be pointless. All of reality is rationally knowable and alterable; given this presupposition, reality does not contain anything irrational or not ideal. [29] This analysis of practical life is thus based on the thesis, considered above, that being can be scientifically known. The latter stipulates the universal cognitive power of reason, the former the universal creative power of reason. Implicitly, the striving to develop both theoretical and practical knowledge presupposes that reality differs only apparently from ideality, stands only seemingly in opposition to ideality, and depends but seemingly on ideality.

There are then three points involved in the negative-dialectical consideration: (a) the entire content of the world of experience is rational and ideal; (b) while the world of things and phenomena is objectively given, its things and institutions are 'absurd' constructs; (c) this leads to the question about the ground of being of this 'absurd' world.

The contentions made here hold only for the introduction to the system, and not for Hegel's system in general. In order to avoid confusion, the relationship of negative dialectic to the system as a whole has to be characterized in greater detail.

(a) Because of its introductory nature, negative dialectic is put at the beginning. However, in the process of double negation, negative dialectic forms the 'second' stage. The 'first' negativity is that of *pure* ideal determinations; it establishes the existence of the 'absurd' things and institutions. *Logic* starts with the 'first' negativity, *Phenomenology* with the 'second', namely, with the world of experience. [30]

(b) Negative dialectic doubtless is the central form of argument in the demonstration of the identity of being and thought. Negative dialectic shows the necessary dissolution of reality and its sublation into the sphere of ideals, i.e., negative dialectic demonstrates that there is a 'process of abstraction' immanent in reality. Independently of human subjects, this process occurs in what is objectively given.

(c) When taken in isolation, negative dialectic can easily lead to false conclusions with respect to Hegel's solution of the problem of universals. (ca) E.g., it is misleading to call Hegel, without reservation, an *extreme realist,* because this is only true of the point of departure of the system. While universals are objective, they — as parts of the absolute whole — are concrete in a threefold way: the universal has an essential tendency to become realized, and what is realized does not exist outside the universal; and in the dialectical process this double relation *grows together (concrescere)* with other relations of the same kind.[31] The *abstract* universals, i.e. the universal as detached from all relations, thus exists but in the human understanding. (cb) For this reason, many of the texts run counter to the view that what is abstract is objective. However, they are not to be interpreted as a moderate realism. Such a solution of the problem of universals indeed — is diametrically opposed to Hegel's: The Hegelian Universal is not present *in* things and phenomena; rather, the latter exist as moments *in* the universal. (cc) Because the process of abstraction and the objectivity of the universal are taken for granted we cannot concur with N. Hartmann's contention that there are nominalist tendencies in Hegel's system.[32] It is true that in several texts 'absolute being', the 'absolute', 'God', or the like is called an 'empty *word*'; but the only claim Hegel wants to make here is that, at the beginning of the dialectical process, these terms designate '*abstract* contents', the concrete content of which is still to be investigated.[33] (cd) In contrast to Kant's subjective conceptualism, Hegel's conceptualism is objective: The absolute is a thinking subject who, by means of his *a priori* forms, posits and cognizes within himself his objectivity (our world of experience).

(d) Negative dialectic points out several identities of 'ideality' and 'reality', as a result of which these terms acquire several meanings: (da) The ideal universal is what subsists in *reality*; it thus has *real* presence in the world of experience. (db) Moreover, the necessary dissolution of the world of experience implies the reality of what is purely ideal. (dc) Negative dialectic also leads to the identity of the real and the ideal: The content of reality is universal and ideal; what is real merely represents an accidental combination of ideal structures. (dd) As the dialectical process continues, we encounter a fourth meaning of 'ideality' and 'reality': 'True' ideality is only ascribed to the most ideal subject. Everything real or separated, *including separated abstract determinations,* will at the end of the dialectical analysis have completely '*vanished*' and be completely '*sublated*'.

In virtue of these new meanings of 'reality', the common identification of 'reality' *(Realität)* and 'actuality' *(Wirklichkeit)* becomes inadmissible. In most of Hegel's texts 'the real' stands for 'the finite', 'what is separated', 'what is spatially juxtaposed and temporally comes one after the other'. The concept 'actuality', by contrast, is given a particular content in the hierarchy of categories which is determined in relation to 'possibility'. For Hegel, 'the actual' primarily is 'what acts' *(was wirkt,* what effects); thus, it inevitably implies a relation to causality and necessity. In order to complete the list of terminological difficulties in interpreting Hegel, it should also be noted that every term which usually denotes what is objectively given acquires an exactly determined meaning in the dialectical process. The *sensual* world is the spatio-temporal world, the *real* world is the finite world, the *perceptible* world is the world of things and phenomena. 'Actuality' is to be understood as what is effective insofar as it is effective, and 'objectivity' means the totality opposed to the absolute subject. *Each of these 'worlds' has its own negative dialectic.* For the sake of greater clarity, we shall refer to what is objectively given mainly as 'world of experience', 'objective reality', 'world of things and phenomena', and 'objective actuality'; to realized ideality (the Hegelian *universale in re*) as 'the objective universal'; and to *what transcends the objectively given* as 'ideal reality of pure determinations'.

1.3. THE PRESUPPOSITION OF DIALECTICAL METHOD: IDEALIST INDIVIDUATION

Negative dialectic implies a critique of the realist principle of individuation, because it cancels the Aristotelian distinction of *universale in re, post rem,* and *ante rem.* The negative dialectic demonstrates the complete resolution of objective reality into *pure* determinations. The same is true of the positive dialectic which — conversely — shows that what is objectively given results from the necessary synthesis of *pure* determinations. This leads to the property that is so characteristic of the dialectical method: that every analysis of something given is immediately tied to the question about the ground and purpose of its existence.

Aristotle rejected the possibility of explaining reality in terms of pure determinations. A thing is the inseparable unity of an *individual* matter and an *individual* form. These two subsist neither before nor after the existence of the individual thing because there are no general traits subsisting in themselves. Hegel criticizes this account of individuality and contends that Aristotle did not sufficiently clarify the relationship of matter and form,[34] and did not understand the Platonic 'transition from thought to corporeality'.[35]

As P. G. M. Manser shows, the Aristotelian principle of individuation has been vigorously discussed in history. His Thomist interpretation no doubt relies on Aristotle.[36] Let us first try to understand this interpretation of the principle. We shall bracket the question of whether it is the only correct Aristotelian interpretation; we shall merely use it to bring out distinctly Hegel's original position with respect to this problem.

1.31. Basically, the principle of individuation is not a 'principle' in the sense of a law or prescription, as is, e.g., the principle of contradiction in formal logic; it much rather is a ground *(arche)* that is present in the things themselves, determines their individuality, and distinguishes them from mere objects of thought. 'Individuation' designates an activity, but not of something which is; for this would mean presupposing that the principle of individuation could exist *before* the thing, by itself and separate from the form. Therefore, what is acknowledged of individuation is only the result, *unique* individuality.

Whereas the form determines *what* a thing is, the principle of individuation determines the being-*this*-something *(hoc aliquid)*. In its relation to form, the scholastics define the principle of individuation as quantitatively restricted matter *(materia quantitate signata)*. They also distinguish the principle from pure matter *(materia prima)* which is a mere abstraction and does not correspond to anything objectively real. Quantitatively restricted matter, however, is present in the things and combined with an individual form in them. Because of this unity, the essence of a thing is something singular *(incommunicabile)*, i.e., the essence exists in a unique form separate from, and independent of, all other realizations of the same kind. This leads to the property that is so characteristic of analytics: that every thing and every institution is considered as something separate and as something given that exists for itself.

1.32. Hegel's views on the individual can be found in the section *Sense-Certainty, This, and Opinion* of *Phenomenology*, and the book *The Doctrine of Being* in his *Logic*; the former describes the 'this', the latter the 'something'. The 'this' of *Phenomenology* is spatio-temporally determined being, the 'something' of *Logic* is generally determined being. Both then are more specific determinations of 'absolute being' which in Hegel's system plays the role of pure possibility of determination, or *materia prima.*[37]

(a) The 'this' is determined by its spatial and temporal dimensions or 'negations': it is here and now. The 'here' and the 'now' are present in 'this' not individually, but as general traits. The 'now' is first night, then noon. The universal, 'now' in the present case, persists and transcends the limits of the 'this' which first was 'night', and now is 'day'. Time is not a form of being of things; it rather runs through these different stages.[38]

In the same way, the 'here' is not individual in or through the 'thises', and is not *incommunicabile*. It remains the same uniform and manifold 'here' which simultaneously exists in all 'thises'.

The *here* itself does not vanish; it rather *is* and remains in the disappearance of the house, tree, etc., and is indifferently house, tree.[39]

The same 'indifference' of space as such and of time as such is present in all 'thises'.

The position of moderate realism, according to which time and space are mere abstractions from objectively given duration and from objectively given quanta, suffers as *'reversal'* here: Time and space do not exist in the 'thises', but rather the 'thises' exist in those forms and by virtue of them.

(b) Likewise, the analysis of 'something' in the *Logic* conflicts with moderate realism. 'Something' owes its determinateness to a series of pairs of categories, namely, being – not-being, qualitative infinity – finitude, one – many, quantitative infinity – finitude, and measurelessness – measure. The unity of abstract being as pure potentiality for determination and not-being as fundamental negation results in the 'determinate being' *(Dasein)* of 'something'.[40] Not-being delimits the 'something' from the 'other'. Analogously, the amalgamation of the two categories infinity – finitude yields the 'finite something' which, by its *end (Ende)*, is delimited from the 'other'.[41] In the same way, the 'something' is more specifically determined by the unity of the other pairs of opposite categories. In each case, the second, *negative* category functions as determination of the first, *positive* category which plays the role of a potentiality for determination. In each of the various spheres of determination of 'something', the 'indifference' of being recurs in a new shape: all positive categories are boundless and without determination, and are thus a possibility of determination. We can see here a distinct analogy to analytical Aristotelianism. On each level of an Aristotelian analysis, *materia prima* is present in more and more concrete form: quantitatively restricted matter *can* be determined by form, the unity of matter and form *can* be realized, and this reality *can* be more specifically determined by accidents. Just as Aristotelian *materia prima* finds expression in various kinds of potentiality, so does the indifference of Hegelian being in the various potentialities of the positive categories for determination.

By its thesis of the 'invincibility' of being' *(Unüberwindlichkeit des Seins)*[42], however, Hegel's *Logic* differs essentially from the Aristotelian analysis of objective reality. The potentiality of the positive categories for determination, while being determined in an objectively real manner, is not individually determined by the unity with their opposites; in each case, this unity transcends the bounds of 'something'. We have met with the same approach, deviating from Aristotelianism, in the *phenomenological* analysis of the 'this'. To sum up, the difference can be formulated as follows. Whereas in the Aristotelian analysis the individual points beyond itself only through its relations, the positive constituents of 'this' and 'something', for Hegel, transcend the limits of 'this' and 'something', and even the totality of all 'thises' and 'somethings'.

This theory of the 'invincibility' of being is a straightforward consequence of the objective reality of universals considered above. The universal by its nature is *inexhaustible*; this is why it objectively transcends the totality of its realizations – provided it has found objectification in the world of experience.

(c) Hegel himself regards this interpretation of individuality as contradictory, and points out two kinds of contradictions: (1) The 'something' is determined through delimitation from the 'other'. The contradiction which Hegel tries to establish here is of the same kind as that which was discussed above in the analysis of the independence of the 'thing'. Thus we shall not consider it again.[43] (2) The second kind of contradiction can be expressed by the following picture: The boundless potentiality of all positive categories for determination can be imagined to form a line. On this line there are points representing boundaries between 'something' and 'other'. This picture illustrates the coexistence in a unity of what is boundless and what is bounded. In this unity there are boundaries, the points, which at the same time are transcended. *The boundaries are there,* since 'something' is distinguished from 'other', *and they are at the same time not there,* since the categories transcend these boundaries, and this is the contradiction. Each unity of all the above-mentioned pairs of categories involves an antinomy which can be illustrated by this picture that is frequently used by Hegel.[44]

Since the structure of 'this' and 'something' is contradictory, it cannot exist on its own; its determinateness is such that it would have to 'vanish' necessarily, or should not exist at all. This reaction of Hegel to the 'perception' of a contradiction is revolutionary. A contradiction will cause the analytical thinker to check his analysis. Hegel, however, on finding an absurd and contradictory structure, tries to discover the ground for the existence of this structure in the ideal reality of pure determinations. The contradiction thus leads to the *dissolution* (*Auflösung*, resolution) of the world of experience, and to an investigation of ideality. In each case, the dissolution involves a *determinate* content: The spatio-temporally determinate 'this' is resolved into 'being' in general and the 'nothingness of this';[45] in the *Logic,* 'something' is resolved into 'indifferent being' and 'the sum total of all negations'.[46]

The theory of dissolution has a double significance: as for epistemology, the absurdities of the world of experience lead to the analysis of pure determinations; as for ontology and ethics, the absurdities would in fact dissolve the world of experience if the ideal *(das Ideale)* were to discontinue its founding activity.

The theory of dissolution faces the following counter-arguments among analytical thinkers: (1) In virtue of the principle of individuation, objectified being does not contain anything universal. The resolution of what is objectively given into universal determinations can, for them, only take place in the mind where it loses its individuality. (2) The assumption of 'absurd' and 'contradictory' structures in the world of experience comes into conflict with formal logic. The principle of individuation enables moderate realists to avoid most of the contradictions established by Hegel. The universal of moderate realism — because of said incommunicability — cannot at all be illustrated by the picture of a continuous line. This principle, then, fundamentally distinguishes Hegel's position from the analytical position.

We have seen that the following points are characteristic of idealist individuation: (a) The individual is the unity of abstract, boundless determinations and their boundaries ('negations'). Within the limits of the 'this', or the 'something', the universal does not possess strict incommunicability, for it transcends the negations. Moreover, it is not exhaustible by the totality of its realizations. (b) The founding activity of pure determinations saves the world of experience from complete dissolution. (c) Since, for analytical thinkers, objective reality does not contain anything universal as such, there cannot be for them any *real* (but only an *intentional*) resolution outside the mind. Hegel partly overcomes this difficulty by assuming a process of abstraction in the absolute whole. (d) The contradictions are in part due to the elimination of individuality, and they bring about the resolution of what is given into pure determinations. This confirms our hypothesis that Hegel's theory of contradiction is essentially connected with the problem of universals.

CHAPTER 2

POSITIVE DIALECTIC

An analysis of texts in which Hegel describes his method (Section 2.1), and an examination of the methodological principles which he borrows from German philosophy (Section 2.2) will enable us to comprehend the nature of his dialectic (Section 2.3). Our discussion of negative dialectic will be supplemented in this context: negative dialectic does not only figure as a presupposition — as in the preceding chapter, but also as a moment of the dialectical movement.

2.1. HEGEL'S DIALECTIC AND ITS ORIGINS

2.11. *'Dialectic', 'Dialectician'*

In philological history, the term 'dialectic' derives from the Greek verb *dialegesthai* which originally means 'to pick out' *(dialegein)*. Homer already uses this verb for a higher mental activity. E.g., he has Odysseus say: "But why does my heart *deliberate (dielexato)* about these matters?" In Greek and Jewish literature, 'deliberating' is often associated with the 'heart' which then was taken for the organ of the activity of thinking. In Homer's poetry the term thus means: 'to think', 'to deliberate', or 'to sort out the arguments regarding some issue'.[1]

To which thinker does the term owe its technical philosophical meaning? Historical sources, Aristotle and Diogenes Laërtius, name Zeno and Plato.[2] We shall leave aside the question whether Zeno or Plato was in fact the first dialectician, since Hegel also leaves it unanswered.[3] More important for us is the fact that in describing his own dialectic Hegel always refers to Greek thought in general and that of Zeno and Plato in particular. Our first task will therefore be a summary examination of Greek dialectic.

2.111. *Heraclitus and the Eleatics*

Parmenides was the first Greek to work out a methodology. He distinguishes two ways of inquiry: The first leads to truth and rests on the principle that being is and cannot possibly not be; by contrast, the presupposition that being may also not be leads to mere opinion. Parmenides here makes the distinction which later on becomes characteristic of dialectical thinking: that between truth *(aletheia)* and opinion *(doxa,* seeming truth).[4] Opinion is changeable and unreliable like the given world of things on which it relies. Its fickleness and uncertainty is due to the mixture of being and not-being in changeable things. For not-being is unknowable and ineffable. Truth can therefore not be obtained from the given world; truth is based on absolute being which has not come into existence — otherwise it would have originated from not-being — and is one, undivided, and incorruptible. If being were to include many things, then the one *would not* be the other; this dissimilarity would thus presuppose the reality of not-being. Multiplicity, therefore, has to be considered as mere illusion.[5] Through his distinction between ideal and real being, his formulation of the principle of contradiction, and his posing of the epistemological problem, Parmenides has become the father of Western thought.

Parmenides' disciple Zeno developed his famous doctrine of antinomies in order to defend the theory of motionless being against public criticism and irony.[6] His master had described the ascent to the highest principle of being and thought in a mythological way, speaking of a chariot drawn by wise horses which drives up to the goddess who reveals the truth. The transition from given reality to motionless being still lacked rational justification.[7] This is why Zeno attempted to establish the necessity of this transition by means of his doctrine of antinomies. This doctrine is supposed to show that knowledge which is based on multifarious and moving reality cannot possibly contain the truth, since plurality and movement are contradictory.[8]

According to Aristotle's testimony, Heraclitus did not require that the world of experience be free of contradiction either.[9] For him, the contradictory unity of being and not-being, i.e. becoming, pervades the structure of the changeable world. In the all-governing process of becoming, a circular movement occurs: *The way up (hodos anoo)* is combined with *the way down (hodos katoo)*.[10] Thus, there is neither beginning nor end. The universe has not been set in motion by either god or man; without beginning and end, it exists and lives by virtue of the eternal fire which kindles and extinguishes itself *'in lawful regularity'*.[11] This circular movement runs through various stages. Having extinguished itself, fire becomes earth and water; from water vapor rise the souls of plants, animals and men.[12] The unity and the strife of opposites are the source of all motion in these diverse realms. The end of strife is peace, but peace is death, the dissolving into fire. The process of cooling down and burning up does not take place haphazardly; it is controlled by *logos,* by harmony. This harmony is primarily to be attributed to the divine fire; in the world, however, everything is dissonance. The all-embracing becoming, then, takes place in an alternation of unity, friendship, fire and harmony, on the one hand, and strife, opposition, disharmony, on the other.

Heraclitus differs from the Eleatics in that he primarily treats of the visible and audible; the Eleatics are solely concerned with being, the limits of which by far surpass our visual and auditory purview. However, the opposition between Heraclitus and the Eleatic school is not *per sic et non*. Both hold the view that the structure of changeable things is antagonistic, and that eternal truth transcends the world of experience.

2.112. *Plato and the Sophists*

Anaxagoras attempts to reconcile the Eleatic absolute being with Heraclitean becoming. Historically, he is the bridge between these schools and the Sophists who followed. He is the first in the history of philosophy to use the concept of finality to explain motion and change. Supreme being, *Nous*, is both the ultimate cause and the measure and goal of the development of all things. *Nous* forms the world from primordial matter. For Anaxagoras, this primordial matter – which was regarded as being simple elements like water, air, etc., by the cosmologists – consists of a multiplicity of primordial particles *(ta spermata)*.[13] In contrast to the Heraclitean becoming which presupposes a direct origination from, and a direct return to, the divine fire, Anaxagoras thought that things arise from particles which previously were constituents of some other thing. He explains becoming by his theory of the association and dissociation of *spermata*.[14] When something changes or is annihilated, its *spermata* become part of the structure of a new thing. Thus the relationship between the world of things and the principle of their motion, *Nous*, is looser, and the separation between the two greater, than in Heraclitus. For this reason, Catholic scholars have looked upon Anaxagoras as a precursor of the doctrine of divine transcendence.[15]

With the Sophists, human *Nous* takes the place of absolute universal reason as goal and criterion for the being and not-being of things. The 'sophistes' were itinerant wise men who taught practical – especially political – knowledge. The rise of the Sophists was made possible by the social structure of Greek cities in the 5th century B.C. At the time, a politician could gain influence only when he was well-educated. The resulting demand for general education was met by the Sophist schools, in which, apart from rhetoric, political science and fine arts as well as philosophy were taught. However, since the main interest was in politics, man became the starting-point and goal of all activities, and the central subject matter of science. For Greek thought, the breakthrough of Sophism meant – expressed in modern, though not quite adequate, terminology – the transition from ontological to subjective idealism.

Protagoras must be named as the most important representative of Sophism. He made the individual the supreme criterion: Man is the measure of all things *(pantoon chrematoon metron estin anthropos)*. By 'measure' is meant both *what determines the significance of something* and *the goal of something*. Protagoras reinterpreted the entire methodology which had so far been worked out in Greek philosophy in an anthropocentric way. Whereas for Heraclitus and the Eleatics, antagonism is present in the things themselves, Protagoras believes that it has its origin in the relationship of man to things and in the inadequacy of knowledge.[16] Since man can neither rise above this relationship nor avoid inadequacy, it is his right and duty to determine on his own what is rational and good.

Socrates opposes to this individualistic ethics his theory of the absolute good. Socrates attempts to bring out this opposition in the private aspirations of men by using this famous method of 'irony'. When teaching about absolute value, he would – pretending to be ignorant – ask citizens and artisans about the goal of their activity and for a justification of this goal, with the intention of making them affirm the exact opposite of what they had started with. In this way, the confused interlocutor would be taught the maturity necessary to acknowledge the general good as supreme value.

Socrates' most famous pupil is no doubt Plato. Just as Zeno developed his doctrine of antinomies to justify his master's conception of being, so it is Plato's intention to give support to Socrates' doctrine with the dialectic of his early writings. Later, especially in the *Republic* and in *Parmenides,* he attempts to give an ontological foundation to Socratic ethics, identifying the general good with the true being of ideas, the origin of all things.[17]

Like the Socratic 'irony', the dialogue form – one of the best-known features of Platonic dialectic – aims at a pedagogical goal: dialogue is meant to rid reader or listener of his narrow judgments and lead him to focus on the true core of the matter. In postulating the good and true as existing in-and-for-itself, the Platonic position agrees with the Eleatic. For Plato the true and good is that which is permanent and persistent, just as being is for the Eleatics. In contrast to these Italian-Greeks, however, he does not want to deny all positive value to changeable things; he gives them the meaning of copies *(eidola)*. This gives rise to the problem which is so specific for Plato's dialectic: the problem of participation *(methexis)* in the being of true form *(eidos)*, which is the model *(paradeigma)* for objective reality. The dialectician masters the art of ascending to ideal being, starting from things that are given. This ascent is dealt with especially in the *Republic,* where Plato puts forth his well-known demand: the statesman must at the same time be a philosopher. A general Sophist education, which is confined to arithmetical, geometrical, astronomical and political knowledge, does not suffice for ruling the state and arriving at a knowledge of justice. In addition, the statesman will have to attain knowledge of the true and good which exists in-and-for-itself — this precisely constitutes dialectical knowledge — before he can devote himself to the task of bringing about justice in the state. This knowledge is the grasping of the absolute by means of concepts.

And when I speak of the other division of the intelligible, you will understand me to speak of that other sort of knowledge which reason herself attains by the power of dialectic, using the hypotheses not as first principles, but only as hypotheses — that is to say, as steps and points of departure into a world which is above hypotheses, in order that she may soar beyond them to the first principle of the whole; and clinging to this and then to that which depends on this, by successive steps she descends again without the aid of any sensible object, from ideas (concepts), through ideas, and in ideas she ends.[18]

Dialectic is the faculty of human resaon *(nous, logos)* to discover the absolute essence in concepts abstracted from things and taken by themselves, and to recognize it as the origin of all things. Reason does not reflect upon the universal as it is realized in things. In this, it differs from the understanding *(dianoia)* which, though being also concerned with what is universal, does not analyze its function of founding being. Reason, then, is a *pure* cognitive power, i.e., reason cognizes what is true and good in-and-for-itself in the universal determinations as such.

Later in the same dialogue, in describing the famous simile of the sun, Plato resumes the same line of thought: As, with our eyes, we recognize the sun as the source of all shadows and colors,

so with dialectic; when a person starts on the discovery of the absolute by the light of reason only, and without any assistance of sense, and perseveres until by pure intelligence he arrives at the perception of the absolute good, he at last finds himself at the end of the intellectual world, as in the case of sight at the end of the visible.[19]

Thus, long before Hegel, Plato tries to discover in pure determinations the ground of being for the world of things.

How does reason come to consider universals no longer as constituent parts of things, but as being in-themselves? Why does it strive to find the origin of all things in the unity of self-subsisting determinations? In Plato as in Zeno, the ascent to the universal, existing in-itself, is caused by the contradictoriness of things. Plato distinguishes between two kinds of objects:

some are sufficiently apprehended by perception; others remain mysterious and stimulate thought and inquiry because they evoke two contrary sense impressions at the same time.

And surely, he said, this occurs notably in the case of one; for we see the same thing to be both one and infinite in multitude.[20]

For Plato as for the Eleatics, the multiplicity of things together with the unity of the universal is contradictory.

In *Parmenides,* Plato again takes up the contradictoriness of things. In this dialogue, Zeno is the first to speak and attempts to show that the plurality of existing things involves a contradiction.

Do you maintain that if being is many, it must be both like and unlike, and that this is impossible, for neither can the like be unlike, nor the unlike like – is that your position?
Just so, said Zeno.[21]

Young Socrates objects to this conclusion and proposes using for the unlike an *eidos* other than that for the like. This prompts old Parmenides to interfere in the conversation, and he refutes the young man who, at the end of the dialogue, is reproached: his technique of dialectical thinking is still wanting. There are divergent opinions among contemporary Plato scholars about the interpretation of *Parmenides*; yet all agree that in this dialogue Plato's Eleatic tendencies stand out strongly. Hegel, too, has interpreted the *Parmenides* in this way.

Hegel's positive evaluation of the dialectic in Plato's *Parmenides* was criticized in the last century by E. von Hartmann, and was more recently misunderstood by L. Sichirollo.[22] The former concedes that this dialogue may suggest a denial of the principle of non-contradiction, but maintains that such an interpretation is not permissible, because Plato acknowledges the principle in other dialogues. This is why, as E. von Hartmann thinks, Hegel is unable to carry out a uniform interpretation of Plato when he relies on the *Parmenides* as an historical witness for his dialectic of contradiction.

E. von Hartmann, however, does not examine the question of whether Plato thinks that the principle holds for both sensual being and ideas. Contemporary Plato scholars – we shall name only E. Hoffmann, G. Prauss and H. Gundert[23] – believe that they perceive in Plato a double meaning of the principle of non-contradiction. For them, Plato indeed implicitly acknowledged and expressed the principle as formulated in its final form and systematically worked out by Aristotle, but he ascribed to it a meaning differing from Aristotle's. Aristotle made 'saving of phenomena', which occupied Greek thought since the Eleatic refutation of reality, the main goal of his investigations; and, in opposition to the Eleatic method, he stipulated that judgments about the sensual also be free of contradiction. Plato, however, when writing his dialogues, was still in agreement with the Eleatic tradition.

Sichirollo, who, like Hoffmann, Prauss and Gundert, arrives at this assertion as well, contrasts it with Hegel's judgment.

As is known, Hegel calls the *Parmenides* the 'most famous masterpiece of Platonic dialectic'. This claim is difficult to maintain regarding the context of the Platonic text. The dialectic under discussion is that of Zeno ...

The author overlooks the fact that Hegel's positive judgment about the *Parmenides*, in almost every case, is accompanied by the remark that the dialogue leads only to 'nothingness'. Yet Hegel's *Logic* begins by showing that Eleatic being is identical with 'nothingness'. Therefore, Hegel's judgment has to be rendered as follows: while being a masterpiece of dialectic, the *Parmenides* fails to go beyond Eleatic dialectic. Sichirollo then is wrong when he thinks that Hegel's interpretation of *Parmenides* differs from his own.

Thus there is agreement today that Plato interprets the principle of non-contradiction in the Eleatic sense. Further, his method presupposes the possibility of pure thought and the being-in-self *(An-sich-Sein)* of pure concepts. The goal of the method is to discover the unconditioned essence as the ground of all things in the realm of these concepts existing in-themselves. To the extent that he propagates Eleatism anew, Plato is a precursor of Hegel's negative dialectic; insofar as he does not pass beyond Eleatism, he is criticized by Hegel.

2.113. *From Aristotle to Kant*

In the *Parmenides*, Plato stated that the dialectic would be completely precluded if the being-in-self of certain forms were denied.[24] It is precisely this view which is impugned by Aristotle in his *Metaphysics;* he maintains that there are no forms apart from the things. In addition, he stipulates that the freedom from contradiction be without exception. He still does not deny all meaning to dialectic and retains it in its Socratic form: opinions of one's predecessors should only be accepted after a dialectical-critical analysis. By comparing contradictory opinions, one can distinguish what is improbable in them from what is probable. For Aristotle, 'a dialectical inference' means 'a probability inference'.[25]

The Stoics as well as medieval philosophers do not attribute any particular significance to dialectic. In Immanuel Kant's transcendental logic, dialectic again occupies a central place. Its negative task consists in demonstrating the contradictions contained in traditional metaphysics of being. Kant calls the dialectic in this sense the *logic of illusion (Schein)*; it has to expose the *semblance* of truth in the unfounded presumptions of the understanding and the contradictions in the views of hyperphysically speculating reason.[26]

After our knowledge has been purified of metaphysical sophisms, the positive task of the dialectic follows: the elaboration of the doctrine of ideas. The objects God, world and soul, which former metaphysics regarded as existing objectively, are replaced by three ideas which are nothing other than postulates requiring the synthesis of empirical knowledge. These syntheses, however, provide only provisional and *probable knowledge, belief.*[27] Thus we again find in Kant the Socratic-Aristotelian meaning of the dialectic: after contradictory opinions have been discarded, dialectic provides probable knowledge.

The Kantian dialectic and the *Critique of Pure Reason* in general have, on the one hand, exerted a great influence on Hegel's dialectic; on the other hand, they are sharply criticized by him. A better insight into Hegel's dialectic is prerequisite for understanding this double relationship. Before we return to Hegel's dialectic, let us summarize the result of our analysis. (a) The Eleatics, Plato, Aristotle and Kant accept the principle of non-contradiction. (b) For these philosophers, dialectic is the method of bringing out the essence of something or a universally valid judgment after contradictory opinions or phenomena have been discarded. (c) While all of these philosophers accept the principle of non-contradiction, they appraise it differently, one reason for this being their different conceptions of reality. According to the Eleatic-Platonic interpretation of the principle, what is given by the senses is contradictory and thus has but the *semblance* of being; the non-contradictory essence of the supersensual world must be searched for. The Aristotelian interpretation of the principle requires unrestricted freedom from contradiction. Protagoras and Kant consider contradiction an inevitable defect of our knowledge.

2.12. *Criticism, Sophistry, Dialectic*

Hegel distinguishes between different kinds of dialectic. The property they all have in common is *'to totter what is firmly fixed.'*[28] The 'firmly fixed' primarily refers to the common opinion that things are independent substances, that the absolute is a thing existing in itself and separate from the world of experience, and that our sense knowledge is an adequate representation of what is. Dialectic in general, then, is directed against 'so-called common sense.' This kind of sense is the *misunderstanding* which considers genuine being to be something *tangible* like a thing.[29]

(A) Hegel distinguishes the kinds of 'dialectic' according to their goal:

(a) *Skeptical dialectic* is directed against knowledge in general. This method yields only *'the pure nothingness'*, i.e., it is unsuitable for delineating boundaries. Skepticism endeavors to show the relativity and subjectivity of all knowledge, and substitutes

universally, in knowledge, for being the expression *appearance.* [30]

Being in itself remains unknown; all knowledge is subjective illusion.

For Hegel, Skeptical dialectic includes that of Kant, since it stops with the negative result that the finite alone is knowable and the absolute unknowable. Kant — as Hegel claims — was not aware of the contradiction involved in this result. Knowledge of an object must include insight into its contrary. Therefore, it is contradictory to regard the finite as knowable and the *in*-finite as unknowable.[31]

The mistake of Skeptical dialectic in general lies, for Hegel, in its tendency to show only what is relative and negative in knowledge without discovering in this very negativity the motivation for ascending to the absolute.[32]

(b) *Sophist dialectic* totters 'the firmly fixed' for the sake of the individual subject.

If the field of reasons, that which consciousness holds to be firmly established, is shaken by reflection, what is one now to take as his *ultimate purpose?* For there must be *something fixed* for him. ... With the Sophists, the satisfaction of the *individual* himself was now made ultimate, and as they made everything totter, the fixed point became this: 'It is my pleasure, vanity, glory, honor, *particular subjectivity,* which I make my end.'[33]

Both Hegelian and Sophist dialectics aim at an absolute freedom. The latter serves only the individual subject, while the former intends to conform the individual to the absolute subject.

(c) *Eleatic and Platonic dialectics* establish an ideal reality which is given prominence as true being. As our analysis of negative dialectic has suggested, Hegel evaluated this form as being the most positive among the historical forms of dialectic.

We here find the beginning of dialectic, i.e. the pure movement of thought in concepts: thus the opposition of thought to phenomena or sensual being ... and in the objective existence the contradiction which it has in itself — dialectic proper.[34]

Dialectic proper, then, comprises two elements: (aa) it is purely conceptual thinking, and (bb) it assumes the objectivity of contradiction. In contrast to Sophist dialectic which only focusses on the limitations of our knowledge, Eleatic dialectic aims at the *immanent contemplation of the subject matter itself.*

One puts oneself right into the thing, considers the object in itself, and takes it according to the determinations which it has. In regarding it thus, it will show from itself that it contains opposed determinations, and thus cancels itself ... The result of this dialectic is null, the negative; the affirmative in it does not yet appear. With this true dialectic may be associated the work of the Eleatics. But in their case, the destination or nature of understanding had not yet progressed far; they rather stopped at the fact that through contradiction the object is a nothing. [35]

Does this text not involve a paradox? Is not *pure* thinking, since it *abstracts from what is given through the senses,* diametrically opposed to the immanent contemplation of the subject matter itself? The paradox dissolves if one takes into account that the mode of thought in question rests on this contemplation. What is meant by 'immanent contemplation' is the discovery of a contradictory structure and the ensuing ascent to ideal reality. Convinced of the negativity of the object as given by the senses, the Eleatic dialectician analyzes what is universal, hence permanent and persisting — which, as an other *(ein Anderes),* is distinct from sensual multiplicity.

The imperfection of this dialectic lies in its exclusive and rigid concentration on pure ideality, on the nullity of what is given. Explaining reality, the proper task of philosophy, is thus neglected. This inadequacy does not keep Hegel from valuing Eleatic dialectic, because of its epistemological realism, more highly than any Skeptical critique. Both kinds of dialectic consider phenomena to be mere illusion. However, the deficiency of phenomena causes the Eleatics to deal only with what is different *(dem Anderen)* from phenomena, with being as one and without differences, while Skepticism renounces the objectivity of our knowledge and becomes engulfed in epistemological speculation. [36]

Although several Platonic dialogues — for instance, *Parmenides* — do not reach a higher level than the Eleatic dialectic and only stress ideal reality, the general tendency of Plato's dialectic is, for Hegel,

further to determine this universal in itself. This determination is the relationship which the dialectical movement in thought bears to the universal; for through this movement the idea comes to these thoughts which contain the opposites of the finite within themselves. The idea, as the self-determining, becomes the unity of these differences; it is thus the determinate idea. The universal is hence determined as that which resolves and has resolved the contradictions in itself, and hence is the concrete in itself; thus the sublation of the contradiction is the affirmative. Dialectic used to this higher end is Platonic dialectic proper: as speculative, it does not conclude with a negative result; it rather demonstrates the union of opposites which have annulled themselves.[37]

Obviously, Hegel wants to interpret Platonic dialectic in terms of the law of double negation, the basic law of his own dialectic. In other texts, however, he concedes that one cannot 'expressly' find in Plato all that he attributes to him.[38] Moreover, any comparison of Hegel's presentation of Platonic dialectic with contemporary expositions, like that of H. Gundert or R. Marten, will show that our thinker has curtailed its richness. For our purposes, however, Hegel's omissions in his interpretation of Plato are less significant than the question of whether the elements emphasized by Hegel in his interpretation can in fact be found in Plato, i.e., whether what he calls 'Platonic dialectic' may justly be called 'Platonic'. Plato expressly stresses the contradictoriness of sensual being and the 'purity' of dialectical thought, and attempts, by means of the dialectic, to grasp the essence, the ground, of all things. Furthermore, in several places he speaks of a circular movement taking place in the objective world.[39] It is these theories of Plato which Hegel underscores.

In Hegelian language, then, 'Plato's speculative dialectic' stands for the view that the universal, whose independence and permanence surpass the given world of things, does not remain motionless in its ideality as does Eleatic being. It contains within itself 'the oppositions of the finite' and therefore has to dissolve and vanish — like the sensual. Thus, the universal achieves a double effect: on the one hand, it has *resolved* the contradictions of its reality into negative dialectic and, on the other hand, it *resolves* the contradictoriness of its abstraction. It is only in this double function that the universal is what is truly concrete; what is sensually concrete is thereby degraded to something apparently concrete.

(B) Hegel's descriptions of his *own* dialectic are scanty, difficult to understand, and accompanied by historical remarks equally difficult to understand in the given context. With the help of the results of our historical examination, we are able to eliminate these difficulties in part. Carrying on the Eleatic-Platonic tradition, Hegel rejects Sophism and Skeptic criticism.

(a) Of the three descriptions of his method given by Hegel, we shall first analyze that in the introduction to the *Science of Logic*.

All that is necessary *to achieve scientific progress* ... is the recognition of the logical principle that the negative is just as much positive, or that the self-contradictory does not dissolve into a nullity, into abstract nothingness, but essentially only into the negation of its *particular* content, in other words, that such a negation is not negation of everything and every negation is but the *negation of a determinate subject matter* which resolves itself, and consequently is a determinate negation, ... Because the result, the negation, is a determinate negation, it has content. ...

That which directs the concept in its advance is the already mentioned *negative* which it possesses within itself, it is this which constitutes the genuine dialectical element. ... Even the *Platonic* dialectic, in the *Parmenides* and elsewhere even more directly, aims in part only at dissolving and refuting limited assertions through themselves; yet partly, it has for result simply nothingness. Dialectic is commonly regarded as an external, negative activity which does not pertain to the subject matter itself, having its ground in mere conceit as subjective itch for unsettling and dissolving what is fixed and true, or at least does not lead to anything but the worthlessness of the object dialectically considered. ...

It is in this dialectic as it is here understood, that is, in the grasping of opposites in their unity or of the positive in the negative, that *speculative thought* consists.[40]

(aa) Hegel's dialectic differs from *common*, i.e. Skeptical, dialectic. The latter is an *external and negative* activity which *does not pertain to the subject matter itself,* and which endeavors by means of contradiction to show the worthlessness of the insight into the *object dialectically considered.* By contrast, Hegel's dialectical contradiction is given objectively. (bb) This contradiction *directs the concept in its advance,* i.e., in our endeavor to understand the existence of something, we discover in it contradictoriness or unintelligibility which causes us to examine something else which can explain this existing contradictoriness. (cc) Because the contradiction is objective, an equally objective transition and connection underlies the mental transition to this other thing. (dd) The term 'the negative' is confusing because of its ambiguity; it stands for contradictory structure *(the negative as the self-contradictory),* the resolution of this structure *(the negative as directing the concept in its advance),* and the result of this resolution *(the resulting negative).* These matters form the moments of a unified movement; this is why Hegel refers to them by one term. (ee) The negative as the result of the resolution is *just as much positive* . Its double content is due to the double effect of the resolution, which sloughs off the contradiction and, at the same time, loses the point of departure. (ff) *The result* has a *determinate content* that issues from the resolution of a determinate subject matter. It is on this point that Hegel's dialectic differs from mystical tendencies which attribute to the supersensual a fancied content or a fancied power. (gg) Knowledge is speculative only when it has grasped the unity of the positive and the negative, both in the subject matter from which one has started and in its other *(ihrem Anderen)* to which one has passed over. It is with this methodological postulate that Hegel attempts to surpass Plato who in part still uses an Eleatic method, which *has for result simply nothingness,* and a Socratic method, which *dissolves limited assertions through themselves.*

(b) Paragraphs 79 to 82 of the *Encyclopedia,* which together bear the title *Logic Further Defined and Divided,* contain another general description of Hegel's dialectic.

In point of form, the logical has three sides: (a) the *abstract* side, or that of the *understanding*; (b) the *dialectical,* or that of *negative reason*; (c) the *speculative*, or that of *positive reason.*
   (a) Thought, as the *understanding,* sticks to fixed determinateness and its distinctness from other determinateness; every such limited abstract is taken by the understanding as subsisting and being for itself.
   (b) The *dialectical* moment consists in the self-sublation of such finite determinations and their passing into their opposites.

In what follows, he rejects the Skeptic and Sophist interpretations of dialectic, and continues:

Reflection is first the passing beyond isolated determinateness and relating it, setting it thus in relationship; while its isolated validity is still preserved. Dialectic, however, is that *immanent* passing-beyond by which the one-sidedness and limitation of determinations of the understanding is exhibited as what it is, namely as its own negation. Everything finite is such that it is to sublate itself. The dialectical, therefore, constitutes the moving soul of scientific progress, and is that principle through which alone the content of science is given *immanent connection and necessity* – just as in general it constitutes the true, nonexternal rising above the finite.
   (c) The *speculative* side, or that of *positive reason,* apprehends the unity of determinations in their opposition – the *affirmative* which is involved in their dissolution and their transition. The result of dialectic is *positive*, because it has a determinate content, or because its result is truly not *empty, abstract nothingness,* but the negation of *definite determinations* which are contained in the result for the very reason that it is not immediate *nothingness*, but a result. This rational result, though a thought and abstract as well, is thus at the same time something *concrete*, because it is not simple, *formal* unity, but *unity of distinct determinations.*

In the dialectical transition, three moments are sharply to be distinguished: the point of departure, the transition, and the result.

(aa) Dialectic presupposes the knowledge attained by the understanding. *Reflection*, or the understanding, no longer considers things to be independent and isolated existences, as does the imagination. Natural science, for instance, demonstrates a general connectedness between things. The understanding, however, fails to transcend its world. It apprehends determinations in a *one-sided and limited* way, i.e., it takes them to be determinations of given things.

(bb) This limitation is manifest on the level of *negative reason,* i.e., in the contradiction inherent in its demand for dissolution and transition to the other *(dem Andern).* This *passing-beyond*, i.e. this transition, is caused by the limitations of determinations realized in things, and is thus *immanent in the nature of the subject matter.* However, the abstraction performed by the understanding lies in *its* nature, and therefore, is an *external rising-above*, foreign to the subject matter itself.

(cc) What is *positive-rational,* i.e., what results from the resolution, is a *thought* and something *abstract;* yet at the same time, it is something *concrete,* because it contains in a unity the determinations which have been set free by the resolution. The positive element in the *positive-rational* consists precisely in this unity, which can become the point of departure of a new movement.

(c) Hegel concludes the *Logic* with a retrospect on the method used and again speaks about the three moments.

(aa) In *Logic* the starting-point is always the universal.

But in the absolute method the universal is not taken as a mere abstraction, but as the objective universal. i.e., as that which is *in itself* the *concrete totality,* though not yet this totality as *posited,* not yet as *for itself.* Even the abstract universal as such, considered in its concept, i.e. in its truth, is not merely the *simple (das Einfache),* but as *abstract* is already *posited* as infected with a negation.[41]

The universal as such is both objective and not objective: it is present in what is objectively given, but cannot exist *for itself.* This ambiguity is due to the double movement in the circular figure. There is a necessary resolution into universals, and an equally necessary negation of the universal. The pure universal indeed subsists in the objective whole, but only as a moment. Since it is *infected with a negation,* i.e. contradictory, it is compelled to unite with its opposite. Therefore, the universal as represented by pure determinations is already *in itself* the totality which will develop from it. In contrast to 'being-for-self', 'being-in-self' includes the necessity of a development. That which forms a completely integrated unity is 'for itself'. 'Being-in-and-for-itself' is ascribed to the *totality* which contains the principle of development within itself, and directs all development toward itself.

(bb) The unity of universal determinations and their opposites yields the second moment.

The second determination, the *negative* or *mediated,* is at the same time the mediating determination. ... it is the negative, *but the negative of the positive,* and includes the positive within itself. ... is consequently *as contradiction,* the *posited dialectic of itself.* ...

(Its) negativity constitutes the *turning point* of the movement of the concept.[42]

(cc) The negativity of the second moment is due to the fact that the universal does not change, but only encounters its opposite. The resulting unity of the two moments opposed to one another is contradictory and cannot be permanent. The dissolution of this unity will again yield the original universality.

In this turning point of the method, the course of cognition at the same time returns to itself. As self-sublating contradiction this negativity is the *restoration* of the *first immediacy,* of simple universality ... which can again become a beginning.[43]

The movement thus returns through the second *mediated,* and at the same time *mediating, determination* to the first *immediacy.* The difference between immediacy and mediation, otherwise so difficult to comprehend, becomes relatively easy to understand owing to the preceding explanation of the cycle method. The first moment is apprehended *immediately.* The second, however, results from the first and thus is *mediated* by the first. But the second is also mediating, since it functions as a moment of transition between the original and the ensuing *immediacy.* The whole circle, which came about through this return-into-self, again constitutes an *immediate* starting-point for the following speculation. Hence, beginning and end of the circular movement are *immediate,* the latter being *mediated immediacy* while the former is simply *immediately* apprehended. It follows from the return-into-self that the first *immediacy* has been without mediation merely for us; our thinking just cannot help starting with what is *immediately* given. Since everything exists only in the circular figure, there is nothing *immediate.*

On the level of the true, all circles are interwoven. The starting-point of any given circular movement becomes the point of return, and again starting-point for a new circular movement; hence, all circular forms come together at one point and are inseparably molten together. Any preceding rotation forms the basis for the subsequent one. Hegel's approach can thus be called an 'unrolling of problems', to use N. Hartmann's term. Once a certain universality has been recognized as starting-point and goal of a reality, one passes on to the question about the ground of another reality. Solely the whole is *immediate,* and is *mediated* not through something else, but through its own moments.

The analysis of Hegel's description of the dialectic has led to the following results: (a) The methodical movement which returns again and again to its point of departure aims at the solution of the problem of values and universals: all universalities, in their circular form, are attributed to one single point, the absolute subject. (b) With his dialectic, Hegel intends to continue the ancient Eleatic-Platonic tradition. (c) As a matter of principle, he rejects Sophist and Skeptical dialectic, according to which essence in-and-for-itself is unknowable, and universals are purely subjective.

2.13. *The Circle of Being, the Most Abstract Form of the Dialectic*

2.131. *Technical Description*

After our general description of the cycle method, we shall now show its application in one instance, the movement of being. The circle of being is the most abstract form of Hegel's dialectic.

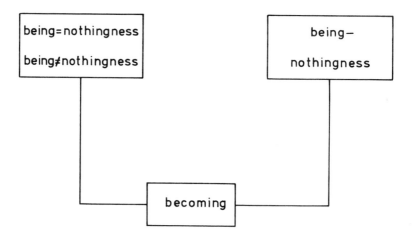

Logic, according to Hegel, begins with 'absolute being', the first attribute of the absolute subject. 'Absolute' — *absolvere* means 'to set free' — is for Hegel abstract reality, freed from all limitations of determinateness; it is thus without determinations, and will be developed only through the development of that which it *implicitly (an-sich)* contains within itself. Hence *absolute being in itself (an sich)* in its pure ideality is not at all a determination which expresses some perfection, but empty and equal to not-being.

Besides this identity with not-being there is the non-identity with not-being; and one merely has to combine these two facts about abstract being in order to discover the contradiction: pure ideal being is *at once* identical and non-identical with nothingness. According to the general law of dialectic, absolute being — because of its contradictoriness — is negated, and the unity with its opposite, not-being, must be postulated.

According to the same law, this unity, *becoming*, contains the positive, being *as such*, although it is united with not-being. Becoming thus contains two opposite determinations: being and not-being. *But such a union destroys itself,* since it is contradictory. Inevitably, therefore, becoming resolves itself so that the two determinations contained in it, being and not-being, become free again.[44]

Both contradictions occurring in the circular movement involve the determinations being and nothingness, although in opposite relationships. In the first contradiction it is their *separation* which is carried to the extreme, in the second it is their *unity.*

2.132. *Presuppositions*

This treatment of being presupposes the negative dialectic which shows both the necessary dissolution of reality and the subsistence and independence of universal determinations. After this has been established in the *Phenomenology,* the *Logic* is justified in seeking the ground of all reality and determinate being in pure universalities.

N. Hartmann's contention that Hegel takes the presuppositions of his theory of self-development for granted, thus evading all accountability and discussion, is not based on an examination of the negative dialectic.[45] For this reason, his criticism is unfounded. Similarly, A. Trendelenburg and L. Erdei believe that the beginning of Hegel's *Logic* has been constructed by means of an abstraction; philosophy ought to begin, not with abstract being, but with sensual-concrete being.[46] This criticism is also unjustified, since, as *negative dialectic* shows, the abstract with which the *Logic* begins is the product of the dissolution immanent in objective reality, and not that of a subjective abstraction.

About the *Phenomenology* in its role as presupposition of the *Logic,* Trendelenburg expresses himself as follows. The *Phenomenology* is either a propaedeutic or a part of the system. If it is the former, then it is not part of the system and cannot have a role in the justification of the system. If it is the latter, then it pertains to the *Philosophy of Spirit* and owes its justification to the *Logic,* which precedes the *Philosophy of Spirit.* We cannot agree with this 'either-or', for the dissolution of reality demonstrated by *Phenomenology* constitutes a moment of the *logical* cycles, and receives through them a second justification. Besides, Trendelenburg confounds a chapter of the *Philosophy of Spirit* with the science entitled *Phenomenology of Spirit.* The former describes the phenomenon of the appearances of the absolute spirit in the human mind, the latter these appearances themselves. The former treats of a property of the human mind, the latter of the content of absolute spirit revealing itself.

The style of the *Logic* and, even more clearly, the controversies in the

Yearbooks for Scientific Criticism indicate that the identity of being and nothingness was sharply criticized by Hegel's contemporaries. Authors of our time display the same negative attitude. C. Nink, for instance expresses himself on this identity as follows:

> The 'pure' abstract being *(Seiende)*, though not defined *in any specific way*, is defined to the extent that it is *not* nothing, and *cannot be* nothing. ... [To the abstract being] thought does indeed not attribute any specific characteristics; its concept is much rather formed by our k n o w l e d g e of what the essence of the abstract being *(Seienden)* consists in. Hence it does not follow that 'pure being' *(Sein)* is 'nothingness'. Absolute nothingness is the negation of all being *(alles Seienden)*; it is not 'simple identity with itself' or 'complete emptiness and lack of determination and content'.[47]

If in interpreting this text one forgets for a moment Nink's Aristotelianism, then these statements are a confirmation rather than a refutation of the lack of difference between being and nothingness as defended by Hegel. For if pure abstract being is not at all *defined in any specific way*, then it cannot as such be objectively given, nor do we *know* any longer in *what the essence of the abstract being (Seienden)* differs from nothingness, whence it is completely empty, without content and identical with nothingness — as defined by Nink. For Hegel, absolute abstract being *(Sein)* in its ideal reality — which has resulted from the *negation* and *dissolution* of all objectively given realities, those becoming and those determinately being — precisely this absolute abstract being is identical with that *negation of all being (alles Seienden)* which Nink describes.

This analysis shows how difficult it is to formulate the difference between being and nothingness. This difficulty is much rather an argument in favor of the Hegelian identity, especially since Hegel holds the view that unstatable differences are to be rejected because there cannot be anything incomprehensible and ineffable for reason.[48]

For a better understanding of the first identity and non-identity, it should be added that they hold only for the *ideal* reality of *pure* determinations, and not for objectively given reality. There is also for Hegel a real difference between the being and not-being of 100 thalers. This difference in *objectively given reality* is expressed in ideal reality by the non-identity of pure determinations.

Hegel's conception of being differs fundamentally from the Aristotelian, and thus also from Nink's. For Aristotelians, nothingness is a *privatio*, it is non-existent, not given and hence *not in any real sense* distinct from being. For them, there is no nothingness at all.

Nink wants to stress — if we have correctly understood him — that 'being' refers to the *act* of being which is above any definition in terms of categories and essence. According to this interpretation of being, there is nothing to be found in objective reality which would coincide with any *concept of being*. Therefore, the dialectical circle of being is not acceptable; objective reality cannot *resolve* itself into the concepts of being and not-being because nothing in it corresponds to these concepts. The *logical* dialectic thus stands or falls with the negative dialectic.

2.133. *Interpretation*

How does one have to conceive of the circle of being? What does it mean, and what does it establish? Where does the circular movement of being take place? These questions have partly been answered by our analysis of Hegel's description of his method. Dialectic is supposed to demonstrate the dissolution, foundation and sublation of seemingly independent and finite reality. Hegel adds some explanatory details to the interpretation of the first *logical* cycle.

It was the *Eleatics,* above all *Parmenides,* who first enunciated the simple thought of *pure being* as the absolute and sole truth ... : *only being is, and nothing is absolutely not.* ... Against that simple and one-sided abstraction the profound Heraclitus brought forward the higher, total concept of becoming, and said: *being as little is, as nothing is,* or: all *flows,* that is, all is *becoming.* [49]

At the beginning of the *Logic* Hegel agrees with the Eleatics, who hold ideal being to be the true reality. This position, however, is subsequently relativized through the identity and non-identity of being with nothingness. While absolute being is that which is most subsistent in the objective whole, it is always tied in various ways to nothingness. Thereafter, Hegel identifies his position with that of Heraclitus, and even claims to have incorporated all of Heraclitus' propositions in the *Logic.* [50] Both ideality and what is objectively given are combinations of being and nothingness, and thus *forms of becoming.* Accentuating his adherence to Heraclitus, he writes

that nowhere in heaven or on earth is there anything which does not contain within itself both being and nothingness. [51]

This statement is borrowed from *imaginative* language, namely, philosophy of religion, and should have no place in the *Logic*, the science of pure thought. Yet it serves well in interpreting the first cycle. As our figure illustrates, both ideal and objectively given reality are formed by a unity of being and nothingness.

The circle of being is the most general and most comprehensive circle; in an abstract way, it describes all subsequent circles, and can already provide an insight into the goal to be attained through the *logical* procedure, the demonstration of the identity of being and thought. This identity means, for Hegel, that all 'somethings', the entire world of things and phenomena as well as objective reality altogether, are but moments in the cyclical activity of synthesis and dissolution of pure determinations. Continuing the tradition of the Eleatics, Anaxagoras and Plato, the *Logic* thus intends to substantiate that everything exists merely as momentary combination of pure determinations, and that true being must be attributed only to the synthetic and analytic activity of thinking of the all-embracing *nous*.

Anaxagoras is praised as the man who first expressed the thought that *nous, thought,* is the principle of the world, that the essence of the world is to be defined as thought. In so doing he laid the foundation for an intellectual view of the universe, the pure form of which must be *logic.* What we are dealing with in logic is not a thinking *about* something which forms a base for itself apart from thinking ...[52]

In contrast to the human intellect which is concerned with objects that stand opposite to it, absolute *nous* creates its objects within itself and out of itself; hence it does not 'think' *about something* which exists *for itself apart* from, or separated from, its thinking.

Universal reason, or the all-pervading activity of thinking, is examined by *Logic* in regard to its *pure form (reine Gestalt);* i.e., in the *logical* process, spatial and temporal aspects of the objective whole are abstracted, and any object-like independence is rejected from the very outset. Indeed, from the very beginning, that which is objectively real is taken to be a combination of two opposite universal determinations.

In virtue of this movement pure thoughts become *concepts,* and are only then what they are in truth, self-movements, circles, they are what their substance consists in, spiritual entities.
    This movement of the pure spiritual entities c o n s t i t u t e s t h e v e r y n a-
t u r e o f t h e s c i e n t i f i c a p p r o a c h.[53]

Hegel distinguishes between pure thoughts and concepts. The latter are universalities regarded in their necessary return-into-self. He thus takes 'concept' *(Begriff)* in the sense cognate to 'comprehending' *(Begreifen):* The givenness of the 'something', of the world of things and phenomena as well as objective reality altogether, is sufficiently 'comprehended' only when the first negativity has been recognized as its ground, the second negativity as its return, and the self-contemplation of the absolute subject — which is based upon the foregoing — as its goal. *For Hegel, the explanation of what is objectively given thus coincides with the examination of the nature of absolute universal reason.*

Consequently, the first cyclical consideration has already provided us with a formal insight into the creative and dissolutive thinking activity of absolute reason.

2.14. *Idealist 'Exposition' of the Absolute*

The circle method essentially determines the nature of Hegel's idealism. Hegel calls himself an idealist because he 'negates' reality. By 'reality' he means 'finitude' or 'alleged independence and existence apart from one another'. The most concise characterization of his idealism is the statement 'Everything finite is such that it is to sublate itself.'[54] In Hegel's 'true' ideality, every apparent independence and every finitude is sublated in the *eternally* returning cyclical movement.

As the analysis of negative dialectic has shown, Hegel denies all individuality and independence to what is finite or objectively given; it cannot exist for itself, nor can it justify its own existence. The *one* finite thing cannot possibly be the ground for the existence of the *other* finite thing, for everything finite by its nature has to perish, or *fall to the ground (zu-grunde-gehen)* into the absolute, where it also has the ground for its existence. Common use of language — so Hegel thinks — already expresses this speculative thesis: When something *falls to the ground* it approaches its *ground (Grund)*.[55] The meaning of the expression *'Zugrundegehen in seinen Grund'* (vanishing into its ground) is clear from the explanation given above: The finite dissolves into the absolute so as to be reestablished anew by it; the absolute is thus both ground and abyss *(Abgrund)* for the finite. We do not think, however, that common language suffices to render this interpretation understandable. Common sense has it that the ground exists before what is established, and what Hegel calls the abyss for something exists after this thing. Yet something can be both 'before' and 'after' some matter only when it is conjoined with it in a circular movement. Hegel's interpretation of this expression then becomes intelligible only in terms of the circle method.

In accordance with the nature of the absolute essence *(das absolute Wesen)* as that which establishes and dissolves existence, there is *a positive and a negative exposition,* or *mode of contemplation.* Enthusiastic about the parallelism between the 'course' of the method and the form of activity of absolute reason, Hegel intentionally uses an ambiguous terminology so as to point up this correspondence. The dialectician provides an *exposition* — i.e. interpretation, explication — of the absolute in the same way in which the absolute *'exposes', 'transfigures', 'expresses',* or unfolds itself. Accordingly, he insists that finite structures are kept from vanishing by the *positive exposition of the absolute.* On the 'falling-to-the-ground' of the finite into its ground, he writes:

> But at the same time this exposition has itself a *positive* side; for insofar as the finite, in falling to the ground, demonstrates that its nature is to be related to the absolute, or to contain the absolute within itself. But this side is not so much the positive exposition of the absolute itself as rather the exposition of the *determinations*, namely, that these have the absolute for their abyss, but also for their *ground*, in other words, that which gives subsistence to them, to illusory being *(Schein)*, is the *absolute* itself. – Illusory being is not *nothingness*, but is a reflection, a *relation* to the absolute; or, it *is* illusion *(Schein)* i n s o f a r a s i n i t t h e a b s o l u t e i s r e f l e c t e d *(scheint).* This positive exposition thus arrests the finite before it vanishes and contemplates it as a n e x p r e s s i o n a n d i m a g e o f t h e a b s o l u t e. But the transparency of the finite, which only lets the absolute be glimpsed through it, ends by completely vanishing; for there is nothing in the finite which would preserve for it a distinction against the absolute; it is a medium which is absorbed by that which shines through it.[56]

(aa) 'Nothingness' designates the pure determinations in their function both as results of the dissolution and as ground for given and dissolving reality. The peculiarity of the text lies in the connection of 'nothingness' with 'illusory being' *(Schein)* which is given a double meaning: The result of negative dialectic, i.e., that reality has but the *semblance (Schein)* of being, leads to a positive insight into the *shining (scheinende)* nature of the absolute subject. Thus, the theory of reality as *illusory (Scheinrealität)* does not lead *to nothing,* but to the apprehension of the absolute. It also states that the objectively given finite is a necessary moment in the *reflection (Widerschein),* or *intro-reflection (Reflexion-in-sich),* of the absolute.

(bb) *The transparency of the finite ends in the complete vanishing of the finite; it is entirely absorbed by the absolute.* This proposition already anticipates the end result of the *Logic;* for only at the end of this science does the dialectician come to know the finite as it is thought by the absolute. It does not have any content which it owes to itself, nor any independence by which it could distinguish itself from the absolute.

(cc) Hegel's intention to continue the Platonic tradition is again evident in the text at hand – particularly when considered in its context. The expressions 'image', 'shine', 'medium', 'nothing' frequently occur in Plato, in the description of the sun simile among other places. The idea of the true and the good gives to all things their existence, as the sun bestows upon them visibility and color.[57] Accordingly, Hegel calls the absolute all-embracing subject, into which the finite *has completely vanished*, the idea of the true and good.

Hegel's Platonism, however, is monistic in two ways. He rejects on principle the duality of universals and the multiplicity which poorly corresponds to them. Moreover, universalities which contain their realization within themselves do not remain juxtaposed and separated from one another; in the spiral movement which always returns back to itself, their circles are chained together into one single subject.

It is now easier to understand the sense in which Hegel professes idealism.

Every philosophy is essentially idealism or at least has idealism for its principle, and the question then is only how far this principle is actually carried out. ... A philosophy which ascribed veritable, ultimate, absolute being to finite existence as such, would not deserve the name of philosophy.... [58]

(aa) *Every philosophy* is idealist *to a certain degree*, since each interprets the phenomenal world by means of a non-phenomenal principle. Even the cosmologists are reckoned by Hegel among the idealists, for water, fire and the other elements in terms of which they explain what is objectively given, are not empirical, immediately given or real elements. Every philosophy interprets the world of experience by means of a principle which is *more permanent* and *more general* than the world of experience itself.

(bb) Because of its theory of *sublation* of everything finite, Hegel's philosophy is an *absolute* idealism. *Every moment* of the whole is denied separateness, independence, reality and finitude. These properties have completely 'vanished' at the end of the *Logic*. Nothing remains but the unitary circle of the all-encompassing, absolute subject.

(cc) On the one hand, there is for Hegel no absolute subject which would exist separate from given reality, since this separation would imply finitude. On the other hand, everything finite in given reality has vanished because it has lost its specific nature: Finitude is *eternalized* and deified. This 'eternalization' is not to be construed as if Hegel deified finite things — each for itself; it is rather finitude *as such* which is an eternal, necessary moment of the absolute. This property is not ascribed to any individual thing. Hegel thus denies both reality as existing separately for itself and a world of experience existing separately for itself: Everything is eternalized, is posited as eternal, and will eternally return without any kind of real independence. Everything is a mere and at the same time necessary moment in the perennial rotation, and thus an *ideal* moment of the all-encompassing activity of thinking. It is in this sense that Hegel calls himself an idealist, for idealism and the denial of reality are to him equivalent.

2.2. FROM SUBJECTIVE TO OBJECTIVE IDEALISM

2.21. *Subject-K-F-H*

Although Hegel's descriptions of his method, the example of the circle of
being, and the characterization of Hegel's idealism provide an insight into
the meaning, effect and purpose of the fundamental law of double negation,
the core of Hegel's methodology is still lacking in our considerations so far.
What must be analyzed in addition is the general schema by means of which
he demonstrates the negative or contradictory aspect of any given object.
Due to the parallelism between method and ontic movement, the structure
of the schema corresponds to the all-embracing being. The terms in which
the methodological schema and the absolute being are described have acquired
their specific meaning in the argumentations with Kant and Fichte.

How can Hegel enter into a discussion with these two epistemologists? He
investigates the structure of being in and for itself, whereas Kant and Fichte
regard ontology in the strict sense as impossible. For them, man apprehends
only what is present in his faculties of knowing, and not objective being in
itself. The subjects as analyzed in the *Critique of Pure Reason* (subject-K)
and in the *Science of Knowledge* (subject-F) differ basically from Hegel's
logical nous (subject-H), since subject-K-F is the human faculty of knowing,
subject-H the all-encompassing activity of thinking. In his polemic against
Kant and Fichte, Hegel neglects this difference because he is not interested
at all in the central question of the *Critique of Pure Reason*, that is, whether
our knowledge derives *'from* experience' or from the human faculty of
knowing. This is why his statements about Kant's and Fichte's philosophies
are for us difficult to understand.

Hegel's contemporaries had to struggle less with this difficulty because
they lived to observe the shift from subjective to absolute idealism. The way
for the transition from subject-K to subject-H was prepared not only by
Fichte, but also by S. Maimon (1753-1800), K. L. Reinhold (1758-1823),
and especially by F. W. J. Schelling (1775-1854).[59] Through the publications
of these philosophers who aspired to achieve a synthesis of subject-K and
Platonism, people in Hegel's time had become familiar with literature in
which subject-K was criticized from an ontological point of view.

Today, difficulties of interpretation can best be avoided if one first focusses
on the basis of the controversies before entering on any further analysis.
Although they hold different views in epistemology, Kant, Fichte and
Hegel deal with a common stock of problems. Subject-K-F is subjective-
idealist; as human subject, it spontaneously posits objective reality within

itself. Subject-H is absolute-*idealist*; as absolute subject, it posits the world of experience which cannot exist outside the absolute subject. Subject-K-F-H posits the objective *(das Objektive)* within itself, and determines the content of it. Hegel's critical discussion of Kant's and Fichte's views is warranted only to the extent that all three of them represent an idealism.

The development from subjective to absolute idealism involves a shift in meaning, especially as regards the terms 'ought', 'thing-in-itself', 'identity', 'immanence', and 'matter'. Taken out of their epistemological or ethical context, they are used in the *Logic* for ontological descriptions. This shift of meaning will be analyzed in what follows.

2.22. *Argumentation with Kant*

2.221. *The 'Impulse From Outside' and Immanence*

Kant deals with the same problem as Plato and Hegel, namely, with the question to what extent phenomenal things are the subjects of their universal attributes. For Kant, the laws of science, the so-called 'synthetic judgments *a priori*', cannot have their origin in the world of experience because, in its manifold, accidental and variable plurality, it stands in opposition to the simple, necessary and eternal content of laws. Kant's solution of the problem is dualistic: (1) The unity and necessity of scientific judgments have their foundation in *a priori* forms which, before any experience, are given in the human faculty of knowing. (2) The source of the manifold plurality lies outside the human subject; it derives from matter as given by the thing-in-itself. The thing-in-itself as such remains unknown; we merely cognize the unity of matter and subjective forms.

The laws of *mathematics* are based on the *a priori* forms of space and time, those of natural science on the categories of the understanding. The understanding, however, does not form the objects all by itself, nor exclusively out of *a priori* forms. Its independence is impaired by the activity of the thing-in-itself. Interpreting Kant, Hegel calls this activity, assumed to take place outside the subject, 'the impulse from outside'.[60] His criticism of this theory can be summarized in four points: (a) As the absolute and all-encompassing whole, subject-H, unlike subject-K, cannot depend on an activity alien to itself. It autonomously posits its objectivity within itself. Therefore, Hegel's methodology demands that the ground for externalization be discovered in the subject-side of absolute *nous* (subject-side-H) — i.e., in the unified totality of all pure determinations. This is just a description of the task of the first negativity in the principle of double negation. It is supposed to demonstrate that it is immanent in pure idealities to become objective and externalize themselves. In the *Critique of Pure Reason,* this positing was explained by means of the spontaneity of subject-K and its activity which remained accidental. The structure and necessity of this positing remained obscure; the independence of subject-K as well as idealism itself remained without foundation. (b) Likewise, as the absolute subject, subject-H cannot take in any content, a matter, *'from outside'.* In several places in the introduction to the *Logic,* [61] therefore, Kant's criticism of formal explanations of reality is refuted.

The content which is missing in the logical forms is nothing else than a solid foundation and a concretion of these abstract determinations; and such a substantial being for them is usually sought o u t s i d e them. [62]

For Hegel, the apparently *substantial being,* the objectively given concrete individual, does not exist outside the universal determinations. Manifold plurality and thus individuality as given by the senses owe their objectivity and content to the synthesis of positive and negative determinations: being *and* nothingness, finite *and* infinite, etc. *Concretion,* or realization, of universals completely determines the object-side-H, whence no matter given from 'outside' is presupposed.

These two points concern the *positing* of the object-side-H, and constitute Hegel's theory of the *'immanent origin of the differences'* which rejects any transcendence of given individuality with regard to formal determinations. The world of experience originates through the movement which is immanent in the subject-side-H. The following two points concern the return to the subject-side-H. (c) According to the law of negative dialectic, the object-side-H dissolves completely, and hence is not something *beyond (kein Jenseits)* for the subject-side-H. In Kant's epistemology, however, the object remains an object that is never apprehended, nor is it ever apprehensible, and thus it is something beyond. [63] (d) In several texts Hegel rejects the beyond, defends immanence *(das Diesseits),* and at the same time — criticizing Kant — postulates a transcendence. [64] Again, these paradoxical statements get cleared up in the cycle theory. Through its dissolution into the subject-side-H, its *transcending to the infinite,* [65] given reality passes beyond itself. This means that while the total *whole,* the moments of which are what is objectively given, *transcends* the world of experience, it is not placed *beyond* the latter. Since the 'dissolution' sublates the boundary of being between given reality and ideal reality, any beyondness *(Jenseitigkeit)* is also sublated. Both realities, as subject-side and object-side of subject-H, are the *partes integrales* of one unitary being.

Relying on this solution of the ontological problem of immanence, Hegel rejects *epistemological* transcendence: The entire content of the absolute idea is *immanent in consciousness (diesseits des Bewusstseins).*[66] Whereas the thing-in-itself remains for the subject-K an unattainable X, the absolute whole — including the transcendent subject-side-H — has for Hegel been *known* all along, or is at least *knowable,* for the ideal *(das Ideale) has* externalized and *will* externalize itself.

2.222. *The Method for Knowing the Unconditioned*

2.2221. *Kant's Criticism of Metaphysics*

The forms of pure intuition render mathematics possible; the pure categories of the understanding render natural science possible; both of them render possible 'empirical science' in general. Not satisfied therewith, man strives to go beyond this kind of knowledge and to grasp the unconditioned. He strives to gain insight into (1) the absolute sum total of the determinations which are at all possible, (2) the sum total of all phenomena, and (3) the absolute sum total of all determinations of the subject. Hypostatizing indiscriminately these concepts acquired through subjective synthesis, rationalist metaphysics calls them 'God', 'world', and 'soul', and does not raise the question of whether things existing-in-themselves could correspond to such concepts. Kant's *transcendental dialectic* shows that human reason can merely obtain three problematic concepts, but no knowledge of things existing-in-themselves.

(1) Of the *proofs for the existence of God,* Kant considers the ontological as the most basic because it has the sum total of all possible determinations for its subject matter. This is why the *Critique of Pure Reason* is mainly directed against this proof. Although we can form a concept of the sum total of all realities, he argues, it still does not follow that they exist, since the mere *representation (Vorstellung)* of an object does not imply its existence. The assumption of a thing-in-itself that corresponds to the conceptual sum total is without justification, for it is not given in any world of experience.[67]

(2) Against *rationalist cosmology,* Kant puts forward his famous doctrine of antinomies. The metaphysician asks himself (a) whether the world is finite or infinite with respect to space and time, (b) whether it is simple or composite as regards its essence, (c) whether it is contingent or necessary, (d) whether it is developing of its own or in dependence on a freely acting cause. Since both the theses and the corresponding antitheses can be established, Kant thinks that the metaphysical problems have been posed in a

mistaken way and that they are unsolvable. Human reason ought to be content with provisional syntheses of the results of cosmological inquiry. The idea of the 'world' as thing-in-itself is illusory.[68]

(3) The 'I think' is regarded as a definite and simple subject, which remains identical with itself in its various mental activities, and differs from the things existing outside the 'I'. *Rationalist psychology* bases its assumption that the soul is immaterial, incorruptible, personal and spiritual on this presupposition. For Kant, these inferences are para-logical and unscientific because they transcend the provisional synthesis of mental experience and the results of empirical-psychological inquiry.

Now to these concepts relate four paralogisms of a transcendental psychology, which is falsely held to be a science of pure reason, which deals with the nature of our thinking essence. We can, however, base this science on nothing but the simple representation 'I' which in itself is without any content. We cannot even say that it is a concept, but only that it is a bare consciousness which accompanies all concepts. Through this I, or he, or it (the thing), which thinks, nothing further is represented than a transcendental subject of the thoughts = X, which is known only by the thoughts that are its predicates, and of which, apart from these, we can never form the least concept.[69]

Speculative psychology is the 'science' of an *empty* representation. Clearly, as far as the soul is concerned, it is not even decided in the beginning whether and how it exists. Still, certain phenomena and mental processes are ascribed to it. The judgments of metaphysical psychology remain statements without content because the subject of the predicates remains a hidden X.

2.2222. *Dialectical Illusion*

The failure of previous metaphysics was for Kant not a reason for ignoring its task. The fact that for centuries metaphysics had been striving without success for a generally acceptable account of the unconditioned is, on the one hand, an indication of its incorrect methodology and, on the other, a sign of the desire rooted in human reason to know the absolute. The ideas of reason are subjective demands to combine our knowledge in a unified synthesis. *Error and illusion* arise only when the result of subjective synthesis is taken to be the essence of something existing-in-itself. Illusion is partly inevitable and even necessary because it is only the *belief* in the existence of such objects which causes us to integrate empirical knowledge in a synthesis. Since the synthesis is indispensable for the systematization of our knowledge, we must proceed in the sciences *as if* these objects actually existed.[70]

If 'illusion' will not cease, and is even requisite for systematization, what sense is there then in exposing it? The quintessence of Kant's dialectic consists in the demonstration of the ineluctable incompleteness of our insight into the absolute, and it intends to safeguard the imperative that our empirical knowledge ought to be expanded forever. This is connected with the positive evaluation which the thing-in-itself gradually receives in the analysis of the *Critique of Pure Reason.* Whereas the *Analytic* gives expression only to the thing-in-itself as the unknowable and inapprehensible, in the *Dialectic* this negativity is associated with a more positive task. The matter of the thing-in-itself acquires through the imperative the significance of an inexhaustible potentiality for determination by the categories of the understanding. *This infinite determinability introduces the practical element into the concept of experience:* The matter *o u g h t* to be more specifically determined. Thereby, the antinomies and paralogisms also acquire a positive effect. They impel an expansion of empirical knowledge so as to make possible a higher synthesis.[71]

The knowledge of metaphysical objects is an asymptotic point: These objects will never be known exhaustively; nonetheless, we have to work under the assumption that we can and ought to come to know them. The difference is subtle: That which *we* will never attain is of itself still not *essentially* unattainable.

Now I maintain that ... the peculiarity of transcendental philosophy is that there is no question concerning an object given to pure reason which is insoluble by this same human reason; ... for the very concept which enables us to realize the question must also give us the power of answering it, inasmuch as the object i s not at all encountered apart from the concept.[72]

While there is no thing existing-in-itself which would correspond to the rational concept (*Vernunftsbegriff,* idea of reason), this concept is of decisive importance for the systematization of our insights. Every element of our knowledge is of scientific value only to the extent that it has a place in the system created by the ideas of reason.

Kant formulates the same thought even more clearly in the methodological discussion which directly follows the *Dialectic:*

The whole is thus articulated, and not accumulated: it may grow from within, but it cannot grow by external addition — just like an animal body, the growth of which does not add any limb, but, without changing the proportions, makes each stronger and more suited to its purpose.[73]

The idea forms the *system,* assigning to each part its role and purpose with respect to the whole, and is thus the *form* which informs the whole. The idea renders possible the *organic development* of our knowledge.

2.223. *The Significance of Critical Philosophy*

Although Hegel remained mainly a Platonist, Kant's philosophy — with which he occupied himself throughout his life — had a profound influence on his thought, and especially on his terminology. In detail, the relationship of the two systems can be characterized as follows:

(1) The meaning of the Hegelian terms 'transcendence—immanence' and 'immanent *(diesseits)*—beyond *(jenseits)*' can be understood only in the context of his argumentation with Kant.

(2) Hegel praises Kant for having connected dialectic with the 'objectivity of the illusion' and the 'necessity of the contradiction'.[74] However, his approval is not given sincerely. Kant and Hegel agree on only one point. Both hold the antinomies to be inevitable. Because of their contradictoriness, Kant regards *our knowledge* of the unconditioned to be a subjective illusion. Unlike Hegel, he does not in any way attribute contradiction and illusion to the *objective whole*. For Kant contradiction is the motive power driving on to further inquiry, for Hegel it is the sublation of reality.

(3) Being ironical about the thesis of the unknowable absolute, Hegel proclaims Kant's philosophy to be a medieval 'handmaiden of faith'.[75] To renounce insight into the absolute is to renounce philosophy.

(4) Kant's Critical psychology prepared the way for the Hegelian concept 'spirit'. In it, the soul is no longer considered to be a substance to which the further determinations, intelligence and the will, are merely added *(accidentaliter)*. Kant reverses the relationship, elevating thinking ('I think') to the primary essence of man which comprises and pervades all psychic and somatic processes. In much the same way, Hegel's absolute 'spirit' comprises the cosmic soul and cosmic life in general.

(5) In Hegel, we encounter again the three Kantian concepts of reason. Yet he considers them to be objective, and synthesizes them into a unified whole. We recognize in the subject-side-H the objective existence of the conceptual sum total of all realities. The ideal being of this latter concept results from the negative dialectic, and in every dialectical analysis one of its elements occurs as presupposition and as goal of the movement. The sum total externalizes itself as *subjective concept*. The totality of all externalizations constitutes the *objective concept* which coincides with the Kantian sum total of all phenomena. The unified movement, proceeding from the subjective concept to the objective, and returning from the objective task to the subjective, takes place in the *absolute concept*, or *absolute spirit*. Thus the dynamic form of spirit comprises the two previous concepts.

(6) These terms, borrowed by Hegel from the Kantian doctrine of

paralogisms and used by him to describe his theory of self-movement, acquire here an essentially different meaning. The 'I think' no longer designates the subject matter of psychological investigation, as it does in the *Critique of Pure Reason,* but that of metaphysical investigation. The same shift in meaning is to be found in texts where Hegel, at the beginning of dialectical inquiry, calls the absolute subject an *empty word,* a *mere abstraction,* and an *empty representation.*[76]

Kant's criticism of rationalist psychology does not hold — so Hegel thinks — for dialectical metaphysics, the *Science of Logic,* which does not define the attributes of the absolute subject by means of human abstraction. The dialectic does not assume that the absolute is a 'fixed point', the content of which is defined in terms of attributes which we abstract and ascribe to it. It is nothing else but what is objectively given which, through the negativity (abstraction!) inherent in it, determines the content of the absolute subject. The absolute is not a dead point, but rather a subject, the content of which — the attributes — is *alive* in the externalizing and dissolving movement.

(7) The idea of reason, according to Kant, renders possible the organic development of reason. Hegel, too, adopts an organic development of thought, not only, however, as regards human knowledge of the absolute, but also in the unfolding of the absolute subject itself.[77]

Hegel's systematization is even more radical than Kant's. He synthesizes *into one* absolute concept the three concepts of reason which remained separate in Kant. Furthermore, the system becomes the criterion for the ontological significance of each and every object: That which does not fit into the systematically developing whole is condemned to 'vanish'.[78]

(8) Matter remains for Kant an unlimited potentiality for determination. The doctrine of ideas concludes with the maxim: The world of experience ought to be determined further and further. Hegel opposes to this 'perennial ought' — which also finds expression in Fichte's philosophy — the completely determined idea of the true and good-in-and-for-itself. Kant and Fichte as well as Hegel regard the contemplation of the absolute essence as the supreme goal of human knowledge. Yet, the absolute-K-F *ought* to be determined by the human faculty of knowing: Man himself creates his absolute, so that the goal remains indeterminate. For Hegel, by contrast, it is the contemplation of the true and good as determined-in-and-for-itself which is the goal of knowledge. The *Phenomenology* is the ladder for ascending to absolute knowledge. The various stages of our knowledge concentrate in the dialectical progress of the *Logic.* The process ends with the contemplation of the eternal and original unity of the absolute concept.

How can the absolute-H be both the absolute as *determined*-in-and-for-itself and still developing? This paradox is resolved when one realizes the twofold shape of the absolute — i.e., the logical-eternal and the spatio-temporal. The logical moves in an eternally identical form, the spatio-temporal is exposed in its development to accidentality.

The logical form is the model; the goal of the temporal movement is uniformity with the logical movement. This can only be achieved step by step in the historical development of human reason. The absolute-H is thus determined in itself, i.e. in its logical form, and *ought not* be determined, as is the case in Kant and Fichte.

(9) Hegel borrowed several kinds of contradictions from Kant's doctrine of antinomies. These contradictions which he demonstrates in the objectively given reality of space and time, of quantity and quality, of possibility, actuality and causality are all based on the same combination of concepts that has already found expression in Kant's doctrine of antinomies: There is a boundary, *and* at the same time this boundary does not exist. However, there is a profound difference here as well. For Kant, the question of whether space and time are finite or infinite remains undecided. Hegel, by contrast, holds these realities themselves to be contradictory, and maintains that they therefore 'fall to the ground into ideality' *(in die 'Idealität' zugrunde gehen)*.

The decisive criterion for Hegel's agreement with, or rejection of, Kant's thought is his Platonic theory of cyclical movement — as is manifest in almost every case. Insofar as Kant's thoughts enrich the complexity of his circle theory, they are adopted; insofar as they are necessarily associated with subjectivism, they are rejected or incorrectly interpreted on purpose.

2.23. *Argumentation with Fichte*

Since Hegel's criticism of Fichte is almost identical with his criticism of Kant, it could be left unmentioned if it were not for the fact that the concept of identity — of central importance for the doctrine of self-movement — is best explained in the context of the dispute with Fichte.

2.231. *Identity in the* Science of Knowledge

Fichte begins his *Science of Knowledge* with the infinite 'I' which — unlike subject-H, for instance — is not to be taken as the absolute whole, but as the abstract subject in its function as precondition of all human knowledge and activity — similar to the transcendental ego in the *Critique of Pure Reason*. While this original I is unlimited and infinite, it is at the same time empty and indefinite. Therefore, its infinity is not a plenitude, but an abstract being-identical-with-itself, which is described by the identity statement 'I=I'.[79]

The process of knowledge cannot result from this infinite I alone, for it requires an object, the 'not-I'. Now the object cannot exist independent of and separate from the subject, since it owes its objectivity to its relation to the subject. On the one hand, in its own identity (not-I = not-I) it stands in opposition to the first identity (I = I); on the other hand, it *ought* to form one identity with the subject. Not-I is not-I, and *ought* to become I, for only an object which is uniform with the I can be known. In order to overcome the contradiction, the *finite* I is posited, to which is opposed a limited not-I. The empirical I has the task of determining the not-I through its theoretical and practical activity, of negating and idealizing the not-I, so as to reconcile it with the infinite I. As with the knowledge of the unconditioned in Kant, this reconciliation in Fichte remains an asymptotic point: The not-I will never be exhaustively negated and never be completely reconciled with the original identity.[80]

2.232. *Identity and Separation in Hegel's Dialectic*

Hegel evaluates Fichte's attempt to ascribe all activity to one subject very positively, as an attempt, but considers it a failure: (a) The I is posited. Opposite to it, the not-I is posited. To bridge the hiatus the empirical I is posited ... All of the *Science of Knowledge* is but an enumeration of positings, the necessity of which is not shown. The reason why there is a transition from one element to the other remains unclear. (b) The not-I will never be completely reconciled with the original I, for it will always *(perennially)* stand in *opposition* to the original identity. In this way a certain independence is implicitly ascribed to it; the unity of I and not-I will never be achieved; and idealism remains without foundation. For 'idealism' in Hegel's sense presupposes that all being and all activity, both theoretical and practical, is exclusively attributed to one single subject.

To gain greater clarity about the law of double negation, the basic law of the doctrine of self-movement, we shall discuss these two objections in some detail.

2.2321. *Identity and Separation in the Subject-Side-H*

The I can only posit the not-I if the not-I is contained in the I and of necessity emerges from it.

Just as much as identity is asserted, separation must be asserted. Insofar as identity and separation are opposed to each other, they are both absolute, and when the identity

ought to be maintained by nullifying the dichotomy, they will remain opposed to each other. P h i l o s o p h y m u s t d o j u s t i c e t o t h e s e p a r a t i o n i n t o s u b-
j e c t a n d o b j e c t; but inasmuch as philosophy affirms that the separation is as absolute as the identity opposite to it, it has posited separation only conditionally, in the same way as such an identity − which is contingent on the nullification of the opposites − is also relative. F o r t h i s r e a s o n, t h e a b s o l u t e i t s e l f i s
t h e i d e n t i t y o f t h e i d e n t i t y a n d t h e n o n−i d e n t i t y; it includes at the same time positing the opposite and being one.[81]

Fichte's dualism, the opposition of I and not-I, can be bridged from the subject-side only if the self-identical, abstract and infinite content of the I determines itself, and thus becomes objective. This is why the *Logic* attempts to demonstrate that the pairs of determinations being-nothingness, infinity-finitude, etc., in their abstract form, are identical *and* non-identical. The self-identity and the separation of abstract being are absurd and, therefore, call for their own negation, which is achieved by the dissolution of the separation of being from nothingness. Abstract being, through the synthesis with nothingness, and negations in general, is divided and determined, and becomes objective. The same happens to identity and separation of the other positive determinations of pure ideality.

How can determinations be 'identical' *and* 'separated'? In the subject-side-H they are *abstract*. Abstract being is not being, abstract infinity is not infinite, etc. These determinations are therefore *identical* with their opposites. However, they also are separated from them, since the abstract is that which is detached. For the idealist, what is objectively real is a *combination of determinations*; the dissolution of something is the detachment of these *determinations*. In the subject-side-H the determinations thus are identical with themselves (abstract) *and* separated (detached). Identity and separation constitute the structure of the first negativity which forms the basis for externalization and the positing of the object-side-H.[82]

2.2322. *Identity and Separation in the Object-Side-H*

In Fichte, the object-side remains in absolute opposition to the subject-side. However, philosophy has to do justice − Hegel maintains − to *separation* and *identity* in both the subject-side and the object-side. The *activity of separation* which the empirical I ought to carry out to determine or negate the not-I *must already be given in the objective identity*, in not-I. The separation immanent in the object-side-H finds its justification in the second negativity. Becoming as objectively given, for instance, *unites* two *opposite* determinations, and the dissolution of this unity implies the *separation* of the determinations contained in becoming.

Through the second negativity, the not-I is completely dissolved and turned back to its starting-point, the I. *Separation and identity are thus present in both sides of subject-H.* Insight into this contention is the preliminary stage toward an understanding of intro-reflection.

In short, the difference between subject-F and subject-H consists in the fact that in the former the positive is opposed to the negative, while in the latter the first positivity and negativity is opposed to the second positivity and negativity.

2.3. INTRO-REFLECTION AS THE ESSENCE OF SELF-MOVEMENT

2.31. *The Expressions 'Self-Movement' and 'Intro-Reflection'*

(A) The terms 'self-movement' and 'intro-reflection' *(Reflexion-in-sich)* are ambiguous: (a) 'Self-movement' suggests the *autodynamic* which we find in the elements of the objective whole, in the universalities.[83] (b) This autodynamic is due to the *principle of self-movement,* the contradiction: contradiction drives ideality to realization, and dissolves objective reality again.[84] (c) The absolute whole is a *subject moving in itself* (aa) which is the source of all activity and content, (bb) outside which nothing can exist, and (cc) into which everything will return.[85] (d) Hegel uses the term 'self-movement' also for the *method* by which one gains knowledge of this self-moving subject.[86]

(B) 'Reflection' means 'turning back', 'radiating back', and 'the faculty of pondering, or reflecting on, something' (the faculty of knowing). The *Logic* ascribes these three properties to the absolute essence *(das absolute Wesen):* (a) What is objectively real *turns back* — as the *Doctrine of Being* demonstrates — into the absolute essence from which it has started. (b) It is the nature of the absolute essence to reflect its content into the world of things and phenomena[87]. But the world of things and phenomena — as the *Doctrine of Essence* shows — does not exist outside or independent of the absolute essence. Hence the absolute essence *mirrors (widerspiegelt)* itself in itself, i.e. in its externalized content.[88] (c) Through intro-reflection the absolute essence knows itself. Since every moment and activity is absorbed in this intro-reflection, the origination, existence and perishing of all things and phenomena has but one single purpose: self-mirroring or self-contemplation of the absolute. This self-cognition is the subject matter of the *Doctrine of the Concept.*[89]

2.32. *Determinations of Reflection*

The theory of the determinations of reflection, though difficult, is an impor-

tant part of Hegel's philosophy, for it is the core of the dialectic of this
philosophy. Hegel summarizes the totality of all determinations of reflection
under the concept 'contradiction' or 'the self-contradictory'.

What is a 'determination of reflection'? The term 'determination' has a
very general meaning. Hegel uses it to refer to 'being', 'nothingness', 'infinite',
etc. While these determinations 'determine' *the content* of the cyclical
movements, the determinations of reflection 'determine' the various *moments
of the circular form.* He also calls them 'essentialities' *(Wesenheiten)* because
they concern the *essence* of the dialectic.

The total set of determinations of reflection consists of the following:
identity, non-identity or absolute difference, distinctness, opposition, and
contradiction. Their meaning can be pointed out by considering any attribute,
since Hegel ascribes all attributes, in circular form, to the absolute subject.
We shall give as an example the first circular form of the *Logic,* because it
has already been analyzed above.

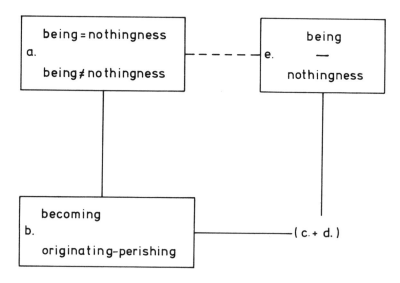

The first negativity of this figure forces abstract being to unite with
its opposite so that becoming originates as the unity of being and nothingness.
This becoming comprises all of given reality.

The negative dialectic reverses the construal of the individual in moderate
realism. It is not seen as the subject existing-in-itself, to which determinations are added. Rather, the objective universal is substantial and subsistent,

and it is determined by the particular and individual in a variable and accidental way *(accidentaliter)*. Accordingly, *becoming* comprises the total objective reality, and forms the identical 'substantial' process which is 'accidentally' determined by more concrete processes, namely, origination and perishing. However, this totality of becoming, originating and perishing is contradictory, for the 'accidents' of the identity of becoming, originating and perishing are opposed to one another. This contradictory structure destroys itself.[90]

According to their determinations of reflection, the circles can be re-presented as follows:

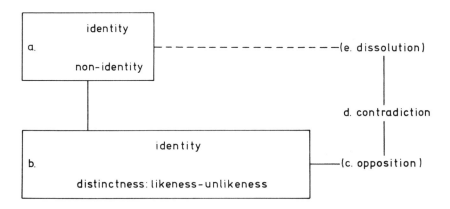

(a) In ideal reality — in the *essence* which in the logical process develops into the subject-side-H, the absolute *I* — the pure determinations are governed by the relations of *identity* and of *absolute difference*, i.e., of *non-identity*. The unity of these relations functions as first negativity, as original source of all activity and externalization, and is the ground for realization, or externalization and 'objectivization', of the entire abstract content.

Difference is the whole and its own *moment,* just as identity is as much its whole as it is its moment. — This is to be considered as the essential nature of reflection and as the *determinate original ground of all activity and self-movement.*[91]

(b) *Distinctness.* Not only the determinations of content — being-nothingness, infinite-finite, etc. — but also the determinations of reflection which are contained in the subject-side-H form a contradictory structure: the *unity* of identity and difference. This is why they externalize themselves, as do the determinations pertaining to content.

Now this external identity is *likeness*, and the external difference is *unlikeness*. [92]

Likeness and unlikeness together constitute *distinctness (Verschiedenheit)*.

Every philosopher will approve of this description of distinctness; distinctness indeed presupposes some correspondence or likeness, and without it any comparison and distinction is impossible. The peculiarity of Hegel's view of distinctness is that its elements are the result of the externalization of identity.

(c) *Opposition* is characterized as

the unity of identity and distinctness; its moments are different in one identity, and thus are *opposites*. [93]

The structure of opposition consists of one more general determination and two more concrete opposing determinations. Together they form one reality. 'Origination', for instance, cannot in reality be *separated* from 'perishing'; the two of them form *one* unity of subsistence. There is no *distinctio realis* between the two processes, because they take place in unified *becoming*. Likewise, father and son, right and left, etc., also form *'one subsistence'*. Hegel views these examples in the same way as origination and perishing. *'Being-father' and 'being-son' are not accidents which have their 'being-in' (esse in) in the substances of the persons 'X' and 'Y'. For Hegel the matter is just the reverse. There is a definite fatherhood which includes the 'being-father' of 'X' and the 'being-son' of 'Y'.* If Hegel's ontological views are disregarded, it is impossible to understand why Hegel finds contradictions in the examples mentioned. To be sure, the person X has many more determinations than 'being-father-of-Y'; but they *subsist in* other definite relationships. Thus, the relation itself is the carrier or subject of the determinations, and not the things, which merely are illusory substances.

How does distinctness differ from opposition? Originating and perishing, father and son, right and left, are determinations which, in each pair, are *distinct* from one another. Opposition comprises the *subsisting unity* of distinctness and distinctness itself: fatherhood *and* father and son, becoming *and* originating and perishing. The different elements form an organic unity of subsistence: 'one identity', 'one subsistence'. *One* being (*viz.*, that of the hypostatized relation of fatherhood) contains within itself two *distinct* kinds of being: being-father and being-son.

(d) *Contradiction.* This conception of opposition is contradictory, not because real opposition has been wrongly conceived, but because its objective reality is contradictory *in itself*. Its structure is constituted by *one* being *(Sein)* with two opposing determinations.[94]

(e) *Dissolution* (resolution). That which contradicts itself ought to dissolve ideality, i.e., it ought to 'fall to the ground' into the ground from which it started.

All that is necessary *to achieve scientific progress* ... is the recognition of the logical principle ... that the self-contradictory does not dissolve into a nullity, into abstract nothingness, but essentially only into the negation of its *particular* content.[95]

The dissolution of a definite contradictory structure does not result in *abstract nothingness* which stands at the beginning of the *Logic* and is both identical with abstract being and distinct from it, but rather in *nothingness which possesses a particular content*. Hegel uses the term 'nothingness' for pure negations or determinations in general. Nothingness as the result of a definite dissolution comprises in itself *all* the determinations of the returning circular movement. The first circular form dissolves into nothingness and potentiality for determination, pure being. Other circular movements take place in a similar way. The content of the absolute essence (the point of departure and point of return of each cycle) is the *unity of all the determinations which are at all possible (nothingness) and the very possibility of determination (being)*.

What is meant in the quoted text by the phrase 'the self-contradictory does not dissolve into nothingness'? Why does Hegel not speak of double negation or double contradiction? The first and second contradictions form a unity: the first contradiction results in the second, which dissolves. The essential characteristic of the circular movement consists in the change of the form of contradiction and in its dissolution as return. *The expression 'the self-contradictory' or 'the contradiction' means the totality of all determinations of reflection.* The sentence 'the self-contradictory dissolves' thus expresses the entire movement of reflection returning-into-itself.

2.33. *Intro-Reflection as the Nature of the Absolute Essence and as the Essence of Dialectical Method*

The logical principle stating that the self-contradictory dissolves into the negation of the determinate subject matter defines Hegel's method of self-movement; the method — as well as the all-encompassing self-movement of the whole — has been illustrated by the schema of the determinations of reflection. This schema is the foundation on which the entire system is erected.

(a) *Reflection in the Logic.* The description of the determinations of reflection occupies a central place in the *Logic.* It provides a retrospect on the route covered so far, for the *Doctrine of Being* shows that the pairs of determinations being-nothingness, finitude-infinity, unity-plurality, quantity and its limits, measurelessness-measure realize themselves, and return, according to the schema of reflections. The description of the schema employed is already part of the *Doctrine of Essence* and prepares the way for its further development. Intro-reflection, on the one hand, externalizes itself into the world of things and phenomena and, on the other hand, establishes *(begründet)* its dissolution or 'recollection' *(Erinnerung,* literally: internalization) into the absolute ground. This recollection becomes clear from the nature of the dialectic as represented in this schema: *all diversities (distinctnesses), oppositions, and relationships which are encountered in the world of things and phenomena form themselves contradictory structures or are elements thereof.*[96]

(b) *Reflection in the Phenomenology.* Once the nature of the absolute and the method based on it have been understood, it becomes self-evident why Hegel in his *Phenomenology,* in analyzing objective reality, cannot help discovering nothing but contradictions. Time is an *identity* the *distinct* moments of which are day and night. Space is an *identity* the *distinct* moments of which are tree and house, left and right. Thing is an *identity* the *distinct* moments of which are law and force, etc.[97]

The difference between the logical and the phenomenological method thus consists in the fact that *Logic* starts 'at the top', in reflection, and *Phenomenology* 'at the bottom'; the schema, however, is the same. Both sciences begin with an element of absolute thought: the former with the subject-side, the latter with the object-side.

(c) *Reflection and the Whole.* Our analysis renders intelligible the most famous, but also the most difficult, of Hegel's descriptions of the whole.

[Absolute substance is] as subject, pure *simple negativity*, and precisely because of this it is the dichotomy of what is simple; or, the duplication into opposites which again is the negation of this indifferent distinctness and its opposite: It is only this s e l f- r e i n - s t a t i n g identity, or the reflection into itself in and from its o t h e r *(i m A n d e r s s e i n)* — not an *original* unity as such, or an immediate unity as such — which is true. It is self-becoming, the circle which presupposes its end as its purpose, and has its end for its beginning, and is actual only through being carried out and through its end ...

The true is the whole. The whole, however, is merely the essence *(Wesen)* attaining its completeness through its own development. Of the absolute it must be said that it is essentially *result*, that only at the *end* is it what it is in truth; and it is just in this that its nature consists: to be actual, subject, or becoming-itself. ...

... mediation is nothing but self-moving self-identity, or it is s e l f-i n t r o-r e f l e c-t i o n, the moment of the I as being for itself, pure negativity, or – reduced to its pure abstraction – the *simple becoming*. The I, or becoming in general, this mediating is, because of its simplicity, immediacy in the becoming, and is immediacy itself. – We misconceive therefore the nature of reason if we exclude reflection from the true, and do not comprehend it as a positive moment of the absolute. It is reflection which insures that the result will be the true ...[98]

The movement of intro-reflection pervades the whole. Its *twofold* negation is reduced to one, a simple negation, since the separation and the ensuing opposition between the negations would also lead to a contradiction. This is why the whole movement is a *simple* becoming.

Each circle starts with the simple immediacy of the I and returns back to it. The terms 'I', 'immediacy' and 'identity' or 'simplicity', though very different in meaning, possess the same kind of ambiguity and refer to the same facts: (a) The starting-point is the *simple* and *immediate I*; (b) the movement returns to it via the mediating not-I; (c) the whole movement takes place within the all-embracing I and forms a whole: the *immediate,* solely self-mediated, *simple* and absolute I.

It is not only the logical movement, but also the spatial and temporal development which takes place according to the given schema. The schema of the determinations of reflection is thus manifest in every objective movement; it also is the abstract schema of the dialectical method, and constitutes the skeleton of Hegel's system.

CHAPTER 3

THE SUBJECT MATTER OF DIALECTICAL PHILOSOPHY

The problem of the relationship of dialectic and its subject matter includes three questions: (1) How is the dialectical method related to the starting-point of philosophy? (2) To what extent is the movement in human reason an adequate rendition of the developing whole? (3) What is the difference between the goal of the dialectical method, i.e. the system, and the objectively existing absolute? Does Hegel regard his system as the adequate and final representation of the absolute?

3.1. DIALECTIC AND THE STARTING-POINT OF PHILOSOPHY

Philosophy starts with *conceptual determinations (Denkbestimmungen)* or *conceptual forms (Denkformen)*, i.e. general concepts, laws and essential entities, which contain an objective image, a *conceptus objectivus,* of what is objectively given. From scientific research and everyday experience, the content of these conceptual forms is *known* to us. It is the task of philosophy to *cognize* this known and abstract content in its significance as constitutive element of the absolute essence.[1]

Hegel never takes things for the starting-point of philosophy. He frequently emphasizes that the philosophical analysis has from *the very beginning* been present in absolute knowledge. From the start, what is objectively given is regarded as the *reflection (Widerschein)* and *transfigured essentiality (verklärte Wesenheit)* of the absolute.[2] Has he simply imposed his theory of intro-reflection onto the world of experience by way of interpretation? N. Hartmann and C. Nink point out in detail that Hegel cannot be charged with apriorism on the basis of these statements. Hartmann even goes as far as to call the *Logic* an empirical science.[3] Hegel does not deny experience, but the independence of the world of experience: He *experiences* that the world of things *'vanishes'*. The first task of the dialectical philosopher is to crystallize the positive and permanent universal traits which are being preserved in the accidental world.

Like the cosmologists who regarded water and fire as constitutive principles *(arche)* of the world, Hegel considers the *universal (das Allgemeine)* to be the building block of everything that is.[4] The universal has a double existence: it is an element of subjective thought and an element of absolute reason. In both forms of existence, it is subject to the dialectical circular movement, though in different ways. Whereas, in human thought, it initially exhibits an *abstract* movement, it constitutes, in the objective whole, a circular form which is sublated into the *concrete* totality of all circular forms. Yet, its first existence *ought* to become adequate to the second.

3.2. THE 'SOUL' OF DIALECTICAL MOVEMENT

3.21. *Possibility of a Dialectical Logic*

Objective thoughts constitute the *arche* of everything that is, whence a law of *thought* – namely, Hegel's principle of contradiction – can also be a law for every objective movement. This leads to the difficulty of distinguishing the subjective law of thought from the objective. Hegel circumvents this problem, and brings up this method as an issue only when, at the end of the *Logic*, the human modes of cognition have become adequate to the absolute mode. While the modes of cognition still differ as to their subject – since human reason is not absolute reason – they no longer differ as to their content. The method, as the human mode of knowing and thinking, can finally be equated, as regards content, with the 'soul', the 'substance', of the mode of being and thinking of the absolute itself.[5]

Since Hegel chose not to analyze explicitly several epistemological and methodological questions, contemporary interpretations of Hegel still struggle with, among other things, the difficult question about the meaning of dialectical contradiction. The solution of this question is made even more difficult through the development of formal logic, the basic law of which is the principle of non-contradiction. If it in fact was Hegel's intention to point out objective contradictions, does not the exact scientific approach of modern logic amount to a refutation of his system?

Even today, the answers to these questions still diverge greatly. Some interpreters affirm, others deny, the objectivity of Hegelian contradiction; some reject dialectical logic because it is contrary to formal logic, others attempt to protect it against attacks by formal logicians. An exhaustive account of all solutions ever offered is not yet available. Our account, too, is incomplete, but it will suffice to show the complexity of these problems.

First Interpretation

Hegelian Contradictions are Objective

A. *Their Objectivity*[6]

A. Vera and C. Stommel compare Kant's antinomies with the Hegelian contradictions; they believe that the latter, in contrast to the former, are to be interpreted as objective. Agreeing with this view, A. Brunswig maintains that in Hegel contradiction and the law of the dialectic govern the world. H. A. Ogiermann, too, asserts

> that this process (namely, the rise and the dissolution of contradiction – *A. S.*) is thought to be the 'own doing' of ontological entities; this is why one must not regard negation as being like a subjective capacity of the knower – it is the ontic dynamic of the very being of what is.

Likewise, R. Garaudy is convinced that, for Hegel, contradiction constitutes the inner nature and source of development of things themselves.

Unfortunately, these authors forgo an examination of the problems resulting from such assertions.

B. *Objectivity and Genuineness of Hegelian Contradiction*

(a) A. Phalén and E. Coreth[7] assert that Hegelian contradiction is *genuine,* i.e., opposed to the law of formal logic.

> The dissolution of the contradiction, however, was its nullification, and the nullification presupposed its actuality; it does directly imply this actuality. The contradiction must therefore subsist in its nullification and, moreover, it must subsist as unresolved ... Actuality then is both contradictory and non-contradictory.

This interpretation of the problem of contradiction by Phalén itself involves a contradiction!

Coreth defines the opposition between formal and dialectical logic with acumen. He points out that this opposition is mitigated by two circumstances: (1) The Hegelian contradiction is not pure, and (2) it will be sublated.

> Insofar as the negation is specified, it is no longer just any non-A which can take the place of A, but only a definite B. The principle of non-contradiction is thus not negated in the whole domain of its validity, but in each case, only in regard to a fully determinate other thing. This other thing, however, remains non-A; hence there will also continue to be a contradiction.

According to the classical schema as developed by Aristotle, Hegel's contradictions are not contradictions in the strict sense, but merely antinomies; in other words, they are not formed in terms of contradictory statements, but merely in terms of contrary statements. Despite this qualification the difference with respect to formal logic remains. A sublation occurs when

the contradictory content is elevated onto a higher level, in such a manner that it undergoes an essential change. The original contradiction was well-founded and existed objectively, but only on the respective level of being and thinking.

Dialectical contradiction exists necessarily and objectively; in the dialectical process, it changes essentially. Being as such is contradictory through its distinction from nothingness and through its identity with nothingness. In reversed form, this contradiction occurs in *becoming*, and in more concrete form, in the *subjective concept*, which contains and, at the same time, does not contain pure being within itself. Contradiction, *then, undergoes a fundamental change.*

Yet Coreth's analysis leaves some open questions as well. Could the absolute whole be contradictory after all? At which point, and for which thinking, was the contradiction, say, between being and nothingness *well-founded and objective?* Disputing Coreth's interpretation of the determinately existing *(daseienden)* contradiction, Grégoire maintains that pure being, pure nothingness, and the *contradiction* allegedly occurring between them *are never objective*, because they constitute merely the initial moment of the dialectical analysis.

(b) Even a superficial insight into Hegel's system speaks against the following assertion by A. Guzzoni:[8]

By existing as *movement,* however, the absolute as such is not there, but is always on the way to itself, and only *becomes* at all times what it *is*.

Hegel sharply distinguishes being-in-self *(An-sich-Sein),* which the absolute *is*, from being-in-and-for-itself *(An-und-für-sich-Sein),* which the absolute *becomes.* Yet, this distinction in fact expresses the most fundamental contradiction. (Our analysis has shown that *every* distinction becomes a contradiction when one thinks dialectically). This fact is also confirmed by the more concrete dialectical analyses. At the beginning, the absolute is merely given, mere being, whose content is mere nothingness. But it *ought* to be all-encompassing being. Analogously, because it is without end and determination, the unlimited and infinite absolute initially is finite itself, while it *ought* to be the all-encompassing true infinite. Guzzoni's characterization, therefore, is a subtle and general definition of the dialectical contradiction. Its relationship to formal contradiction, however, is neglected by the author.

(c) N. Hartmann and W. Sesemann[9] emphasize the genuineness and objectivity of the Hegelian contradiction. However, they unanimously reject the dialectic of concepts that is used in Hegel's *Logic*, and propose in its stead a dialectic of reality as the most successful method for philosophy. According to them, this method is to dispense with contradiction as determinately being, and is to assume only a 'real repugnance' *(Realrepugnanz)* in the subject matter, or a 'mutual penetration of the opposites' in reality. (aa) Sesemann maintains that Hegel's way of thinking differs from any previous way of thinking, because both each single fact and being as a whole are regarded as thoroughly contradictory. (bb) Hegelian contradiction is based on the assumption that there is *isolation* in reality, i.e. 'negation' or 'abstraction', which

posits what is in itself indeterminate (or not univocally determined) as something quite determinate.

(cc) Sesemann denies the reality of this isolation and, consequently, the scientific character of the Hegelian 'dialectic of concepts'. The latter is at best sometimes useful as an auxiliary means for discovering a hidden dialectic of being. Sesemann's concluding remark is relevant to an evaluation of his interpretation:

A limiting case of the dialectic, indeed one of enormous significance, has been disregarded in our analysis, namely, the *coincidentia oppositorum* in the *absolute*. This is justified because a fruitful discussion of the dialectic of the absolute, in our opinion, is possible only when one has first gained clarity about the dialectic of finite empirical being.

Thus, Sesemann implicitly conceded that dialectical contradiction arises precisely, where it is supposed to arise according to Hegel's methodology: in the analysis of the absolute, the sole subject matter of philosophy. If one wants to 'gain clarity about the dialectic of finite empirical being', philosophically, he will inevitably be confronted with its *difference* from, and *thus also its contradiction* with, infinite and universal being.

(aa) For N. Hartmann,[10] as for Sesemann, the Hegelian contradiction is 'meant to be genuine'. That which in ordinary logic is

an indication of incorrectness and would first have to be overcome in order legitimately to claim validity, is in the dialectic quite consistent and cannot be taken as an indication of factual invalidity. If one keeps this in mind and screens Hegel's dialectic for inconsistencies, he will simply find none. His dialectic proceeds everywhere smoothly and consistently, it truly satisfies its own formal law, and does by no means give offense. [Under the conditions mentioned, it is] flawless and without blemish.

N. Hartmann distinguishes formal logic from dialectical logic; the latter is consistent only when freedom from contradiction is no longer required without exception. (bb) The term 'sublation' is to be taken literally as well. In sublation the contradiction is not resolved; otherwise it would not be objective. The coexistence of 'A' and 'non-A' is 'nailed down' by the synthesis of thesis with antithesis. (cc) However, not all Hegelian contradictions are eternalized; some are resolved, hence are not genuine.

Among them, i.e., those which are not genuine, are no doubt many from the *Phenomenology* as well as from later parts of the system. In the *Logic* they should be represented only in small number. When Hegel's dialectic is up to par ... the cases concerned are presumably all genuine antinomies. This is so for good reason: contradiction that is not genuine could hardly call forth moving force and life. –

It is hard to make sense of this remark because the dialectic of the *Phenomenology*, *History of Religion* and *History of Philosophy* is speculatively on a 'par' with that of *Logic*, since history for Hegel is the struggle for insight into the *logos*. Accordingly, his approval of the identity of the sum total of all realities with being in the metaphysics of the understanding, taken *together* with his approval of the Critical non-identity, does not merely constitute a description of an ideological controversy, but it also means the assumption of a dialectically contradictory fact. Since Hartmann did not analyze the opposition between logic and dialectic in any greater detail, Coreth and Grégoire, who hold opposite views, were able to appeal to him.[11]

Hartmann's expressions 'a nailed-down coexistence of two opposite elements' and 'a genuine contradiction that sublates itself and remains resolved' require further explanation. If the analysis has resolved a contradiction *permanently* and finally, then the contradiction is *not genuinely* present in the objective whole, and would be but a moment in subjective thought.

In addition to the authors mentioned, E. H. Schmitt[12] considers Hegelian contradictions as genuine and objective, but his publication, which is directed against Michelet, does not deal with this problem in any detail.

C. *Formal Logic Versus Dialectical Logic*

While the preceding group of interpreters insist only on the objectivity of the contradiction and the opposition between dialectic and logic, M. Aebi, Ja. A. Berman'', J. J. Borelius, I. H. Fichte, E. von Hartmann, A. Trendelenburg, and F. Überweg – all of them opponents of Hegel's system – go further and reject dialectical logic because of its incompatibility with traditional Aristotelian logic.

I. H. Fichte considers Hegel's chief mistake to be the determinately existing contradiction. M. Aebi criticizes the concepts 'identity' and 'distinctness' which underlie Hegel's theory of contradiction. Trendelenburg and

Überweg claim that Hegel confuses 'contradiction' with 'real opposition' and Borelius thinks that Hegel has abused the term 'contradiction'. For the last-mentioned author, 'A' and 'non-A' form a contradiction only when 'non-A' means the denial of 'A'.

Instead, however, Hegel expressly attributes a positive meaning to not-A; it is even one of the main points of his philosophy that the negative is just as much positive.

The statement that the negative is just as much positive is used incorrectly here. For Hegel, the negative, e.g., that of pure being, is just as much the positive because negativity brings about the movement that returns to itself. For Borelius, by contrast, the pure not-being of the beginning, for instance, would be composite and would *contain* being. In this case, there would in fact be no contradiction; 'nothingness' would be identical with being in one respect, and non-identical with it in another respect. However, Hegel expressly rejects this distinction of respects.

In blaming Hegel for having misunderstood 'contradiction', Aebi, Borelius. Fichte, Trendelenburg and Überweg[13] are defending formal logic. Berman" and E. von Hartmann[14], however, attempt to achieve the same goal in a different way, by pointing out the difficulties associated with the affirmation of a contradiction that determinately is. The publication by Ja. A. Berman" is directed against the 'metaphysical' materialists, J. Dietzgen, G. V. Plekhanov and Lenin, and tries to show that dialectic in general, and materialist dialectic in particular, are untenable. By assuming that contradiction is completely lawful and rational, so Berman" argues, Hegel gets into an impossible situation because he must also acknowledge the principle of non-contradiction in order to be able to express any determinateness, any property, or any difference in the developmental moments of the absolute.

Going into greater detail, E. von Hartmann attempts to lead the assumption of a dialectical logic alongside traditional logic *ad absurdum*: (aa) On the basis of a thorough analysis of Hegelian texts he comes to the conclusion that the denial of the principle of non-contradiction is *conditio sine qua non* of the dialectic. In particular, he stresses that in common opinion the self-contradictory is impossible, whereas in Hegel's view it is 'nothingness'.

Nothingness [however, is] a quite *determinate*, not at all impossible, *result.*

Analytical thinkers quite generally regard a contradictory structure as impossible. For Hegel, however, its objectivity leads to a 'not at all impossible result', namely, nothingness. This just means, they say, that Hegel has denied the principle of formal logic. (bb) Debate between dialectician and analytician is impossible; the former cannot be accused of any mistake because of his fundamental denial of the principle of non-contradiction. (cc) For the same reason, any discussion among dialecticians is impossible; they lack a 'criterion of truth'. (dd) Without this criterion of truth, there cannot be *any* knowledge, thus no dialectical knowledge either. (ee) Hegel's theory of contradiction rests on a confusion of actual with possible infinity. (ff) E. von Hartmann considers the *delimitation* of the domain of validity and invalidity of the principle of non-contradiction as unfounded. He emphatically rejects dualist psychology which separates the laws of the understanding from those of reason.

However one distinguishes reason and the understanding ... this much is certain: that it is *one and the same* intellect which, a c c o r d i n g   t o   t h e   s a m e   m o s t   g e n e r a l l a w s of efficacy, turning here to this object, there to that object, operates here in this way, there in that way.

On the last-mentioned point, the author contradicts himself, since distinctness of objects may involve distinctness of their laws. If the boundary between the domain that is free of contradiction and the contradictory domain can be exactly determined, then the refutations by E. von Hartmann as well as Berman" will be invalidated. The task of delimiting dialectical logic has been unsatisfactorily solved by Hegel interpretations so far. As to point (ee), it should be added that Hegel does not *confuse* possible infinity with actual, but assumes the presence of the infinite in given finite reality.

Second Interpretation
Modification of the Requirement of Non-Contradiction[15]

Nink holds that Aristotle and Hegel have conceived non-contradiction in different ways. Hegel's views of being call for a new interpretation of this logical principle,

and to that extent one can say that he built his system in opposition to the principle of contradiction in the Aristotelian sense.

Like Nink, A. Devizzi and L. Pelloux also assert that the changed view of reality in Hegel implies a new interpretation of said principle. The distinction, emphasized by K. Fischer, R. Kroner, G. Maggiore, and D. Sfard, between the speculative, rational and necessary contradiction *(contradictio in adiecto)* and the empirical, 'understandable' and impossible contradiction *(contradictio in subiecto)* underscores Hegel's original view of the principle of non-contradiction, for according to the analytical approach there are no *necessary* contradictions in *any* domain of our knowledge. However, Hegel's qualification of the principle is not clearly expressed in the authors mentioned because they fail to determine the boundaries more specifically. A mere hint at the distinction between the understanding and reason does not suffice as a justification of dialectical logic; for E. von Hartmann, for example, there is no psychology that could warrant this distinction.

Third Interpretation

No Restriction of the Principle of Non-Contradiction

A. *Hegel's Logic Does Not Deny the Principle of Non-Contradiction since It Demands the Resolution of Contradiction*[16]

This or similar assertions can be found in the accounts by W. Albrecht, G. Lasson and W. T. Stace. In them, however, the complexity of the problem does not find adequate expression. Albrecht, for instance, states that dialectical philosophy, though not in the beginning — because of the claim that things are contradictory — but in the end, complies with the rules of formal logic.

There is then good reason for hoping that dialectic, which deals with contradictory things, will in the end prove compatible with logic.

The author overlooks the fact that the wrong starting-point would have a disastrous effect on the entire dialectic.

B. *Dialectical Contradiction Is Not a Formal Contradiction, since the Absolute Develops and Changes from Thesis to Antithesis*[17]

C. R. G. Mure, who holds this thesis, considers the accusation that Hegel has violated the principle of non-contradiction as unfounded. To be sure, the antithesis contradicts the thesis:

But though they both claim to characterize the Absolute as a whole, they are not, in fact, competing for the same position; for the subject which they characterize *develops* in the transition from thesis to antithesis. Despite Hegel's occasionally misleading language, the antithesis is not just the negation of the thesis: it is the negated thesis.

(aa) The dialectical violation of freedom from contradiction is not only emphasized by opponents of Hegel's system, but also by Hegel himself. (bb) Being is not first identical with itself, and only then identical with nothingness. For Hegel, the content of abstract being is *identical with its opposite:*

nothingness. This one statement implies two judgments that contradict each other: being is being and nothingness. (cc) The contradictory situation of abstract being is negated; thereby occurs the transition to becoming. If the antithesis (being = nothingness) is established only *after* the thesis (being = being), then the motive force — attributed by Hegel to contradiction — remains unexplained, for no contradiction at all is present in this conception of the process.

C. *Dialectical Contradiction Actually Is a Mere Opposition*[18]

(a) The *Old-Hegelians* — A. Bullinger, C.L. Michelet, K. Rosenkranz — assert, on the one hand, the genuineness of Hegelian antinomies and — defending Hegel against the analyticians — emphasize, on the other hand, that the term 'contradiction' designates only a real opposition. Bullinger, for instance, starts his book by assuming that the Hegelian contradiction is 'something given in objective thought, in reality'. To specify the nature of dialectical contradiction, he raises the question whether for Hegel man is also not-man, acid is at the same time not-acid, and answers:

That would be pure nonsense. It is not with respect to its external, corruptible reality, but rather with respect to its inner potentiality, its essence, that it [acid — *A.S.*] is the negation of itself.

In our view, there is no contradiction between the self-identity of an acid and the possibility of its being negated in the future. If the Aristotelian distinction between the potentiality and the real actuality of something is maintained, as in the quoted text by Bullinger, then no mutually contradictory judgments can result from an analysis of motion. For him, the contradiction between an acid and its base dissolves into salt. However, it is not clear from his explanation why the relationship between said elements is contradictory.

According to Michelet, Hegel only apparently comes into contradiction with formal logic, for he does not assert the unity of contradictory concepts — like horse and not-horse — but that of contrary concepts — like light and darkness.

Two contrary opposites, like light and darkness, black and white, are both determinate, each is the negative of the other, yet positing its own positive through this very negation. This unity of the positive and the negative is the indeterminate, color and gray in our case, which just as much dissolves both opposites as it makes them subsist: thus preserving their sublation. However, one cannot say this of contradictory opposites. Horse and not-horse are not two determinate things which could form a unity; hence they do not have an intermediate. In this case, the law of excluded middle is valid; and Hegel did not sin against the law of contradiction. We are witnessing how one single word mentioned in the right place at the right time procreatively elicits ever new thoughts. On me at least, it has had this effect.

The dialectical process, for Michelet, consists in the meeting of the opposites, which are encountered in a given case, *in* an 'intermediate', like the union of light and darkness at dusk, etc. Horse and not-horse, however, must not be united. Hegel, on the contrary, even unites being with not-being, the finite with the not-finite, etc. Michelet's account also fails to explain why Hegel protests against *sophistry* which wants to keep contradiction away from the things themselves.

For Rosenkranz, dialectic demands the unity of two opposite predicates; otherwise, however, he follows the law of formal logic: no subject is to be ascribed opposite predicates.

(b) Like the Old-Hegelians, the contemporary interpreters I. Il'in and F. Chiereghin identify 'contradiction' with 'opposition'. According to Il'in, Hegel by no means intends to defend the legitimacy of contradiction against formal logic; he only intends to restrict the general requirement of freedom from contradiction. In addition, the author stresses that Hegel uses the term 'contradiction' in place of 'difference', 'distinctness', etc., and he draws the conclusion that by 'dialectical contradiction' is meant a real opposition and not a formal contradiction. But how can Hegel do away with the general validity of the principle of non-contradiction if he uses the term 'contradiction' in a sense that deviates from the formal-logical sense, and takes it to designate merely a real opposition?

Chiereghin begins his analysis — as does Devizzi — with the statement: a contradiction can never be given or enunciated.[19] The interpreter concludes from this statement that the examples of contradictions considered typical by Hegel are not contradictions at all. Hegel calls those terms contradictory which in reality are mere contraries. This starting-point of the author is not evidence of an objective analysis. If he himself considers a violation of freedom from contradiction as impossible, he must not put forward this impossibility as a general principle for interpreting Hegelian texts. Because of his extreme-realist ontology, Hegel regards the relationship of father and son, right and left, as contradictory. Chiereghin's theory of the reduction of the contradictory to opposites is the reversal of Hegel's dialectic.[20]

D. *Dialectical Contradiction Is Based on Human Abstraction, and Is Not to Be Attributed to the Objective Whole*[21]

For J. McTaggart, Hegelian contradiction is due to the human manner of contemplating the object.[22] This interpretation does not differ essentially from H. Glockner's statement that dialectical contradiction rests on the separation of the understanding from reason, owing to which human consciousness is inwardly split when confronting its world.

But because this world is itself never anywhere else but in our consciousness, it appears as contradictory as this consciousness. Moreover, this contradiction is already from the beginning exhibited in the fact that this world, on the one hand (for the understanding), is indeed 'merely' the world of our consciousness – and yet, on the other hand (for reason), it is at the same time the 'full whole world' ... .

Contradiction is thus said to arise from the task of discovering the *absolute* within the *confines* of the world given to us. However, we do not know to what extent Glockner takes his own Hegel interpretation seriously. While in the context of the quotation he attributes this theory to Hegel, he states nine pages earlier that he does not intend to render Hegel's lines of thought in a historically faithful manner because one could 'not enter them without a residue of Kantianism'. J. Maier, too, believes that Hegelian contradiction is present only in the human faculty of knowing; a category becomes contradictory only through abstraction from the whole.

Starting from the thesis that, for Hegel, the whole is the true, Fr. Grégoire attempts to establish the following: (aa) Hegel intends to demonstrate by means of his theory of contradiction that the realization of some object presupposes that of its opposite. The first realization would be contradictory without the second: the finite without the infinite would be contradictory, like a father without son. (bb) The realization of the two opposite determinations never leads to the formal identification of the two. (cc) In Hegel's system, things by their nature are related to their other *(das Andere)*; if isolated, they would become contradictory and impossible. (dd) Hegel frequently uses the term 'counter-struggle' (*Widerstreit*, conflict) ('I am the struggle') literally: the serf, e.g., wages a (counter-)struggle with his lord. (ee) Hegel's treatment of the principle of non-contradiction is sterile and banal. (ff) Grégoire would agree with Coreth's interpretation of the determinately existing contradiction if, according to Hegel, being as such, nothingness as such, and their contradictory relationships existed as such. Yet being and nothingness are not realized as such, but only as elements of becoming. Logically speaking, they would be contradictory only if they were real as such. That which is logically contradictory does not exist, according to the Hegelian dialectic.[23]

In our view, Grégoire's position is untenable. As to (aa): Hegel not only demands the realization of opposite determinations, but he also shows that, in their objective reality, they are opposites in one unity, or identity, and thus are contradictory. As to (bb): While Hegel does not identify *all* opposite determinations, *every* real opposition, in *dialectical* analysis, is contradictory. As to (cc): Grégoire maintains that things become contradictory through the denial of their relatedness. Dialectic has for its goal the demonstration of the relativity of things. However, we have seen above that matters are just the other way around. For Hegel a thing is contradictory because by its nature it is independent. Yet independence = being separated = relatedness = dependence. This contradiction is not resolved — as Grégoire thinks — by assuming the universal relativity of things. For Hegel, the contradiction of the thing rests precisely on its independence *and* relatedness. *Together*, these properties constitute the contradictory structure of the thing. As to (dd): Does Hegel in fact see a genuine contradiction in the struggle between lord and serf, or did he want to mislead the reader by the word 'counter-struggle', as Grégoire claims? Before Hegel, in the *Phenomenology*, analyzes the relationship of lord and serf, much has already been unrolled in the dialectical process. The circle of the spatio-temporal 'something' has been sublated into the circle of the thing, and the latter into the circle of phenomena. The entire biological nature, including the lower levels — e.g., physical and chemical processes — constitutes the object-side of the absolute understanding. In the section on lord and serf, the question arises as to what extent individual man, by virtue of his *self-consciousness,* is able to evade the operation of this absolute *understanding.* By his self-consciousness, his work and knowledge, man ranks qualitatively higher than the absolute understanding which governs the lawfulness of nature. However, man contemplates and manipulates nature not as an individual, but together with other men. In this society, the lord rises above the serf and makes the serf handle nature for him. The reality of this society comes into contradiction with its essence, since the lord, who grows more and more stupid, remains the representative of self-consciousness, whereas the serf, who *educates* himself in his confrontation with nature, must recognize the lord, who is inferior to him, as superior and leader. This society then comes into conflict *(Widerstreit)* with its essence. *'Widerstreit'* is here taken in the scientific, not in the literal, sense. As to (ee): Grégoire considers the sections on contradictions in the *Logic* as 'banal and sterile'. As was shown above, however, these sections describe the schema by which Hegel discovers in the ideality and in the reality of all determinations the contradiction and source of movement. As to (ff): As concerns 'sublation', the interpreter has obviously overlooked that, in every case, the logical contradictions are sublated into a more concrete form, and *return again* in this new form, so as to become finally a part of the all-encompassing contradiction, and of the equally universal logical and temporal movement of the absolute concept.

At the center of the misunderstanding is the question about the meaning of Hegel's statement 'The self-contradictory is nothingness', which Grégoire interprets as follows: 'The self-contradictory is not'. E. von Hartmann has already shown the incorrectness of this rendition.[24]

After having considered the solutions offered so far, we can say: (a) Dia-lectical contradiction is opposed to the formal-logical *principle of non-contradiction (NKpNp and DpNp)*. (b) Hegel's theory of contradiction makes sense only when the boundaries between the contradictory domain and the domain free of contradiction can be sharply delineated. (c) The theory of the objectivity of Hegelian contradiction is tenable only when, in the dia-lectical analysis of the subsisting structure of being, the contradiction is not completely resolved, but is only sublated; otherwise, the contradiction would only be a moment of subjective thought.

3.22. *Hegel's Theory of Contradiction*

3.221. *KpNp as Determinately Being*

For Hegel — as has been emphasized several times — things are contradictory, since their independence *is* dependence. The attempt to avoid this contra-diction by distinguishing different respects is called 'sophistry' by him.

Opposites, therefore, contain contradiction insofar as they are, in the same respect, negatively related to one another ... and are *indifferent* to one another.[25]

The independence of the thing differs from (and, therefore, is related to) its dependence. A father is father *insofar* as he is identical with himself, is 'indifferent', and differs from the son 'in the same respect', namely, is *negatively related* to him. Or, more simply, the father is himself *insofar* as he is related to the son, or, he is himself *insofar* as he is related beyond himself. Every determination which attributes independence to a subject is thus at the same time and in the same respect its dependence.

The statements which express this relationship always contain an *insofar*. On this point, Borelius writes:

'Insofar' can mean necessary conjunction, and when taken in this sense it is not a contradiction in the Aristotelian sense to say that an object can only be for itself insofar as
it is at the same time for another, i.e., that its being-for-self and its being-for-other are
conditional on one another. If, however, 'insofar' is to mean the same as in one and the
same respect, or in one and the same relation, then it is indeed not only contradictory,
but also counter-sensical, to maintain that the object is for itself insofar as it is for
another; for the very words *for itself* and *for other* express a difference of respects
(relation to itself and relation to an other).[26]

Hegel's *insofar* has been most clearly analyzed by this opponent. Hegel
uses the term in the second, anti-analytical sense as discussed by the author:
something is something for itself *insofar* as, in the same respect, it is for an
other — i.e., not for itself.

In this context, we must point out an objection by M. Aebi[27]. Appealing
to Aristotle, she attempts to show that anything can be 'identical with itself'
and, *apart* from that, 'opposed to something else'. For her, the contradictory
relationship between unity and opposition, which is assumed in Hegel's
system, rests on a confusion and impermissible identification of the property
'self-identity' with the relation 'opposition'. Thus, Aebi adopts the first
meaning of *insofar* discussed by Borelius, and separates in this way identity
from opposition, being-determinate-in-itself from being-related. In our opinion, however, Hegel by no means confuses the two determinations, but
brings them together on purpose so as to attain the contradiction; this is why
his view differs from Aebi's Aristotelian view of being. The experience that
we do not come to know things which are *essentially* identical with themselves, but only things that vanish speaks in favor of Hegel's construal.
Because reality is 'counter-sensical' it necessarily dissolves into 'nothingness'.

By this 'nothingness' — as has been pointed out several times — Hegel
means the result of the dissolution of reality, namely, the universal determinations which are contained in reality, or, in other words: *the sum total of
all realities.*

It is usually shown, first of all, that this determination [namely, this 'sum total' —
A. S.] is possible because it is free from *contradiction,* reality being taken only as
reality without limitation. We remarked that this sum total thus becomes simple indeterminate being, or if the realities are, in fact, taken as several determinate beings, it
becomes the sum total of all negations. When the difference of reality is taken into
more specific account, it develops from difference into opposition, and thus into
contradiction, so that the sum total of all realities simply becomes absolute contradiction within itself.[28]

Even the unconditioned sum total is contradictory because each determination contained in it is pure only *insofar* as it differs from its potentiality
for determination, from pure being. Dialectical-logically, the *difference* is

analyzed as follows. The pure determination is pure and opposed to its opposite *insofar as* it is related to, i.e. connected with, its opposite, i.e., *insofar as* it is not pure. Since this *insofar* applies to all determinations of reality in general, the sum total is the *absolute* contradiction. Thus, the law of negation of negation twice presupposes *KpNp*.

The most important texts which argue for the contradiction as *determinately being* are those in which Hegel describes the basic principles of his ontology. According to his own statements, the fundamentals of his conception of being are identity, distinctness, contradiction and its dissolution into the ground.[29]

Hegel rejects the analytical-ontological interpretation of the formal-logical principle of contradiction, according to which objective contradiction is impossible. Reason and common sense have discredited this interpretation.[30] Thinking reason *'sharpens the blunt difference'*[31]; this refers to the Hegelian 'insofar'. Even common sense gains the insight

that at least *there is* a *host* of contradictory things, contradictory insitutions, etc., whose contradiction exists not merely in an external reflection, but in themselves.[32]

In this text, Hegel not only expressly stipulates the objectivity of contradiction; he also gives us a hint as to the intention underlying this doctrine. The institutions — sometimes state and church are given as examples for such contradictory arrangements[33] — never correspond to their ideal, they are in contradiction with it, whence they change or vanish. Everything that *determinately is* was once an idea, and is now in contradiction with its essence. *Speculative logic, then, is nothing else but the establishment (Begründung) of the practice of the absolute spirit.* It leads to the assumption that every reality presupposes an ideal activity as its ground and, in turn, causes ideality to establish a new reality, because it is itself so negative and wanting. Contradiction, understood in this sense, is the 'root of all movement and vitality'.[34]

Still a second conclusion is imperative: *Hegel is opposed to formal logic insofar as its requirement of formal freedom from contradiction should imply the same requirement for given reality and ideal determinations.*

3.222. Sublation

The relationship between formal and dialectical contradiction cannot be determined without insight into the problem of 'sublation'. For if 'sublation' meant 'complete annihilation', then the alleged 'mistake' of dialectical contradiction would no longer be present in the end result of the dialectical analysis.

3.2221. *Logical Sublation*

To sublate (aufheben) has a twofold meaning in language, in that it means to preserve, to *maintain,* and at the same time it means to make cease, *to put an end to.* [35]

This is one of the many[36] paradoxical assertions of Hegel. How can a contradiction be resolved and, at the same time, be maintained? Again, insight into the circular form of movement makes the paradox disappear. To answer the question, let us once more come back to the example of Hegel's cyclical method discussed above: the circle of being.

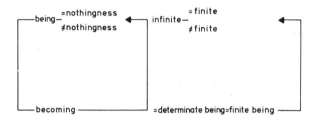

Becoming dissolves and 'vanishes', but not without returning, since the same ideal determinations (being and nothingness) as well as the result of of its nullification constitute the starting-point of its realization.

Return-into-self is not completely pointless. It would be non-sensical only if it led to unchangeable repetition. Through return, however, the whole changes. Since the becoming disappears into that from which it started, it will eternally return: *it endures.* But 'becoming which endures' is *'determinate being,* the stable unity of being and nothingness'. Determinate being is absolute being which, through the unity with nothingness, has been *limited* and *made finite* and, by the return-into-self, has acquired a limited subsistence; as such, it is the *finite.* The 'sublation' of becoming into determinate being leads to the problem of finitude. This present example shows how Hegel forges the various circles together. What happens now to being and nothingness in the new circle of infinity?

The more precise meaning and expression which being and nothingness receive, now that they are *moments*, is to be ascertained from the c o n s i d e r a t i o n o f d e t e r m i n a t e b e i n g as the unity in which they are preserved.[37]

The consideration of finite being ('determinate being') will more precisely determine the significance which *being* and *nothingness* have with respect to the whole. It will show that the relationship between the infinite and the finite is nothing else but a *more concrete* form of the circle of being.[38] The *sublation means, then, that the more abstract circle is incorporated into a more concrete one. In this way, Logic becomes a process of rolling up circles one into another. At the end of this science, the most concrete circle emerges: the logical idea.* Every *logical* contradiction and every *logical* cycle thus exists objectively, but not in the abstract, finite, isolated form in which it is considered, since 'sublation' binds up all circular forms with one another, and unites them in the one rotating movement of the absolute idea.

The *Logic* investigates the idea in its eternal movement, independent of spatial and temporal externalization and return; figuratively speaking, it is the description of God before the creation of nature and finite spirits.[39] *Our* concepts, by contrast, are taken from spatial and temporal actuality, and we are unable to imagine how their content can subsist in an absolute, unified form. According to common conviction and practice, all determinations exist separate from one another and 'for themselves'. The *Logic* refutes this belief, and grinds off finitude and *'separateness' (Aus-einander-Sein)* from our concepts. In this way, it leads to the contemplation of the absolute circular form that embraces in its eternal and unified movement every content and every activity, which otherwise appear as separated and successive in spatial and temporal reality.

The idea ... is the dialectic which forever divides and distinguishes the self-identical from the differentiated, the subjective from the objective, the finite from the infinite, soul from body, and only on those terms is it eternal creation, eternal vitality, and eternal spirit. In thus being itself the transition or rather translation of itself into the *abstract understanding*, it also forever remains *reason*; [secondly − A. S.] it is the dialectic which makes this mass of understanding and diversity again understand its finite nature and the illusory independence of its productions, and leads it back to unity. Since this double movement is not separate or distinct in time, nor indeed in any other way − otherwise it would again be only the abstract understanding − it is the eternal contemplation of itself in the other.[40]

A double and eternal movement takes place in the logical idea: What is united in a contradictory way in the sum total of all realities − subjective-objective, soul-body, finite-infinite, being-nothingness − is *distinguished*, and the result of this distinction, which is an actual separation, is at once brought back again to the unity of the point of departure, so that there is *no* temporal break between the separation and the reunification. The logical idea represents the absolute spirit which externalizes within itself the content united in unified subjectivity, and immediately dissolves it again. Through this dissolution, absolute spirit contemplates itself within itself. *Thus, there also is in logos itself an eternal moment 'of the abstract understanding', hence of the dialectically contradictory,* be it but as moment.

3.2222. *Spatial and Temporal Sublation*

In addition to the *eternally* returning world, the sum total posits the physical world in which its content is realized as spatially asunder and in temporal succession. Whereas the inner, divine world is *eternally* contradictory, the physical world contains the contradiction *always* and *everywhere*. The sum total thus posits its second objectivity:

> The *object* in general [is] the *one* whole still indeterminate in itself, is the objective world in general, God, the absolute object. But the object is also instilled with the difference, falls in itself apart into indeterminate multiplicity (as objective *world*), and each of these *isolated* parts is also an object, a determinate being that is concrete in itself, complete, independent.[41]

Because of the double externalization of the conceptual sum total, the Hegelian terms 'world' and 'nature' are ambiguous. In the *logical* idea, the world is 'God', the 'Son', the 'objective concept'. Its contradiction would be imperfect if it would not immediately and eternally return; through this eternal dissolution, it becomes a moment in the logical vitality. The *external* world, by contrast, assumes the temporal appearance of an independent reality. However, this appearance is momentary, since the spirit does not only eternally dissolve the contradiction within the logical idea, but also everywhere and always those of the physical world. In this way, the spirit reconciles the Son (the objective concept) as well as individual, physical being with their point of departure, the Father.

In addition to the eternal and the spatio-temporal sublation, both of which are *objective*, an *intentional* circular movement takes place in human spirit which is constantly on the way toward a better insight into the absolute. Altogether, then, a threefold sublation occurs which can schematically be represented as follows:

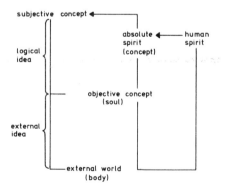

3.2223. *The Non-Contradictory Whole*

Sesemann claims that the Hegelian whole is contradictory through and through. Our analysis of the various dialectical forms seems to confirm his assertion, for we have shown that every element of the whole contains contradiction and, therefore, moves. The ever-returning movement leaves no hope of encountering an element free from contradiction. But how can the whole, which for Hegel is the 'true', still be contradictory?

In agreement with Sesemann, E. Weil characterizes Hegel's position as follows:

The dialectic *'is* this movement' between the train of thoughts and reality revealing itself: it is not designed by the mind. For this very reason the dialectic ends with the knowledge that it is the non-contradictory totality of contradictions.[42]

While he recognizes that for Hegel everything is contradictory, Weil regards the totality as non-contradictory. Yet he fails to explain the leap from contradictory to non-contradictory ('true') totality. Hegel himself describes the totality of contradictions in a very poetic way:

The true is ... the bacchanalian revel where no member is not drunken; and because every member immediately dissolves as soon as it detaches itself, it is just as much the transparent and simple repose. ... The activity of separating is the strength and work of the *understanding*, the most astounding and greatest, or rather the absolute power. The circle which rests closed in itself and being substance, holds its moments, is the immediate, and hence not astounding, relationship.[43]

If all the elements of the whole are contradictory, how can the totality of all these contradictions be non-contradictory? To solve this problem, one has to recall once more the relationship, pointed out above, between the Eleatic school and Hegel. According to Zeno, plurality and motion are contradictory. With this theory, he supports the claims of his master Parmenides, who regards being that is motionless, one and all-encompassing as solely true. Hegel's position is similar: Everything *within* the whole is contradictory and in motion, whereas the *whole itself is at rest in itself* as the circle which is closed in itself and embraces everything. The members are contradictory, since they *'detach themselves'*, the whole, however, cannot detach itself from anything.

The speculative reason for the fact that the whole is free from contradiction is its unrelatedness. It does not possess any 'being-for-other'. Yet the Hegelian contradictions — as we have seen — rest on the 'insofar' between 'being-for-self' and 'being-for-other'. This 'insofar' then is not applicable to the whole. It is only the whole for which the principle of complete 'self-identity' $(A = A)$ holds true.

This principle of identity, posited identity, or identity which is in itself, is thereby exempt from the dialectic; this identity cannot be sublated, since it has itself completely sublated all sublation, all relation to anything else.[44]

Since the whole comprises within itself all activity and all content, it is free from any external influence and any external activity, thus remaining identical to itself. *It cannot be sublated into something else, for it itself sublates all motion and contradiction into itself.*

3.223. *Knowledge of the Understanding that Is Free from Contradiction*

After having shown which elements in Hegel's ontology are contradictory, we can delimit the analytical, formally consistent domain of knowledge from the dialectical.

3.2231. *Human and Absolute Understanding*

A double activity of abstraction and dissolution takes place in absolute being. Both the ideal unity of the determinations in the sum total of all realities and the unity possessed by the determinations in real things and phenomena are *dissolved* by this activity.[45]

In addition to the ontic resolution of contradiction, Hegel recognizes an intentional resolution. While the activity of the universal understanding forms one aspect of the creative and dissolutive vitality of the absolute whole, human understanding *dissolves intentionaliter* — not really, as does the universal understanding — objects given by the senses into abstract determinations. However, there is a correspondence between the two kinds of activities of understanding: both absolute and human understanding dissolve given reality into pure determinations. The universal understanding carries out this activity of 'separating and distinguishing' because the rational and contradictory unity compels it to do so. Human understanding is driven by natural spontaneity to the activity of abstraction. Schematically, the relationship between the two activities of the understanding can be represented as follows:

The universal understanding   *The human understanding* ⟵⎯⎯⎯⎤

The rational, contradictory
unity of the sum total   is the faculty of abstracting
of all realities is   concepts and laws from what is given
dissolved.   ↑

↓   and of judging the world ⟵⎯⎯⎯⎯
                                  of experience.
The objective world
of things, because of
the contradictions con-
tained in it, is *d i s s o l v e d.*   Starting-point: the world of things ⎯⎤

The relationship between absolute understanding and human understanding is explicitly determined by Hegel.

It [namely, the understanding – *A. S.*] has the right to point out contradictions through
the distinction and its intro-reflection; but it is just God, pure spirit, who eternally
sublates this contradiction. He has not waited for this understanding which wants to
remove the contradiction and those determinations containing the contradiction. It is
his nature to remove them, but also to posit those determinations, and to distinguish
them by diremption. The understanding sets abstract universality, unity, in opposition
to this diremption. Unity, however, is just another mode of contradiction, which the
understanding does not know and, for this very reason, does not resolve ...[46]

The distinction and its intro-reflection. In the subject-side of the absolute
nous, the distinction of the absolute understanding occurs as absolute
difference, in the object-side as unlikeness. While human understanding
perceives the differences and dissimilarities, it leaves the rational unities, or
identities, out of consideration.

The text quoted shows: (aa) that the activity of the understanding is a
contradiction-resolving activity; (bb) that *one* activity of the understanding
is performed in the absolute spirit; (cc) that this absolute understanding
is a power governing the whole, which on the one hand dissolves the contradictory reality and, on the other hand, posits it again by uniting ideal
determinations;(dd) that human understanding gathers from objective reality,
which came about by *diremption* (severance), the abstract universal and
opposes it *intentionaliter* to objective reality, without becoming aware of
the contradiction contained in the abstract universal, since human understanding in no way assumes the objectivity of pure determinations. Only
reason can gain this insight through the negative dialectic, since reason alone

sees universals and their absurd combinations, whereas the understanding regards what is objectively real as 'firmly fixed'.

For our purposes, the first and the last assertions in the quoted text are the most important; they show: *Dialectic presupposes a faculty which is related to a domain f r e e f r o m c o n t r a d i c t i o n.* This presupposition has not been taken into account in previous interpretations of Hegel.[47]

What is the function of reason with respect to the knowledge of the understanding? Hegel settles this question at the end of the *Logic*.[48] Reasonless cognition of the understanding does not go further than the position of the mere subjectivity of our general concepts, it does not lead to insight into the subsistence which universal determinations have in the objective whole, and it clings to the fleeting thing-like and institutional realizations of the ideal. The understanding considers the ideal as unreal and does not 'dare' to compare institutional ideality with its realization. Reason reveals the objectivity of ideal being, and what is posited on the basis of its negativity. This insight of reason, however, presupposes the abstracting and *contradiction-resolving* activity of the understanding. *Dialectic thus presupposes a knowledge which complies with the basic law of formal logic, the principle of non-contradiction.* This domain of knowledge has to be defined more precisely.

3.2232. *Dialectic and Knowledge of Facts*

Knowledge of the understanding includes 'beginning' philosophy, all sciences, and factual knowledge as 'the daily ways and doings of consciousness'.[49] We shall first examine the relationship of factual knowledge and dialectical logic.

'My father is alive and dead.' Can Hegel's system be refuted by an appeal to such untenable propositions? Dialectical-logically considered, the being of my father is to be described as follows. My father's existence is contradictory and, therefore, ought to dissolve; it is kept from dissolving by the contradiction immanent in true essence. Factual knowledge is only interested in what obtains *here* and *now,* and not in what obtains *most generally*; it totally neglects the relationship of things to true and ideal being. *For Hegel, this relationship constitutes the essential and only subject matter of philosophy.* It is only when the questions about the origin of objective reality and about the reason for its vanishing are posed that the principle of non-contradiction must be violated. Dialectical logic deals with these problems. It attempts to grasp all-encompassing reason and the ground of material movement and social development. Daily practical life is not concerned with such problems. Since daily and dialectical knowledge differ fundamentally in their subject matter, they can conform to fundamentally different principles. This difference, when applied to the existence of a father, is harmlessly speculative and neutral. But it gains in practical significance when realities like 'democracy', 'socialist world', 'the free West', are analyzed according to this double method.

3.2233. *Dialectic and Natural Science*

Borelius claims that Hegel's philosophy runs counter to the practice of empirical science. He is overlooking the fact that Hegel, in accord with the *'practice'* of natural science, demands that it be free of contradiction. Hegel sharply distinguishes between the domain of natural science and that of philosophy, avoiding in this way any possible conflict between the two.

For him, philosophy deals with the question of whether the source of all content of reality and reality itself are free from contradiction. This question of a purely ontological nature *cannot* be decided *by any natural scientist* or *by any formal logician* unless he were to transgress the limits of his field.

What do natural scientists study? Where does their investigation, for which freedom from contradiction is required, lead? The laws which constitute the goal of scientific research are non-contradictory, ideal, eternal, immutable, necessary, and neither temporal nor spatial. Objective reality with which the philosopher is concerned does not possess any of these properties, for there is no empirical science which attempts to demonstrate the necessity of the realization (limitation, making finite) of ideal determinations.[50]

Dialectical logic shows the general validity of a law concerning the foundation and dissolution of reality. This law demands that the ground of reality and reality itself be contradictory. If this dialectical law holds for ontology, can then the natural scientist afford to employ contradictory claims in his field? His investigation is to yield non-contradictory and immutable laws, whereas philosophical inquiry is to yield the interpretation of *contingent* reality. Insofar as the latter is concerned with the *contingent* existence of the immutable, it deals with something contradictory. Natural sciences comply with the rule of non-contradiction insofar as it furnishes *absolutely certain (feststehende)* knowledge of universally valid laws.

3.2234. *Dialectic and Formal Logic: Truth and Correctness*

Formal logic requires that our knowledge be rational, meaningful, and hence consistent. It by no means requires, nor can it require, the rationality of *reality itself;* otherwise it would no longer be the science of the rules of our knowledge. Hegel is far from ascribing rationality to every moment of the objective whole. Is there a contradiction between the rationality of our knowledge supplied by the understanding (formal logic) and the assumption of the irrationality of reality, namely the claim that there is an element in reality which does not comply with the rules of our knowledge (dialectical logic)?

Hegel's doctrine of contradiction is closely bound up with his view of universals and values, and is indeed a necessary consequence of it. If ideal, abstract being is actually present in reality, it must be there in contradictory form, because eternal, necessary and motionless being is appearing in time, in contingent form, and in motion. The task of the understanding is to resolve these contradictions. His system, therefore, in no way contradicts formal logic, the science which is concerned with the rules of *correct* inference. Formal logic *ought* to require consistency, since ideal being and consistent laws can only result from the *resolution* of the contradictions contained in objective reality. But it *ought not* prohibit that the *realized ideal* be regarded as contradictory.

In his criticism of Hegel, E. von Hartmann comments on the present questions as follows:

It would be equally inadmissible to attempt to apply Hegel's remark 'the formulae which are the rules of inference ... concern merely a *correctness*, and not a truth, of knowledge' — the attempt, I say, to apply this remark on *syllogisms* to the 3 supreme laws of thought, especially to the law of contradiction; for the fixed distinction between correctness and truth would turn out to be just as impossible as that between representation *(Vorstellung)* and concept.[51]

The author thus rejects both distinctions, that between 'representation' and 'concept', and that between 'correctness' and 'truth'. One need not, however, be a Hegelian in order to accept these distinctions. 'A concept' is 'a generality', while 'a representation' is 'a concrete image'; only traditional empiricists will reject this. No serious philosopher will assent to the identification of 'correctness' with 'truth' either. An inference can well be correct without having any correspondence to reality; in this case, the premises do not agree with reality. *It is precisely in this opposition between correctness and truth that formal logic differs from dialectical.* An argument is 'correct' when it obeys the rules of formal logic, and thus complies with the requirement of non-contradiction. Thoughts are 'true', when they correspond to their object.

One can approve of the principle of non-contradiction as formulated by Aristotle without adopting his view of *being*, according to which given reality, too, is free from contradiction. The requirements which hold for the knowledge of non-contradictory, *motionless* and ideal laws and determinations are not necessarily the principles of reality *in* motion. Dialectical logic, therefore, will not have violated the formal-logical principle of non-contradiction when it shows that ideal being is not in accordance with its content, and is present in real, limited objects in a limited and contradictory way — ideal being as such being unlimited and universal! Every real object contains two incongruous elements (two opposite determinations), whence it will necessarily dissolve. *The dialectical way of thought traces the path of dissolution to which all reality is subject, and ascends — in thought — to ideal being which — in the objective whole — will be the result of the deliverance of the object.* This dialectical analysis is fundamentally different from formal-logical analysis which only ascertains and checks the rules involved in arguments.

No philosopher in history has distinguished as clearly as Hegel between philosophy of logic and formal logic, and also between ontological laws and rules of thought.

As regards the real *philosophical value* of Aristotelian logic, it has received in our textbooks a position and significance as though it gave expression only to the activity of the understanding as consciousness and, therefore, was an instruction in how t o think c o r r e c t l y. Thus it appears as though the movement of thought were something independent, not concerned with what was thought about.... The manner of this knowledge has merely a subjective significance, and the judgment and the conclusion are not a judgment and a conclusion about the things themselves...Thought in this sense becomes something subjective: t h e s e j u d g m e n t s a n d c o n c l u s i o n s a r e i n a n d f o r t h e m selves q u i t e t r u e, o r r a t h e r c o r r e c t — t h i s n o o n e e v e r d o u b t e d; but because they lack content, it is said, this judging and concluding does not suffice for knowing the truth.[52]

(aa) To understand this text, one must be aware of the ambiguity of 'judgment' *(Urteil)* and 'conclusion' *(Schluss)* in Hegel's language. A thing comes to be by an *'Ur-teil'* (original division), by the 'diremption' of the sum total explained above; its end, its perishing, is its *'Schluss'* (conclusion), its dissolution into ideality.[53] (bb) For Hegel, too, it is formal logic alone which provides the rules of *correct* knowledge. Yet it analyzes merely rules, and not ontological laws. (cc) Formal logic makes possible a correct argument, and not one which follows the way of the 'dissolution' of things and institutions; the form of movement inherent in reality belongs to ontology. Without knowledge of the objective process, we cannot make our mode of cognition correspond to the objective development. This process will remain 'something subjective' as long as the dialectical movement of being and thought has not been grasped. (dd) Formal logic, as viewed by the dialectician, requires that our understanding resolve the contradictions present in reality; a similar activity takes place in the objective thought process. However, since formal logic is a mere moment of this process, Hegel criticizes the view that there *cannot but be* knowledge which resolves contradictions. Resolution of contradictions is merely a part of the cognitive process by which we grasp the developing whole. (ee) Hegel asks about the *philosophical value* of formal logic and concludes his examination with the statement that it does not suffice for knowing the 'truth'. *Every* logician will assent to this assertion: Correctness of inference is by no means sufficient for an adequate knowledge of reality. Formal logic even expressly neglects the question of *ontological* truth. Thus, it would be misunderstanding Hegel if one were to see in his texts a refutation of formal logic. He merely wishes to indicate its limits, of which formal logic itself is aware. When proposing a mode of thought which conforms to the circular movement immanent in the things, he does not violate logic, but rather surpasses the confines of its limited task.

No one ever doubted, as Hegel stresses, that the rules of formal logic must be observed for the sake of the *correctness* of all inferences. He explicitly emphasizes the significance of formal logic once more:

However little this logic of the finite may be speculative, yet we must make ourselves acquainted with it; for it is everywhere discovered in finite relationships. T h e r e a r e m a n y s c i e n c e s, s u b j e c t s o f k n o w l e d g e, e t c., t h a t k n o w a n d a p p l y n o o t h e r f o r m s o f t h o u g h t t h a n t h e s e f o r m s o f f i n i t e t h o u g h t, w h i c h c o n s t i t u t e i n f a c t t h e g e n e r a l m e t h o d f o r t h e f i n i t e s c i e n c e s. Mathematics, for instance, is a continuous series of inferences; jurisprudence is the subsuming of the particular under the general, the uniting of these two sides ... Aristotle is thus the originator of the logic of the understanding; its forms only concern the relationship of finite to finite, and in them the truth cannot be grasped.[54]

Every science must observe the rule of non-contradiction; to violate it would mean to renounce correctness, *universal* validity, formalism, which are intended by the rule. There must not be any contradiction at all as long as one is dealing with what is separate, 'finite'. The formal rule applies to simple statements, like: Caius is human, and also to the determinate laws of the various sciences.[55] It is only when one gets to the question about the 'true', about the relationship between ideal and real determinations, that contradictions become inevitable, that it will turn out that both pure ideality and objective reality are wanting and limited.

3.2235. *Dialectic and Its Justification*

Like the natural sciences, dialectic cannot completely circumvent the principle of non-contradiction. The demonstration of contradictory facts itself is to be given in a non-contradictory way. A faulty and *incorrect* proof lacks all power of conviction. The requirement that the explication of dialectic be *free from contradiction* is implicitly acknowledged by Hegel when he asserts that the rules of formal logic are the prerequisite for correctness in science. The accusation that Hegel attempted to refute the principle of formal logic by assuming contradictory structures in absolute being *rests on a confusion of the subject matter of a representation with its form.* Hegel would have offended against this principle only if he had declared the principle of non-contradiction to be invalid with respect to the *form* of presentation. He would have violated it, but would not have refuted it. Formal logic cannot be refuted by any ontology. This principle holds good also in its converse form provided that ontology has been *correctly* established.

The assumption of *irrational* and contradictory structures in objective being can be *true* and is quite compatible with the requirement that knowledge be correct and rational. The formal-logical principle of non-contradiction *(NKpNp* and *DpNp)*[56] thus holds only for the *formal content,* and not for the *whole content,* of our thought. The non-philosophical sciences deal only with the formal contents of the objective whole. Factual knowledge avoids contradictions by explicitly pointing out, in each case, the 'now' and 'here', or the respects involved. Factual knowledge, therefore, represents but sections of the whole. It will inform us, for instance, that in a certain place and at a certain moment politician X acted undemocratically in a certain respect. However, in knowledge that embraces the whole, factual knolwedge can engender a contradiction: The totality of this state which — objective-idealistically speaking — is the realization of the democratic ideal is at the same time undemocratic. In this way, the ontology that considers the finite as a realization of the infinite, can also declare what is given as contradictory.

3.2236. *Ex falso sequitur quodlibet*

To elucidate Hegel's doctrine of contradiction, we shall make use of a partially fictitious objection.

According to A. Phalén, Hegelian dialectic leads to the conclusion that 'the true is false, and the false is true'.[57] This contention seems to be corroborated by our analysis: Hegel asserts the irrationality of objects existing separately, because they do not conform to the rules for correct knowledge of the understanding. He even states explicitly that immediately given reality is 'false', and that dialectic makes the false disappear in order to grasp what has first been regarded as 'false' as a 'moment of the truth'.[58] This falsity is the contradiction, and from its presence the dialectician infers the dissolution of reality. Yet, according to formal logic, anything or — what amounts to the same thing here — nothing can be inferred from what is false. Is this principle not a serious objection to dialectical logic? Allegedly, it is directed against negative dialectic, the starting-point of the system.

This objection rests on a confusion. The Hegelian terms 'the true' and 'the false' indicate ontological relationships. The 'false' has only the semblance of being. In formal logic, the *falsum (Np)* in the principle *CNpCpq* means: what is said by the statement p is not the case. This kind of absurdity is essentially different from the 'absurdities' which man encounters in actual reality and cannot cope with. Through his assumption of absurdities in absolute being, Hegel becomes an irrationalist.[59] But at the same time — however paradoxical this may seem — he is a superrationalist in virtue of his attempt to grasp and demonstrate the essence and the necessity of the absurdities. From every aspect of reality he shows its absurdity which consists in the fact that it unites in itself two incompatible elements; therefore, he calls for the dissolution of this unity, which yields a result that also contains two incompatible elements. The circular form does not rid the several moments of their absurdity, but provides us with an insight into the necessity of their existence. Only a confusion of ontology with logic can make one oppose formal-logical correctness to the demonstration of this kind of absurdity. *The assumption of an absurd reality need not be formal-logically absurd.*

3.3. THE GOAL OF DIALECTICAL METHOD

The goal of the dialectical method is the system, the representation of the the absolute in its various 'shapes'. How is this goal related to the ontological whole?

3.31. *The System*

(a) *In the Phenomenology*, individual man turns to spatial and temporal actuality. The goal of the *Phenomenology* is the knowledge of the absolute, which is the primordial ground *(Urgrund)* of *all and every* actuality. Actuality in general comprises logical actuality and spatial and temporal actuality.

Since the subject matter of the *Phenomenology* is both the temporal and the logical, it tends to present the entire system exhaustively.[60] It differs from the *Logic* to the extent that it analyzes immediately *given* reality.

(b) *In the Logic*, pure and ideal determinations are taken as the point of departure. The determinations of any spatial and temporal actuality are considered only in their eternal and immutable form of circular movement, which takes place within the logical idea — that alone is truly concrete.[61]

(c) *The Philosophy of Nature and that of Spirit* analyze the external realization of the logical idea. They presuppose the knowledge obtained in the *Logic*, the insight into the difference between what is absolutely concrete and what is apparently concrete.[62] While the *Logic* concentrates mainly on the absolute concrete, the *Philosophy of Nature* and that of (human) *Spirit* study everything that is spatially and temporally concrete with respect to its purposiveness. These sciences inquire into the *goal* of external objectivity, which presupposes all lower purposes, 'sublates' and encompasses them: the reflection of the absolute in human reason. In this way, the *Logic* is the starting-point and the point of return.

This is also a kind of return-into-self: Starting from the *eternal* and spiritual intuition, one proceeds to the forms of space and time, and returns to the temporal and spiritual self-intuition of the absolute in man. The absolute does not only recognize its content eternally within itself, but also in its externality, in human reason. The *Logic* as presupposition of the two other sciences differs from 'Philosophy', the final chapter of the *Philosophy of Spirit*. While the latter considers *logical* knowledge as a form of human knowledge and as the supreme form of realization of the absolute, the *Science of Logic* is the analysis of the *content* of absolute reason itself.

3.32. *The Development of the Absolute and the Development of the System*

Hegel has been called the philosopher of 'evolution'. Everything in this system has the property of motion or development. There is nothing static. Yet he is not a 'Darwinist'; his view of 'development' is a far cry from the common one.

'Evolution' is usually understood as meaning that 'everything gets better', and that 'there is nothing absolute'. What is absolutely established cannot evolve. If the absolute were to reach a qualitatively higher stage in the future, then it would not now be absolute, because it would be lacking a perfection to be attained later.[63]

Hegel, on the contrary, maintains that the unfolding of the absolute does not contradict the concept of the absolute. If the absolute is to be that which is utterly perfect, then internal self-identity and rigidity must not be ascribed to it, since vitality and development are perfections. The fact that everything moves and develops is not contrary to the thesis that all movement and development has to be ascribed to one single subject. As every animal both remains identical with itself and develops, so does the Hegelian absolute.[64] The only difference is that an animal receives the material for its growth from outside, whereas the absolute in Hegel's system obtains the material for its growth from within itself. An external development, however, cannot be ascribed to the absolute, for, as the comprehensive whole, it has sublated all relations to things other than itself.

A theory of development does not call the objectivity of the absolute into question, but rather presupposes it. How could one speak of a 'development' and of a 'qualitatively higher stage' if there were not a uniform criterion for judging the progress? If it were not the *same* man who first is a child and later a man, one could not say that the reason of this subject has developed. There is no progress without unity or identity. Accordingly, ontic development presupposes an absolute identity.

This is why Hegel regards as inconceivable any historical reflection on philosophy that does not presuppose the *unity* of the absolute spirit.[65] Without a *uniform* criterion history would remain an inane narration of facts. He who regards multiplicity as the only characteristic of history does not grasp its nature and its dialectic.[66] History is unified by its source and purpose: the absolute.

In accordance with his assuming two kinds of movement and contradiction, Hegel also assumes two kinds of development: the *logical* and the *historical.* They have in common that both obtain their movement from the subjective concept and are oriented toward the self-contemplation of the absolute concept. Because of its *eternity,* logical development differs from historical progress. Despite the eternity of its form, logical development is a progression in the strict sense of the term: the subjective concept becomes something *other,* the objective concept. In this transition the subjective concept *gains* the perfection of movement, and in the return from objective to subjective concept the perfection of self-contemplation.

Hegel denies any development to inorganic and organic nature.[67] In this realm there is movement which always remains *identical with itself.* Nonspiritual nature cannot develop, for it does not move on its own and does not exist for itself. It *is* moved as a moment of the all-embracing spirit. It is only in the spiritual realm that there is development in the strict sense, since it is the spiritual which creates unity.

The spirit develops in its logical and in its historical form. Like the logical form, the historical development has its *source* in the subjective concept; historical being presupposes the externalization of the subjective concept. This is not one *single* creation, for every movement and every activity in spatial and temporal being presupposes an externalization.[68]

The historical externalization has *as its goal* historical self-contemplation. In its spatial and temporal externalization, logical reason reveals its essence and strives for its adequate self-contemplation in human reason. This development takes place in the history of philosophy. Philosophical systems are *different* formulations of the absolute which are in accord with the stage of development of a given period and of a given people. In Hegel's view, however, there is only *one* human, collective spirit and only *one* philosophy which comprises all other kinds of human knowledge within itself in synthetic unity. Thus, the *various* systems form a contradiction. In one 'identity', in the *one* philosophy, they are opposed to one another.[69] Because of their contradictory structure they will necessarily be dissolved and will just as necessarily evoke a new formulation of the absolute which sublates the preceding into a higher synthesis.

The history of philosophy develops in accordance with the human process of knowledge in the *Science of Logic*. In the *Logic*, every circular form is a formulation of the absolute; each circle is sublated into the next. The last circle, which unites the subjective, the objective and the absolute concepts, is the most concrete formulation of the absolute being. Philosophy has developed, and will develop, in the same way: *At each subsequent stage, the logical subject comes to know itself and reflects itself more concretely in its spatial and temporal externalization* (in human reason), and is determined more precisely.

Hegel never expressed himself on the question of whether this process would ever come to an end in history.[70] To be sure, he claims that in history the absolute spirit *strives* for a completely adequate self-contemplation and complete freedom, i.e., for its liberation from the unconscious and the physical; yet this does not imply that this goal will ever be attained.[71]

We are only certain, as Hegel states, that the logical *nous* will completely externalize itself in spatial and temporal form. What is this certainty based on? Sometimes he speaks of God's goodness, stressing that we must not attribute any envy to the absolute.[72] The technical reason for this certainty is to be found in the negativity inherent in what is logical, namely, in its abstraction from its spatial and temporal externalization.[73]

Why does philosophy develop? Why does the logical absolute not externalize its total content all at once? In its logical circular form, this content is for Hegel fully concrete: this circular form combines all possible content in an inseparable unity. Logical realization (the objective concept) does not permit any separation; return-into-self immediately and eternally follows upon realization. *The historical externalizations, however, are necessarily separate in space and successive in time.*

In all its forms, therefore, the goal of the dialectical method in general is the grasping of the absolute being in its most concrete circular form.

PART II

DIALECTIC AND METAPHYSICS

DIALECTIC AND METAPHYSICS

To analyze agreement and opposition between Hegelian and metaphysical methodology is very important for gaining insight both into Hegel's philosophy and that of today, for in his main work, the *Logic*, Hegel criticizes traditional metaphysics in order to replace it with a new form of metaphysics. The most influential representatives of contemporary non-analytic philosophy take this criticism of traditional metaphysical ideology as their starting-point. Heidegger, for instance, makes his dialectic subservient to metaphysics and ontology so that, along with Hegel, he can 'bid farewell' to these sciences. In his criticism of Confucianism, Mao Tse-tung relies on Hegel, but reproaches him for his metaphysical tendencies. Soviet philosophers, too, praise Hegel for his refutation of all traditional 'metaphysics', and at the same time they blame him because of his new form of metaphysics. With them the term 'metaphysics' becomes even more ambiguous, because they intensively criticize positivism, which rejects all metaphysics. In Marcuse's personalistic Marxism, the term is just as misleading as in Soviet philosophy, since he is critically opposed to the same positions. Sophisticated criticism of 'metaphysics' and the terminological complications associated with it started to some extent with Kant, but began in earnest with Hegel.

'METAPHYSICS' – A PHILOSOPHICAL DISCIPLINE

1.1. 'METAPHYSICS'

Andronicus of Rhodes (70 B.C.) gives to the sixth book of his collection of Aristotle's works the title 'The Post-Physical' *(ta meta ta fysika),* since it follows the book of physics *(fysike akroasis).* It is only since the late Middle Ages that *all of* philosophy or one of its disciplines is designated by Andronicus' term. Aristotle (384-322 B.C.) himself speaks of 'wisdom' *(sofia),* 'first philosophy' *(prote filosofike)* or 'theology' *(theologike).*[1] For him, this science deals with being *qua* being. He calls it 'first philosophy' because it investigates the eternal and *first* causes and principles of being,[2] and he sometimes refers to it by the title 'theology' because he considers God as one of the first causes.[3]

Aristotle distinguishes the objects of the sciences in terms of their independence and with respect to their relationship to motion: The science of nature deals with movable and independent being, mathematics with immobile and dependent being, and first philosophy which immobile and independent being which is not subject to any movement. For Aristotle, it is thus absolute being and essence, the cause of all that is, which is 'metaphysical'.[4]

In defining the subject matter of first philosophy, he speaks, on the one hand, of 'being *qua* being' and, on the other, of 'first causes'. Are there for him two kinds of subject matter? Does his characterization anticipate the rationalist distinction between ontology and natural theology? Although the Peripatetic defines the subject matter in two ways, it would be incorrect to attribute to him a double metaphysics. Being *qua* being in the absolute sense is God, the explanatory ground for the subsistence of being. Without this discussion of the first causes, the general study of being would remain meaningless.[5]

Although Thomas Aquinas (1225-1274), in his commentary on Aristotle's metaphysics, insists that *one and the same* science study both the separated substances, i.e. the essences in divine thought, and being in general, he is accused by S. Moser of having laid the basis for the rationalist view of 'metaphysics' as a *trans*physical science. By his doctrine of *analogia entis,* Thomas is said to have saved metaphysics from a pantheistic interpretation, but at the same time, to have separated absolute being from physical being, and transferred it into a world beyond.[6]

Thomas Aquinas attempts to explain why we cannot come to know essences except in their immobile and eternal original source. For him, this fact is due to the nature of scientific knowledge, which is restricted to the necessary, which is also immobile and immutable.[7]

While empiricists assume a negative attitude toward metaphysics, rationalists attribute to this science a central significance. R. Descartes (1596-1650), through his chief work *Meditationes de prima philosophia* (1641), and G. W. Leibniz (1646-1716), through his work *De primae philosophiae emendatione et notione substantiae* (1694), restore to honor the Aristotelian term 'first philosophy'. For Descartes, it is both the science of the supreme and indubitably established principles and that of the immaterial objects: God and soul. For Leibniz, by contrast, it deals with being as such and with first being. In the system of B. de Spinoza (1632-1677), metaphysics constitutes a part of ethics.[8] C. Wolff (1679-1754), through his division of metaphysics into ontology, natural theology, cosmology, and rational psychology, became the originator of the separation of the study of being from that of the absolute causes.[9]

Impressed by the multiplicity of differences of opinion in the history of metaphysics, rationalists seek a new method for this science. Descartes founds his system on assertions that are established beyond doubt – for example, *'cogito, ergo sum'* – and which are not doubted by anyone.[10] Leibniz, Wolff, and Spinoza design methods that conform to mathematics.[11] Hegel in part continues this tradition which searches for an exact method.

For I. Kant (1724-1804), metaphysics derives from an inborn desire to gain insight into God, world, and soul.[12] This aspiration can either degenerate into sophistry or develop into a critical mode of thought. In this way, the term acquires a positive and a negative sense. (a) *Dogmatic,* or rationalist, metaphysics judges objects which exist in themselves; it is 'transcendent' and 'transphysical', since it 'flies beyond' the limits of our experience (of *physics*) without sufficient scientific justification.[13] (b) *Critical* metaphysics, i.e. Kant's own, deals with the first principles of our knowledge, and renounces insight into an absolute existing-in-itself.

All true metaphysics is taken from the essential nature of the faculty of thinking itself and is by no means therefore invented, because it is not borrowed from experience, but contains the pure operations of thought, and hence contains concepts and principles *a priori*, which first of all bring the manifold of *empirical representations* into lawful connection, whereby this manifold can become *empirical knowledge,* i.e. experience.[14]

Thus Kant, reduces metaphysics to a critique of knowledge; it is only concerned with epistemological problems and attempts to show that it is impossible to make any reasonable statement about objects-in-themselves.

In Hegel, we again encounter the two senses of 'metaphysics' mentioned, though with some modifications. We shall see how and why he – continuing the ancient tradition – restores ontology and natural theology as integral parts of dialectical-logical metaphysics. Partially agreeing with Kant, he calls this metaphysics a logic.

1.2. THE LOGIC IS A METAPHYSICS

1.21. *The Metaphysical Content of the Logic*

In the catalogue of the university at Berlin, Hegel announced the topics of the *Logic* under the title 'Logic and Metaphysics'.[15] In many texts he calls the logic a metaphysics;[16] in others he calls it a rational theology.[17] Are ontology and natural theology separate sciences in their own right in his system – as in Wolff's system before him? Is the *Logic* merely a rational theology, or does it also include ontology?

In the 'General Division of Logic' we read that this science is divided into two parts:
(1) *objective* logic takes the place of all previous metaphysics and includes ontology – 'that part of this metaphysics' which investigates 'the nature of *ens* in general'.

Furthermore, objective logic also comprises 'the rest of metaphysics' which deals with the forms of thought: God, world, soul.

(2) The subject matter of *subjective* logic is the concept; the concept is 'the essence which has sublated its relation to being or its illusory being, and in its determinations is no longer external but subjective – free, independent and self-determining, or rather it is the *subject* itself.'[18]

The description of the circular forms pertaining to being, infinity, unity, quantity, and measurelessness, that is, the *Doctrine of Being,* takes the place of all previous *ontology.* This part elucidates the concept of an absolute being ('God') which realizes its content through self-negation and which, in each circle, is restored through the negation of the realization.

The *Doctrine of Essence* shows that this theory does not only apply to the afore-mentioned determinations, but also to the 'world' of things and phenomena. The absolute 'soul' comprises in one unity the absolute essence together with its externalization.

After finding that nothing can exist independently of the absolute being, and that this being, together with its externalization, forms the all-embracing subject, one can proceed to the *Doctrine of the Concept.*

Hegel, while distinguishing ontology (doctrine of being) from natural theology (doctrine of essence), does not regard them as independent fields:

both of them form part of the unified science of *logos*. Ontology is sublated into theology, and theology into the doctrine of the concept.

1.22. Why Does Hegel Call His Metaphysics 'Logic'?

1.221. Kant's Influence

In his justification of the idea that metaphysics is to be a critical logic, Hegel appeals to Kant.

The latter has 'already turned *metaphysics* into *logic*', without, however, bridging the opposition between subject and object.[19]

The meaning of this assertion, which contains both agreement and rejection, is not immediately understandable.

The transcendental logic studies the cognitive conditions of experience, which are from the outset given in the understanding as categories (transcendental analytic) or in reason as ideas (transcendental dialectic). As noted, Kant considers this logic as a 'metaphysics'; today one would call it a 'metaphysics of knowledge'. On the one hand, Hegel approves of this Kantian interpretation of 'metaphysics': it is to be a science of the conditions of knowledge. On the other hand, he stresses that it is not the human cognitive faculty, but solely *absolute* reason which contains the conditions of the world of experience in its subject-side. This is why *metaphysics* primarily has to deal with the conditions, presuppositions, positings and dissolutions by means of which absolute reason creatively thinks the *world* of experience.

Kant was unable to bridge the opposition between subject and object, and did not advance beyond the position of subjective-idealist and epistemological transcendence. Hegel's *Logic,* however, shows that what is objectively given constitutes the object-side of absolute reason and exists solely by being posited by the subject-side. Objective actuality is *subjective*, i.e., it is totally immanent in the absolute subject. Everything is rational in a twofold sense, for there exists nothing outside all-encompassing reason, and nothing is unknowable to human reason. Thus, the remark about Kant's logic is to be understood as follows. Kant already elevated metaphysics to the status of logic, and dissolved the theory of being into a theory of knowing. However, he was unable to advance beyond the merely subjective-human mode of knowing, and considered the transition from human thinking to an all-comprehensive thinking as impossible, because the opposition of subject and object appeared to him as absolute. Hegel's metaphysics, the *Science of Logic*, is thus Kant's 'metaphysics of knowledge', or 'logic', transferred to the ontological level.

1.222. 'Logic' – 'Logos'

Metaphysics is the science of the *logos,* the absolute universal reason. Several texts indicate that, among other things, it was the term *logos* which caused Hegel to call his metaphysics (doctrine of *logos*) a *logic.*[20]

1.223. *The Metaphysical is Logical*

Logical Being is being in thought. Yet for Hegel, things exist as moments of absolute thought. Therefore, their existence is logical being. It is not foreign and extrinsic to them to be thought, known, and judged as a moment existing in the absolute subject.

Moderate realists sharply distinguish between being and thought, between the ontic and the logical. They believe that things can be ascribed only ontic relationships, and no logical relationships, since it is foreign and extrinsic to things to be known and thought by a subject.

In *Hegel's system,* these matters are changed: Since things are moments of *thought*, it is proper to them to appear both in ontic and in logical relationships. Metaphysics, the science of being, thus 'coincides' with logic, the science concerning the laws of absolute thought.[21]

1.224. *'Sublation' of Metaphysics of Being into Logic*

Kant's criticism of the metaphysics of being has no doubt had an immense influence on Western thought. In his book *On the Foundation of Ontology*, N. Hartmann asserts:

Old metaphysics after all was a discipline of delimited content: God, soul, the totality of the world were its subject matter. This conception persisted from ancient times up to Kant. Yet it was this metaphysics which had to give way to the critique of knowledge. It ... never stood on solid ground.[22]

With his *Logic,* Hegel intends to undermine this significance of the Kantian critique and, at the same time, to render rationalist metaphysics of being more scientific by incorporating the positive elements of Kant's logic into his new form of metaphysics. This presupposes a common basis of discussion.

We encounter here an example of Hegel's tendency to concede a limited validity to any thesis advocated in the history of philosophy. The significance of this tendency is most evident in the present case. Through limited agreement, he provides for a basis common to his and former systems, and thus for the possibility of coming to terms with them and 'sublating' them. Accordingly, he welcomes the Kantian endeavor to dissolve metaphysics of being into a theory of knowledge. But in contrast to Kant, he claims that to sublate metaphysics of being is not to nullify it; it remains intact as the necessary stage in the comprehension of the concept. Hegel admits that things as such cannot be the subjects of their determinations and laws, and that determinations and laws have their objectivity only within some faculty of knowing. But this does not amount to a refutation of realist Platonism in epistemology or of absolute-idealist ontology. The subject whose moments of thought constitute things is the absolute whole and not the human cognitive faculty.

It is the endeavor to synthesize and sublate rationalism and Kantianism which causes Hegel to call his metaphysics a logic. It is the science which 'sublates' both traditional metaphysics and transcendental logic.

1.225. The Demythologizing of Metaphysics

As is clear from his treatment of Plato's philosophy, for instance, Hegel considers mythological language as unsuitable for expressing speculative thought. Metaphysics should not make use of any language of imagination, since it studies objects of thought, and not objects of imagination. We encounter here another reason why he called his metaphysics 'logic'. He wants to indicate that his metaphysics is no longer concerned with the traditional intuitive and religious problems, but rather with the concepts and laws of science.

The *point of departure* of the 'logic' is completely non-religious. It starts from the categories with which all human thought operates, and analyzes their necessary connections. The 'logical' *problems* are equally non-religious in character. They concern the comprehension of the logical relationships which are immanent in things. The intention is to comprehend the all-comprising soul as the vital pulse and ground of movement in perceptible reality;[23] an edifying effect is in no way intended.

Hegel at times speaks of God in order to facilitate insight into the subject matter of logic by means of religious language.[24] This image, however, is not used as an end in itself but solely as a means: he wants to educate the reader to grasp the absolute through pure thought, not to grasp its mere fanciful image. He expressly excludes the imaginative representations 'God', 'world', and 'soul' from dialetical-logical thought.[25] Although the intention of the *Logic* is non-religious, it does not remain without significance for the philosophical analysis of religion. Hegel even blames Kantian logic for not possessing this property. How is this possible? How can the *Logic*, on the one hand, abstract from religious problems altogether and, on the other, be of relevance for them? This paradox is resolved as follows: *The Logic* takes over from rational theology the task of investigating absolute being, the absolute essence and the absolute subject by means of pure thought, and thus without use of the faculty of imagination. In this way, rational theology has been elevated to a discipline concerning pure thought, an absolute logic. *The Philosophy of Religion* receives in Hegel's system the rational-theological task of comparing the absolute of thought with the absolute of imagination (e.g., with the God of Christianity).[26] Hegel thus strives, on the one hand, for a purely scientific and non-religious investigation of the absolute and, on the other, for an objective evaluation of religions, the absolute of science becoming the criterion of this evaluation. This method has been assessed in diverse ways by interpreters. For C. Bruaire, J. Hoffmeister, and G. Lasson, it signifies the supreme defense of Christianity, whereas for R. Garaudy, A. Kojève, and J. Kruithof, it signifies an undermining of Christianity; F. Grégoire thinks that Hegel's system will lead to a synthesis of all major world religions.[27]

The *Science of Logic*, then, is not a science of God, as former metaphysics had been, but of the objective relationships between the given contents of thought as such. This is why it is named 'logic', and not 'metaphysics'.

1.23. *Does Dialectical Metaphysics Replace Formal Logic?*

1.231. *'Ordinary Logic'*

In contemporary understanding, logic is the theory of the rules for correct inference, and not a theory for the *formation* of adequate concepts and judgments on matters of fact:[28] Logic is not epistemology. It is very doubtful whether Hegel was familiar with this interpretation. In any case, his expression 'ordinary logic' has nothing in common with this interpretation, for he understands by it Kantian logic or sometimes even the common view that things exist in themselves.[29] Yet these issues are ontological and epistemological, and hence not logical according to the modern view.

1.232. *'Formal Logic'*

At times, Hegel employs the term 'formal logic'.[30] Could he have identified it with 'metaphysics of being' after all? This question has partly been answered above when we dealt with the relationship of formal and dialectical contradictions. We have shown that Hegel acknowledges the value of formal logic for everyday experience, for the non-philosophical sciences, and even for the form of presenting dialectical-logical thought. If one leaves the principle of non-contradiction intact for the knowledge of the understanding, only a vanishingly small *content* of dialectical-logical thought does not comply with the requirement *p/-p*. In fact, Hegel rejects only the transferring of this rule from the domain of formal logic to that of ontology. The rule of thought pertaining to the understanding is not a law of being. Dialectical-metaphysical logic thus by no means absorbs the domain of formal logic as construed today. The principle of non-contradiction *as* a formal-logical rule is not at all refuted or touched by the assumption of irrational structures in objective reality. For this reason, the rule needs to be discussed and justified in its own context. It is true that Hegel himself holds the view that his dialectic stands in opposition to formal logic. As we have shown, however, he only rejects a purely analytical conception of being based on the rules of *formal logic*.

1.233. *Hegel's Logic Is a Metaphysics of Being, and a Metaphysics of Knowledge Based Thereon*

Hegel at times speaks of rules and laws that prescribe how one 'arrives at the truth', i.e., how one attains adequate knowledge of the absolute. Are these the same kind of rules which are the subject matter of formal logic as it is understood today? What was meant by 'laws and rules of logic' in Hegel's time?

> ... for example, that one must think out and test what one reads in books or hears by word of mouth; that when one's sight is not good one should help one's eyes by wearing spectacles. ...[31]

Dialectical logic does away with *these* kinds of rules and investigates the abstract, ideal, real, actual, objective, and absolute content of our concepts and judgments. It is not concerned with the method of *correct* inference, but with the absolute objectivity of our knowledge, that is, an epistemological problem. This critique of knowledge is based on the study of the forms of the absolute in itself, that is, an ontology, or metaphysics of being.

1.3. HEGEL'S ENTIRE SYSTEM IS A METAPHYSICS

According to rationalist methodology, metaphysics of being comprises the study of being as such (ontology), that of absolute being (natural theology), that of cosmic being (cosmology), and that of mental being (psychology). Yet Hegel's *Logic* is an ontology, a natural theology, and, in a certain sense, also a cosmology and psychology. The 'soul', however, is viewed in it as absolute spirit and is therefore no longer identical with the subject matter of former rationalist psychology. The 'world', too, is only considered in its 'eternal' logical form in the *Logic*. This science does not deal with the problems of its temporality and spatiality. This is why two other sciences appear in addition to the *Logic:* the *Philosophy of Nature* and the *Philosophy of Spirit.*

All parts of rationalist metaphysics are thus included in Hegel's system. Their inseparable unity in the new system rests on its absolutely monist interpretation of being according to which the subject matter of every science exists only as a partial aspect of the absolute whole.

CHAPTER 2

METAPHYSICAL METHOD IN GENERAL

In the first chapter of this part it has been shown that Hegel by no means denies the scientific character of metaphysical problems. Aside from his use of the term in the positive sense, however, Hegel also frequently uses 'metaphysics' in a critical sense, as designating an out-dated method of obtaining knowledge about the absolute.[1]

By 'older metaphysics' Hegel means the thought of Greek antiquity, especially that of Anaxagoras, Plato and Aristotle.[2] This metaphysics receives by him a much more positive evaluation than the 'metaphysics of the understanding' of the rationalists: Descartes, Wolff, Spinoza, Malebranche, Leibniz, etc.[3] Medieval metaphysics is not deemed worthy of any serious discussion.[4] It is for him pure theology, a 'formless droning of ringing bells, or a warm nebulous cloud, a musical kind of thinking'.[5]

We shall first analyze the positive value attached by Hegel to the method of the metaphysics of the understanding (2.1), and subsequently turn to his criticism of this method (2.2).

2.1. POSITIVE ELEMENTS IN THE METHOD OF THE
METAPHYSICS OF THE UNDERSTANDING

2.11. The 'View of the Understanding'

It is however only in reference to the history of philosophy that this metaphysics can be said to *belong to the past;* for itself it can be found at any and all times as the view which the *abstract understanding* takes of objects of reason.[6]

The understanding is the cognitive faculty of distinguishing. Its distinctions are by no means denied or questioned by reason, in spite of the tendency of reason to consider everything from a unified viewpoint. Indeed, contradiction is based precisely on the unity of identity and distinctness; yet non-identity, distinctness and opposition are objects of the understanding.

To give an example, reason does not negate the distinction made by the understanding of the finite from the infinite. Apart from this difference recognized by the understanding, however, reason stresses that it is impossible that these determinations exist separated from one another. In each case, reason penetrates to the unity of subsistence of the determinations distinguished by the understanding. The difference between the world of things and the absolute essence – to give another example – belongs also to the domain of objects of the understanding, and is by no means denied by Hegel.[7] Reason elucidates the impossibility that the world of things exists outside absolute being. This necessary unity does not stand in opposition to the difference, but rather presupposes it. How could one demonstrate the necessary unity of subsistence of two elements without first distinguishing them? Hegel's dialectic, then, is not opposed to analytical thought, *but rather presupposes it so as to sublate it.*

Hegel credits the method of the metaphysics of the understanding with having emphasized the difference between reality as it immediately manifests itself and the objects of reason. While for Kant the unconditioned is practically only to be sought in the phenomenal world – for him the absolute can only be represented by a subjective and temporary synthesis – the metaphysical method has stressed the difference between phenomenal and ideal absolute being.[8] On this point, Hegel and the metaphysicians of the understanding differ from Kant.

2.12. *Epistemological Realism*

Although Hegel regards reality as contradictory and as an illusion, he by no means denies its objectivity. Epistemological idealists, he contends,[9] leave the most interesting question of philosophy unanswered, that of explaining the reality of things and institutions. In this point, he concurs with the realist epistemology of the rationalists and opposes Critical philosophy, since the latter fails in the task of saving the objectivity of reality despite its dependency.[10]

2.13. *The Idea In-and-for-itself*

In contrast to Kant, Hegel and the metaphysicians of the understanding consider it possible to come to know the true nature of the absolute essence. In the respective systems, the 'God' of the rationalists and the 'idea' of Hegel's philosophy are taken to be the absolute ideal truly in-and-for-itself.[11]

2.2. CRITICISM OF THE METHOD OF THE
METAPHYSICS OF THE UNDERSTANDING

Hegel's praise for rationalist metaphysics is paired with criticism. His disappointment about the rejection of all metaphysics in Germany since Kant's critique, his identification of the *Logic* with metaphysics, and his decision to restore the honor of the so-called proofs of God[12] in no way mean that he wishes to maintain the rationalist analytical form of metaphysics. The dialectical-logical mode of considering the absolute differs in several points from that of the metaphysics of the understanding.

2.21. *'The Dead Product of Enlightenment'*

How does the metaphysician of the understanding attain insight into the absolute? To him, it first of all is a subject the nature of which is totally unknown at the beginning: it is an 'X'. Thereupon he notices the finitude, the limited goodness, the limited justice and the deficiencies in reality, and he denies that these shortcomings belong to the absolutely perfect being. The latter is infinite and *free (abstracted)* from any finitude; it is infinitely good and *free* from evil; it is infinitely just and *free* from any justice. Thus, the rationalist, according to Hegel's analysis that was inspired by Kant, gains knowledge of the absolute only through subjective abstraction. For Hegel, the result of this rationalist movement *of thought* is a 'point at rest' (the 'X') and an aggregate of abstract conceptual determinations, that is, in his language, 'the dead product of modern enlightenment'.[13] Since rationalists deny to the absolute any limitedness and limitation, they set it in opposition to and separate it from reality. In this view, the absolute lacks the vitality of actuality. Being a dead abstraction, the transcendent absolute of the metaphysics of the understanding is the opposite of developing reality, and is therefore less perfect than the latter.

Hegel confronts this approach with the conception of 'self-movement'. While the absolute being is infinite, it is not severed from the finite. In analogy to the body of a man, which is connected with his 'I' and distinct from it, the Hegelian finite is connected with, and distinct from, the infinite.

As conceived by the metaphysics of the understanding, the absolute lacks all vitality. In the dialectical conception, however, the absolute lives by virtue of its self-negation, i.e., through becoming finite and through the dissolution, or abstraction, of the limits which it has assumed in its finite realization. The dialectical method, the *'self-movement'*, is due to the form of the absolute in itself; metaphysics of the understanding proceeds by way of negation and abstraction, because this approach lies in the nature of *our* cognition. From a dialectical point of view, the all-comprising absolute itself restores its inner ideality and transcendence by negating reality. Real ideality and ideal reality are the moments of one unified life.

According to the method of the metaphysics of the understanding, the absolute subject is absolutely infinite. According to the dialectical method, there is a momentary absolute infinity which, on the one hand, is the starting-point and, on the other, the result of its self-negation. The absolute has its true infinity in its circular movement.

The subject [in metaphysics of the understanding – *A. S.*] is taken to be a fixed point, and to it as their support the predicates are attached, by a movement belonging to him who knows about it, but not looked upon as belonging to that point itself; only such a movement, however, could represent the content as a subject. Constituted as it is, this movement cannot belong to the subject; but when that point has been presupposed, this movement cannot be otherwise constituted, it can only be external. T h i s   a n t i - c i p a t i o n   t h a t   t h e   a b s o l u t e   i s   s u b j e c t is therefore not merely not the actuality of this concept, it even makes its actuality impossible; for it posits this concept as a static point, while the actuality is   s e l f - m o v e m e n t.[14]

Since the method of the metaphysics of the understanding – in effect, so as to avoid the contradiction of a finite infinity – presupposes that *solely* an absolute infinity lacking any finitude must be ascribed to the absolute subject, it is of no use for acquiring knowledge of self-moving, auto-dynamic actuality. For it demands the separation of living actuality and the absolute, and precludes their unification from the very outset.

2.22. *Dependency on Imagination*

While the faculty of imagination can to a limited degree represent the *movements, changes, and modifications of things* by means of its sensual and thing-like images of objective reality, its nature is by far surpassed by the thesis 'There are no things, but only contents of thought.' Since the theory of the *all-encompassing movement of dialectical thought* presupposes this thesis, the theory must remain inaccessible to a mode of thought which has been unable to free itself from the faculty of imagination. Yet the understanding is a faculty of thought which necessarily refers to the faculty of imagination. Thus, the dialectical unity of all being is inaccessible to metaphysicians of *the understanding.*[15]

2.23. *Mathematical Metaphysics*

For Hegel, the rationalist attempt to correct metaphysics by adopting the mathematical method is bound to fail, because the two sciences differ fundamentally in their subject matter. Mathematics tries to mediate a concept of *magnitude,* metaphysics a concept of *being in general.* He shows the discrepancy of their subject matter using Pythagoras' proof as an example:

The movement of mathematical proof does not belong to the subject matter at hand, but is an operation *external* to the matter. Thus, the nature of the right-angled triangle does not take itself apart in the manner set forth in the mathematical construction which is required for the proof of the theorem expressing the relations of its parts. The entire process of producing the result is a procedure and a means of cognition [of human understanding – *A. S.*]. ... The means taken, construction and proof, no doubt contain true propositions; but all the same we are bound to say that the content is false. The triangle in the above example is dismembered, and its parts are allotted to other figures which are constructed about the triangle. Only at the end is the triangle with which we are really concerned restored; it was lost from view during the process and was present merely in fragments that belonged to other wholes.[16]

The auxiliary lines needed for the proof cannot be deduced from what is given alone, namely, the right-angled triangle. Nor do they possess any ontic relationship to the result; while every right-angled triangle possesses the property attributed to it by the Pythagorean theorem, it does not possess the auxiliary lines needed for the proof. Mathematical mediation, then, is external to the starting-point and the result.

Metaphysics, on the other hand, cannot afford 'auxiliary mediations'. It cannot possibly start from provisional assumptions, for it has to deal exclusively with the essence of *what is present*. For example, metaphysics must discover in the nature of the finite the relationship of the finite to the infinite. The transition from the finite to the infinite – and conversely – is not of the same kind as the transition from the right-angled triangle to the result $a^2 + b^2 = c^2$; the former rests on an objectively given relationship, the latter on relationships which are not necessarily *present*. In the proof of the Pythagorean theorem, for instance, it is not a necessary fact that three squares border on the triangle; nonetheless, they are indispensable elements in the proof of this theorem.

All this explains Hegel's enthusiasm for his own method: The dialectical methodological transitions coincide with those in objective being. His thought accomplishes the transition from the thought-content 'infinity' to the thought-content 'finitude' *just as objective* infinity necessarily becomes finite. Both kinds of transitions are rooted in the negativity inherent in 'infinity as such'. Both metaphysics of the understanding and mathematics lack such a perfect method.

2.24. *Dogmatism*

Hegel regards metaphysics of the understanding as dogmatic. What he, like Kant before him, calls 'dogmatic' is the tendency to consider the unconditioned as a *thing-in-itself*[17] which exists apart from 'worldly' things. In his dialectic, Kant attempts to demonstrate that dogmatism is untenable: such an unconditioned thing-in-itself is contradictory, and hence cannot exist.[18] Hegel reverses Kantian dialectic: such a being *(Wesen)* exists as a contradictory moment. Because of its contradictory structure, however — Hegel agrees with Kant on this point — it cannot be an object that *exists in-itself.* The negativity is the reason for its externalization by natural necessity, and for the inevitable sublation of the externalized content. Thus, this essence *(Wesen)* does not exist separated from, but rather in necessary unity with, its externalization; hence, as such, it does not exist 'in-itself'.

In Hegel's dialectic, neither the purely ideal essence nor the world of experience are objects in-themselves. They are united in an indivisible form. The infinite as such does not have any being-in-self, but only a being-for-other; it does not subsist in itself, since it is merely *illusion (Scheinen).* Nor does the finite have any being-in-self; it is nothing but a *posited* moment in the circular form.

This is a distinction [namely, that between being-posited and being-in-itself — *A. S.*] which belongs only to the dialectical development and which is unknown to metaphysical philosophizing, which also includes Critical philosophy; the definitions of metaphysics, like its presuppositions, distinctions and conclusions, seek to assert and produce *what has being (Seiendes),* and moreover, *what has being-in-self (Ansichseiendes).*[19]

The difference between the positions mentioned is the following: (aa) Metaphysicians of the understanding consider God and things as being in-themselves. (bb) Kant considers the being-in-self of the separated absolute as impossible, whence also metaphysics of being is quite generally impossible. (cc) In Hegel's view, it is only the all-comprising whole which is in-itself: Every element of this whole is a *moment* in the circle, and hence has no being-in-self, but solely being that is posited by negation.

According to Hegel, dogmatism applies the principle of non-contradiction incorrectly: dogmatism simply presupposes that every element of reality is *in itself* rational and meaningful. However, if one denies the irrationality of every *aspect* of the absolute whole, one will not grasp the unity of the whole, any more than the reason why there occur perpetual movement, change and alteration in this whole.

Now it becomes clear why Hegel defends transphysicalism and rejects transphysicism. On the one hand, the 'absolute whole' in his philosophy transcends every physical *(physikalische),* i.e. thing-like, interpretation of being; on the other hand, Hegel denies that there is any being that exists separate from the physical *(physischen),* phenomenal world.[20] The dogmatist, however, defends the being-in-self of things, and is thus obliged to separate the absolute as a thing from finite things.

2.25. 'Inferences of the Understanding'

The proofs of the metaphysics of the understanding are 'inferences by the understanding'. Let us mention some examples: (1) If the finite exists, the infinite should also exist. Yet the finite exists; therefore the infinite does too. (2) If the contingent exists; the necessary should also exist. Yet the contingent exists; therefore the necessary does too. (3) If there is an infinite spirit, then there should also be an absolute spirit, etc.

Metaphysics of the understanding was unaware of the opposition in these inferences. The metaphysical view of being is contradictory because it considers being both as finite and contingent and as infinite and necessary.[21] For Hegel, there is only one *single* being, absolute being. His criticism of the 'inferences of the understanding' is closely bound up with his monistic interpretation of being. In the mutual transition of the moments of being, the contradictions find their dialectical resolution; true being is to be found in the whole.

The rationalist was either unable to free God from the still positive finitude of the existing world, so that God had to determine himself as the immediate substance of that world (pantheism); or, he remained as an object in opposition to the subject, and in this way, *finite* (dualism).[22]

The metaphysician of the understanding advocated either pantheism, as he focussed on the unity of finitude and infinity, or dualism, as the difference of the two was most evident to him. Rationalism was unable to reconcile the difference of determinations with their unity. Hegel regards both positions as contradictory. The pantheistic rationalist discovers the infinite; the dualistic rationalist assumes a *finite* God, because the finite exists for him outside the divine.[23]

The dialectical method demands the *resolution* of these contradictions. The inferences of the understanding have to be completed by a fourth proposition: If, e.g. the true infinite exists, then the finite has to be denied any being of its own, and must be considered as mere illusion; it can only be a moment of true infinity.

On the basis of his theory of the double externalization, the logical and the temporal, of the absolute, Hegel cannot be accused of dualism, since this double externalization does not call into question the *unity* of the absolute whole. For Hegel, there is only one single and absolute subject which externalizes itself in a twofold way, and there is only one single form which is taken as the vital pulse for both externalizations.[24]

2.26. *Univocal Conception of Being*

In a monistic interpretation of being, the *unitary* being can still be ascribed a wealth of forms. For Hegel, the objective whole contains a multiplicity of modes of being and of moments which are woven *into one unity* by the circular forms that are sublated into one another. The process of cycles passing into one another leads to the idea of absolute being as both multifarious and monistic.

The metaphysician of the understanding recognizes but one form of being. For him, there *is* God, there *is* a thing, there *are* a hundred thalers, etc. Hegel's dialectical methodology, by contrast, requires that one exhibit the 'concrete' significance of every determination in all-encompassing being. Dialectical research is supposed to show the *multilevel hierarchy* of the forms of being.

Being is in general the *first* immediacy, and *determinate being* is the same with the first determination. Existence, along with the thing, is the immediacy that issues from the *ground* – from the self-sublating mediation of the simple reflection of the essence. But *actuality* and *substantiality* is the immediacy that has issued from the sublated difference of the still unessential existence as phenomenon and its essentiality. Finally, *objectivity* is the immediacy to which the concept determines itself by the sublation of its abstraction and mediation.[25]

'Being' means nothing else but 'being given without any further determinateness'; 'determinate being' *(Dasein)* should be reserved for determinate and real being. Something 'exists' *(ex-sistere)* when it has issued from its ground, from essence; it emerged *from (ex)* essence and became phenomenon. Something can be called an absolute *actuality (Wirklichkeit)* only when it has its effect *(Wirkung)* within itself, and thus includes *within itself* all *substantiality*. Under the influence of Fichte and Schelling, Hegel calls being that contains the supreme determinateness within itself *objectivity*. Objectivity is completely determined being, that is, being which is completely determined by the absolute subject.

Because of their undifferentiated conception of being, the metaphysicians of the understanding were unable to explain why and to what extent the absolute subject existed. They started from given finitude, deduced from it the concept of infinity, and postulated the objective being of this concept. The ontological proof of the existence of the absolute subject was based on the claim that absolute perfection must also include the perfection of being. This thesis is attacked by the Critical dialectic: Even though the *concept* of the infinite and the *concept* of the absolutely perfect is given, the object corresponding to this concept still need not exist. I can easily imagine *my* 100 thalers and still not have them. Likewise, the infinite need not exist, even though we can think its concept.

On the one hand, Hegel agrees with this criticism. If one imagines the absolute subject as a quasi-human person, it need not exist any more than the 100 thalers which one desires to have. The metaphysicians' univocal conception of being does not permit a scientific analysis of the absolute subject. If one imagines its existence to be like that of a tree or a house, then it would exist just as accidentally as a certain house or a certain tree.

But on the other hand, Kant's criticism is rejected by Hegel. Insofar as Kant identifies the being of the absolute with that of 100 thalers, he is himself under the influence of metaphysical methodology. There is an implication holding for absolute infinite being which surpasses the necessity of thing-like being: If there is something finite, i.e., having definite potentiality for being determined, then there must also be the infinite, i.e., unlimited potentiality for determination. It was because of its uniform view of being that the method of the understanding provoked Kant's criticism.[26]

2.27. *Multiplicity of Proofs*

The rationalists supplied a disordered variety of proofs. As 'principal moments'[27] of the *Logic,* these proofs are sublated into *one unified progression,*[28] and into the hierarchy of categories. Each circle is woven into the circle of a more concrete category. The objective reality of any circle can be taken as point of departure for the ascent to the absolute subject.

CHAPTER 3

SPINOZA AND DOUBLE NEGATION

Hegel regards Spinoza as the most important rationalist. In confrontation with the philosopher from Amsterdam, Hegel's methodology of self-movement and his criticism of the metaphysics of the understanding find especially lucid expression.

3.1. 'DETERMINATIO EST NEGATIO'

By means of this principle, Spinoza determines the relationship between the absolute substance and its accidents: In the substance, everything is one; the *unity* of its content, which lacks any determinations, reveals itself in determinate form in its negation, namely, in the *plurality* of the accidents.

Hegel uses the same principle to determine the relationship between the 'positive' determinations and reality, that between the absolute essence and the world of things and phenomena, and that between the subject-side and the object-side of absolute reason. Every objective determinateness — Hegel renders *determinatio* by 'determinateness' *(Bestimmtheit)*[1] — results from the negation or limitation of a positive abstract determination; and conversely, every abstract determination results from the negation or dissolution of the limits of a determinateness. Thus, e.g., the determinate being of the 'something' is the negation of absolute being, which is the negation of determinate being.[2]

3.2. 'POSITIO EST NEGATIO'

G.R.G. Mure contends that Hegel, aside from determining negation, has also adopted a determining *positio*.[3] Agreeing with this view, C. Stommel thinks that 'according to Hegel, *omnis determinatio est positio*'.[4]

Neither this principle nor the alleged criticism of Spinoza can be found in the *Logic*. While Hegel is convinced that every determinateness is due to a 'position', he does not oppose the principle in this formulation to Spinoza's philosophy, for every *position is a negation*, namely, a negation of abstractness or determinateness.

As shown above, nothing *in* Hegel's all-encompassing whole is in-itself: everything is posited. Being-in-self is mere illusion. Every element is the reflection of the 'other', and just as much being-for-other. Every element presupposes a negation, hence negation is immanent in all elements.

The method is governed by the law of 'double negation'.[5] Hegel emphasizes repeatedly that double negation implies a *relative* affirmation and positivity.[6] Since every double negation points out another negativity and leads to a new dialectical movement, its affirmative result is but relative. The relationless whole alone is absolutely positive.

Mure and Stommel believe that only something positive can be negated; accordingly, every negation would presuppose a positivity. However, this argument is alien to Hegel's methodology. In his dialectic, the result of any negation is not only positive, but just as much – i.e., in the same respect – negative, and hence it will be negated again. With this cyclical method, he can thus maintain a completely negative way of considering being. The negation of A is B, that of B is A, and that of A and B is C, etc. Genuine positivity would block the process of *self*-determination and *self*-negation.

Haring describes Hegel's speculation on unity and plurality as follows:

The thought of the one is the *concept* in its originality (immediacy), the *thesis,* the *position.*[7]

The identification of immediacy, thesis, and position is easily misunderstood.

In interpretations of Hegel, it is common to describe dialectic as consisting of thesis, antithesis, and synthesis. Kant and Fichte used the schema of this triplicity in order to express their dialectical method; while Hegel's contemporaries, too, frequently used this schema, Hegel himself regards it as being 'shallow nonsense' and 'barrenness'. In the *Phenomenology* and the *Logic* it is totally absent. Hegel stresses explicitly that counting the moments cannot provide any insight at all into his methodology. If one absolutely wanted to *'count'* and work with the triplicity, he states, the identity of being (being = being), for instance, could be called the thesis, the nonidentity (being = nothingness) the antithesis, and the unity of the determinations (being + nothingness = becoming) the synthesis. But one could also consider contradictory being as the first moment, becoming as the second, ideal being and nothingness as the third, and totality as the fourth. In this way, one obtains 'quadruplicity'.[8] Hegel regards the terms of the triplicity and the counting of complexity as irrelevant, since they are inappropriate to the method of self-movement and completely arbitrary. Therefore, immediacy must not be put without further ado on the same level with 'thesis' and 'position'; this would give the impression that Hegelian thought is positing, whereas in fact it only negates, observing in each moment only a negation and discovering its presupposed negation by returning. Even the temporary starting-point, because of its *temporariness,* is not objective, and hence is *negative.* For Hegel, *positio* is thus identical with *negatio.*

3.3. NEGATION AS CONTRADICTION

In Hegel's terminology, 'negation', 'negativity', and 'contradiction' are in many places equated, although they have different meanings as far as the genesis of the system is concerned, whence an intelligible *explanation* of Hegel's philosophy should keep their meanings distinct. The terms designate several moments of the dialectical speculation. The *negativity* of abstract being, for instance, yields the *contradiction,* which leads to the negation of indeterminate being, whereby its lack of determinateness is *negated.* In the objective whole they are moments of one *uniform* movement. In this union of negation and contradiction we encounter the core and basis of Hegel's criticism of Spinoza. Whereas Spinoza regards the wordly multiplicity as a mere, simple negation of the one substance, and the unity of the substance as mere negation of physical multiplicity, the Hegelian negation, by virtue of its union with contradiction, is *self-negation.* Hegel's dynamic negativity is opposed to Spinoza's static negation.[9]

3.4. DOUBLE NEGATION

[According to Spinoza, reality] is not negation *as* negation, not the negatively self-related negation which would be *in its own self* the return into the first identity, so that this identity would then be veritable identity.[10]

In Spinoza, there is no demonstration that the *modi* of the substance, the real determinations, constitute in turn a negativity. Intro-reflection and movement returning into itself are absent in his system. Since objective reality does not negate itself, it becomes a positive element; it possesses some independence with respect to the substance. This makes it possible to interpret Spinoza's system in a dualistic manner.

For Hegel, Spinoza's attempt to demonstrate the unity of substance by means of the above-mentioned principle has been a failure. Since reality – lacking return-in-self – is to some degree independent, the unity of substance falls asunder in it. The 'one' dissolves into multiplicity. That is why the common view which considers Spinoza's system to be a pantheism, is for Hegel to some extent justified.[11]

3.5. AMBIVALENCE OF SPINOZA'S POSITION

In contradistinction to what has been said so far, Hegel in many places defends Spinoza against the accusation that he is a pantheist; Spinoza, Hegel feels, can also be considered an acosmist, since he regards substance as veritable being, and reality as mere negativity of substance.[12] This is the reason why Hegel regards Spinoza's intentions as obscure; one could look upon Spinoza's system as a dualism, as a pantheistic denial of transcendence, and as a denial of reality. In opposition to this ambiguity Hegel sets forth this univocal monism: everything exists and lives but in the all-embracing absolute. The two negations, which are juxtaposed in Spinoza, are unified in *one* movement.

One can say that Hegel has dissolved wordly being into divine being; but one can also say that he has secularized divine being. This does not mean that his system is ambivalent, for he sublates the two allegedly independent realities into one unity.

3.6. SUBSTANCE AND THOUGHT

For Spinoza, thought is an attribute of the absolute substance. Nonetheless, Hegel believes that this substance can be ascribed *neither* thought as such *nor* self-consciousness. However unjustified these objections may seem at first glance, a brief explanation can render them understandable.

The first objection is that the substance is not thinking. Thought is a negating activity. This activity is totally absent from Spinoza's substance, since the two spheres stand in a static relationship of mutual negation; there is no self-negation through which one sphere *passes into* the other. Transitions take place only in the human faculty of cognition. Thus, *thought-activity* is extrinsic to the substance. Within itself, it contains but negation 'at rest': the not-being of 'an other'.

Since intro-reflection is absent from Spinoza's substance, one cannot — as Hegel thinks — attribute self-consciousness to it. In addition, it is not the result of a self-negation, but merely the negation of 'an other'; this is why it does not possess self-determining thought, nor self-contemplation. By inserting negativity as activity into the Spinozistic absolute, and thereby elevating it from the level of a thoughtless substance to that of a self-cognizing substance, Hegel sublates the metaphysics of the understanding and of being into the discipline of pure spirit.

PART III

DIALECTICAL METAPHYSICS

DIALECTICAL METAPHYSICS

The circular movement, intro-reflection, is the essence of the dialectical method (Part I); it is the starting-point for Hegel's criticism of rationalist metaphysics (Part II); and it is also — as we shall see — the most abstract schema, according to which he constructed his new metaphysics. We shall confine ourselves to the topics which Hegel calls the *principal moments of the Logic,* namely, (a) the problem of infinity, (b) that of absolute necessity and of absolute substance, and (c) that of the absolute concept.[1]

CHAPTER 1

INFINITY

1.1. THE FINITE AND THE INFINITE

In Hegel's texts, 'the finite' *(das Endliche)* means 'that which has a boundary, an end', or 'the limited in general'. One should not imagine the finite in any more concrete form, for in the concept 'finitude' or 'the finite as such', there is no further specification of what the 'end' refers to. It may be a finite span of time, a finite space, a finite existence, an ideal realized to a limited degree, etc.[2]

The finite presupposes something other than itself in a twofold way: its boundary separates from the other, and it limits the other. Thus, the finite has something other than itself beyond its boundary, and is itself the limited representation of something else. In both cases, this other is the infinite.

(a) The other, which is represented by the finite to a limited degree, is infinite. It *becomes* finite only through the boundary; without the boundary it would be non-finite.

[The finite] does not limit itself, for self-limitation would be the positing of its other.[3]

Self-limitation presupposes a double 'self', namely, the 'self' as the starting-point, and the 'self' as the result, of the restriction. Yet the result is different from the starting-point. *Limiting oneself* is thus *positing an other*. But the other, the limitation of which yields the finite, cannot itself be something finite, for 'the finite' comprises all finitude. The finite, then, can only issue from the self-limitation of the infinite, and not from the restriction of something else that is finite. Therefore, the finite does not *limit itself*.

Is it not possible that everything that is, is finite? If everything that determinately is has an end, then everything is finite and there is nothing infinite! This objection does not apply in dialectical logic. Dialectical logic does not attempt to demonstrate that there is an infinite *thing;* it rather analyzes the infinite insofar as it is exhibited in finite determinate being.[4] To regard given being as *finite* and limited is to presuppose in an implicit way unlimited ideal being, the limited representation of which is what is given. This is why any consciousness which recognizes a boundary has already transcended it. The structure of finite determinate being thus presupposes not only the conceptual content 'finitude' or 'limitedness', but also that which becomes limited and finite: the infinite.

(b) There is still the second way in which the finite presupposes the infinite. The other which is excluded by the end is also infinite. If this other were again something finite, then it would already be contained in the 'finite', since 'finite' means 'the finite in general'.

In this way, Hegel arrives at the traditional metaphysical proposition: If there is something finite, then there should also be something infinite. In turn, the infinite is essentially related to the finite, for infinity cannot be conceived of without its opposite: the infinite is nothing but the abstraction of the finite. In the process of thought, the non-finite, or in-finite, results from the dissolution of the boundary of the finite.[5] One might object that this conditional character of the infinite is purely subjective! And one might say that the truly infinite is free from, and beyond, all finitude, and is incomprehensible, unknowable and ineffable. Hegel rejects these romantic utterances; in the dialectical logic, he argues that nobody has the right to speak of the incomprehensible and unknowable infinite, because it is only *the concept* which gives meaning to words. *The concept* of infinity arises from the negation of the finite, from the abstraction of the boundaries of the finite. Only this infinity is relevant for dialectical logic, the critical theory of pure concepts.

The relationship between the finite and the infinite is analogous to the relationship between the individual and the universal.[6] There is nothing individual without something universal, and no universal without something individual; there is no man without mankind, no mankind without man; no democracy without the ideal of democracy, no freedom without the ideal of freedom, which forever transcends real freedom.

1.2. THE 'BAD' INFINITE

The pantheistic metaphysician believes that the infinite issues from the totality of everything finite; the theistic metaphysician views it as being beyond the finite. Hegel regards both suppositions as 'bad'. The true view is to recognize the double identity and non-identity of finitude and infinity.

1.21. *Infinity as Perennial Ought*

It consists in the repetition of the finite, in that it merely reproduces the former finite, so that the finite posits another finite and so on to bad infinity.[7]

Hegel regards the linear process in the infinite as contradictory: (aa) In this endless repetition, the infinite consists merely of finite elements: hence, it is itself only finite.[8] (bb) Infinity, when taken as the totality of everything finite, presupposes that the infinite can be posited along with the finite! To the objection that it is not the finite itself, but the linear process, which is taken as infinite, Hegel would respond that this means that what, on the one hand, is separated in thought — the process and the finite elements constituting it — is taken, on the other hand, as an undifferentiated unity — the infinite process.[9] (cc) The infinite process is inexhaustible, unlimited and incomprehensible. This incomprehensibility, however, is not a deficiency of thought, but rather one of what is given, which is nothing else but a 'boring' repetition of the same object. The deficiency of the infinite process lies in its incapability of exhausting infinity.[10]

1.22. *Dualistic Infinity*

The dualistic infinite is denied any finitude: it is *only* infinite. This gives rise to two contradictory states of affairs.

(a) Because of the separation of the infinite from the finite, the infinite is itself limited and finite.

The infinite as thus posited as the opposite of the finite, in a qualitative relation *of others* to one another, is to be called the *bad infinite,* the infinite of the *understanding* which takes it for the supreme, absolute truth.

This contradiction is at once present in the circumstance that the finite as determinate being remains opposed to the infinite; thus we have *two* determinatenesses: *there are* two worlds, one finite and one infinite, and in their relationship the infinite is only the *limit* of the finite, and is thus only a determinate infinite, an *infinite which is itself finite.* [11]

Besides, the separated infinite is incapable of providing a solution of the problem posed. The infinite is supposed to be the presupposition of the finite, and to *posit* it. The presupposed infinite is taken as purely infinite. In the positing of the finite, the separation is repudiated. Thus, this dualistic view of infinity involves the same inconsequence as does the conception of infinity as infinite process: a boundary is presupposed, and at the same time denied.[12]

(b)

The finite, in turn, as placed for itself apart from the infinite, is that *self-relation* in which its relativity, dependence and transitoriness is removed; it is the same independence and self-affirmation which the infinite is supposed to be.[13]

Through the separation made in the metaphysics of the understanding, the finite becomes independent. However, this is contrary to the nature of the finite. If it does not return into the infinite, it becomes an independent opposite pole, and thus just as infinite as the infinite itself.

Those, however, who assert the impossibility of any such transition [namely, the dissolution of the finite into the infinite – *A. S.*] will themselves not have it that the finite is absolute, unchangeable, imperishable, and eternal.[14]

If the finite is separated from the infinite, it becomes identical with its opposite – the absolute, unchangeable – and thus contradictory, for, according to its concept, it is supposed to be finite.

1.23. *The Bad and Untrue*

Although Hegel calls the linear process as well as the separate infinite 'bad' forms of infinity, and demonstrates their contradictoriness, this does not mean that he denies them objectivity. 'Bad' and 'untrue' infinity refer both to an inadequate view and to a limited mode of being. These forms of infinity do not correspond to their true and ideal *concept*. Just as there are bad and untrue works of art or friends, *bad infinity is also objectively given.*

The bad and untrue in general consists in the contradiction which obtains between the determination or concept and the existence of an object.[15]

It is this lack of correspondence between its existence and its concept which is characteristic of the finite.[16] Just as everything finite must 'vanish', so must both these deficient forms of infinity; as moments, they are sublated into true infinity.

Which schools in the history of philosophy regarded these 'bad' forms in question as the true ones? Roger Garaudy[17] believes that Hegel had mechanical materialism in mind, as well as mysticism which considers a mode of being separate from given reality as the true one. The expression 'the ought' which is invariably associated with the 'infinite process', however, points in Hegel's language to Kant's and Fichte's theory according to which the infinite ought to be sought solely in, and by means of, the finite, and should not be attributed any further objective existence.

The infinite – in the usual meaning of bad infinity – and the *progress to infinity* are, like the ought, the expression of a *contradiction* which puts itself forward as its final *resolution*. ... The resolution of this contradiction is not the recognition of the *equal correctness* and equal incorrectness of the two assertions – this is only another form of the abiding contradiction – but the *ideality* of both, in which as distinct, as reciprocal negations, they are only *moments*;... In this being which is thus the ideality of the distinct moments, the contradiction has not vanished abstractly, but is resolved and reconciled, ...[18]

(aa) Both the immanent and the transcendent concepts of infinity imply a contradiction which no one ever attempted to solve because it was not even recognized. (bb) Neither is totally incorrect; otherwise the infinite and the finite would not form opposites and would be unrelated. (cc) Nor is either of them totally correct, for contradictory structures cannot subsist. (dd) The form of infinity advocated by Hegel does not make these two self-contradictory forms vanish altogether ('abstractly'); as *'moments'* of this form, they mutually resolve each other, and in this way are reconciled with one another. This new form is the 'true' infinity. Although its components are 'false' in themselves, the true is not composed of the 'false';[19] the 'false' is the abiding contradiction.

1.3. TRUE INFINITY

1.31. *The Finite Is Sublated*

The *sublation of the finite* does not just mean that given reality is considered in a higher context: it changes, loses its finitude, and becomes an eternal moment of the self-moving absolute subject.

Ideality can be called the *quality* of infinity; but it is essentially the process of *becoming,* and hence a transition, ... which is now to be specified. As a sublation of finitude, that is, of finitude as such, and equally of the infinity which is merely its opposite, merely negative, infinity is return into self, *self-relation, being.*[20]

The ideality of true infinity is not something static, but a process in which objectively given finitude becomes the finite infinity of the metaphysics of the understanding, and the latter becomes again finite reality. Since these transitions do not take place separately, but rather form moments of an uninterrupted process, both kinds of finitude lose their specific character and their separateness; both are thereby *negated;* their finitude vanishes, and there remains only truly infinite and unified *being.* In addition to their negation, they find their *preservation* in that being. Since the process is one that returns into itself, they will subsist forever, as moments of this eternal process. The *sublation of the finite* is thus equally related to the objectively finite and to the rationalist infinite.

It is not only the two determinations which are sublated into the moving form, but also the *relationships* holding between them:

This *unity* of the finite and the infinite and the *distinction* between them are the same inseparable union as finitude and infinity.[21]

As the infinite and the finite are present in the subject-side and in the object-side, so are their unity and their difference. The subject-side *unites* the two *distinct* and abstract determinations. The unity of unity and difference is contradictory, whence it externalized itself into the object-side.

The schema of intro-reflection has clearly been manifest in Hegel's analysis of infinity; it finds explicit expression in the following text:

The image of true infinity, bent back into itself, becomes the *circle*, ...[22]

pure ideality

state of affairs: The abstract infinite is finite. logical rendition: the infinite = the infinite   the infinite = finite

realized ideality

state of affairs: The abstract infinite has become finite and determinate. Reality contains the finite and the infinite. This *unity* of opposite *determinations* is untenable.

CHAPTER 2

ABSOLUTE NECESSITY

2.1. ACCIDENTALITY AND NECESSITY

In the same way that he has taken 'finitude' *(Endlichkeit)* literally, namely, as the property of being up to a certain limit *(Ende)*, Hegel takes 'accidentality' *(Zufälligkeit)* literally. The *accidental* lacks in *necessary* connectedness so that it essentially *falls*[1] and *falls onto its other*.[2] The theory of circular movement thus enters the interpretation of these expressions: the accidental separates itself from necessary connectedness, *falls out of* it, and again *onto* it. Just as the finite ends and presupposes infinity, so does the accidental fall and presuppose necessity. Both categories, finiteness and accidentality, by their negativity, point to their opposites. Their circular forms differ only in their abstractness. While finite determinate being is being which is determined by its limits alone, accidentality includes a more concrete complexity of determinations: since the accidental steps outside the necessary connectedness — which among other relations is constituted by *causality* — it acquires a relative *independence*. The relativity consists in that the accidental has the *possibility* of also not being.[3] The most important *ground* for why the accidental falls out of the general connectedness is 'individualization'.[4] Since *individual* beings lack complete connectedness, there arises the possibility that the laws do not always *act* in complete accordance with their necessity. Chance, therefore, is loss in necessity.

Through 'individualization', the accidental acquires a certain independence which is absurd. If something *distinguishes* itself within, and stands *opposite* to, the general connectedness, then it is in *connection* with it. That which steps outside the general connectedness is essentially condemned to fall through and fall back.

The independence of the accidental also contradicts the concept of necessity. Indeed, the necessary is what is independent and subsistent in a process, whereas accidentalities are merely incidental *additions*.

If, nonetheless, the accidental acquires some independence, then the necessity will turn 'bad'.

For the necessity of an existence, we require ... that it stand in connection with others, so that in all respects such existence is completely determined by other existences as its conditions or causes, and is not, and could not be, by itself severed from them; nor should there be any condition, cause, or circumstance of the connection by which it could be so severed, nor any such circumstance as would contradict the others which determine it.

Necessity is thus the process which implies that the result and the presupposition are distinct only as regards their form.[5]

A process is necessary if its preconditions and its results are immediately combined in it. Any separation impairs the necessity of the positing. Any cleavage makes influences from outside possible. Any distance between action and result renders the latter at least partly accidental because the mediation can effect an alteration. This is why the result must not be *severed* from the necessarily determining conditions; this would *contradict* the necessity.

Are we dealing with a *logical* contradiction here or with an extrinsic discrepancy between two properties existing separately?[6] The expression 'contradiction' implies an ontic absurdity which in thought evokes two opposing judgments: *Necessity* becomes contradictory by the separation, for the latter renders it accidental. Being accidental is contrary to the *absolute* necessity which issues from the *negative dialectic* – all conceptual contents become abstract and absolute in the *negative dialectic!* Yet the necessary process becomes accidental when something outside the process – be it necessary or accidental – is effective, for this effect can influence that of the necessary process and thus reduce it to accidentality.

(a) For the metaphysics of the understanding, the accidental exists outside the absolutely necessary. Hegel finds this view 'bad', since the separate mode of being presupposes a boundary, a limit.

Every limitation involves a relation to some other and hence c o n f l i c t s with the determination of the absolutely necessary.[7]

The distinction gives rise to a contradictory state of affairs, for necessity becomes accidental through distinction.

(b) Is the contradiction not resolved by the assumption of unity? It is this unity which Kant defends against previous metaphysics. For him, the absolutely necessary *ought* to be sought in what is accidental. His demand, however, is just as contradictory as metaphysical dualism. The task of Critical reason as perennial *ought* can never be solved because it is itself contradictory. The sum of everything that is relatively infinite can never yield the absolutely infinite. Analogously, the necessary never results from accidentalities. The contention that the necessary is inevitably present in what is relatively necessary, forming with it an inseparably unity, is just as contradictory as the separation made by the metaphysics of the understanding.

Speculation is now confronted with a duality. On the one hand, the *unity* of determinations is contradictory, so that separation is to be required; on the other hand, unity must be required, since the *separation* is just as contradictory.[8] The 'falsity' of these two contentions can only be rectified by a third: The two states of affairs, separation and unity, make up for their lack of ontological truth by mutual transition. Again, this movement — like that concerning *true* infinity — must not suffer any temporal interruption. True necessity repels accidentality, but does not allow it to become an independent existence, for the separation is immediately sublated again.

[Absolute necessity] in mediation with something other, relates to itself; i.e., the other through which it mediates itself with itself is itself. As other, it is thus negated; it is, to itself, the other, but only momentarily — momentarily without, however, introducing the determination of time into the concept, which determination enters only in the determinate being of the concept. — This being-other is essentially a sublated moment; in determinate being, it appears also as a real other. But absolute necessity is that necessity which is in accordance with its concept.[9]

(aa) Only the logical subject, whose return takes place in eternal movement, is truly necessary. It is only in *logos* that a process evolves whose properties coincide with the concept of true necessity. (bb) 'In determinate being', i.e., in spatial and temporal reality, however, nothing is necessary; everything is condemned to 'vanish' without trace. (cc) Hegel's analysis of necessity exhibits anew the schema of intro-reflection. The necessary separates the accidental from itself and becomes thereby — if 'only momentarily' — accidental itself; its externalization into accidentality in turn dissolves immediately. The separation is eternal, because the unity brought about by its dissolution in turn dissolves eternally. Likewise, the unity of the determinations is also an eternal moment of the logical movement.

2.2. ABSOLUTE ACTUALITY

As has been noted, the concept of necessity is richer in content than that of infinity. Of the determinations associated with it, we shall first examine absolute actuality. The latter, according to Hegel, is the unity of internality (absolute essence) and externality (the world of phenomena).[10] The two poles are not united in a static way, for that which is internal *can* externalize itself, and that which is external can 'internalize itself' (*sich erinnern*, remember). Which pole — the question arises here — is the decisive one in the eternal process of living actuality?

Actuality as a whole contains internal and external, pure and realized, essentialities, which are all also 'building blocks' of new actuality. Even on its own, every essentiality possesses some kind of actuality, be it abstract or real.

Everything possible has therefore in general a *being* or an *existence.* [11]

The sum of the pure essentialities constitutes but a *formal* possibility. While all of them, each one taken separately, are possible, their sum is impossible, because it contains opposing possibilities. Formal actuality, therefore, cannot constitute the decisive element in total actuality; it merely is that which is possible in general.

Real actuality is *determinately* real actuality. Whereas the possibility of formal actuality is unlimited and indeterminate, and hence impossible, real actuality contains determinate and limited possibilities as real conditions for the origination of something new. It might seem that real actuality is self-sufficient. Novelty — we commonly believe — evolves from real possibilities. But this self-sufficiency is illusion. Something will necessarily become actual only when *all* its conditions are present. Yet, while *many* conditions taken together can form a real (limited) necessity, they cannot form a totality of all conditions, since 'all-ness' (totality) cannot be exhausted by many-ness' (plurality). What is demanded of real possibility contradicts it and dissolves it. Limited actualities become negations. Absolute actuality becomes an empty abstraction in real actuality, since it can neither be exhausted nor determined by realities.

This *emptiness* of its determination makes it a *mere possibility,* something which can equally be *otherwise* and can be determined as possible. But this possibility is itself *absolute;* ... [12]

This concept of absolute actuality is akin to the Aristotelian *'materia prima'.* The real conditions combine with the inexhaustible potentiality for determination present in reality. Hegel calls this absolute possibility *absolute actuality.* The difference is in part purely terminological. His possibility-actuality is no more a form of being *(ein Sein)* than is Aristotelian *materia prima.* What is characteristic of Hegel, however, is that he assumes the being-in-self of *materia prima* to be contradictory. While *materia prima* as such exists objectively, its objective existence is an absurdity. Thereby, its existence becomes dynamic, *acting (wirkend).* In this sense, *materia prima* is both absolutely acting and *empty* possibility of determination.

Yet how does the whole *act*? The synthesis of the speculation so far provides an answer to this question. *Formal* possibility cannot decisively determine the process of actuality since it is also impossible because of the many opposites contained in it. The process of formal possibility is *accidental*. In every case, only one of two opposite possibilities can be actualized; every result leaves open the possibility of the opposite. This feature is characteristic of accidentality. *Real* possibility, too, remains limited in necessity, hence accidental, since real possibility, composed as it is of limited conditions, can never be absolute; indeed, it constitutes a badly infinite process. However, it *ought* to be absolute in order to act with necessity; this is what makes it 'fall to the ground'. Through this sublation, real possibility passes into formal possibility. The cyclical process, starting from formal conditions and passing to real conditions, and from those back to the formal, constitutes the whole which acts of *absolute necessity*, and cannot be impaired by any outside influence.

Now in self-sublating real possibility, what is sublated is a duality, for it is itself the duality of actuality and possibility. (1) Actuality is formal, or is an existence which appeared as independent and immediate, and through its sublating becomes reflected being, the moment of an other, and thus acquires itself *being-in-self*. (2) This existence was also determined as *possibility*, or as *being-in-self*, but that of an other. By the sublation, then, this being-in-self is also sublated and passes over into *actuality*. – Thus this movement of self-sublating real possibility produces *the same moments which have already been present*, but now each grows out of the other; hence, it is in this negation not a *transition*, but rather a *coming-together-with-itself*. ... Thus what vanishes is this, that actuality was determined as the possibility, or the being-in-self, or an *other*, and conversely, possibility as an actuality which is *not that* whose possibility it is. ... thus this new actuality develops only out of its being-in-self, out of *the negation of itself*.[13]

Real possibility is a *'duality' (Gedoppeltes):* given actuality is at the same time the totality of conditions, the *possibility*, for the new actuality. (aa) The *actuality* of real conditions – existence – is to vanish so as to make room for the new actuality. This is done in the sublation, which reduces existence to 'being-in-self', *or* abstract being. (bb) But existence is equally dissolved, insofar as it is the *possibility*, i.e. abstract being, or being-in-self, for the new actuality. It is sublated into the existence of the new actuality. In this way, the process of total actuality brings about a double movement rotating within itself.

In the view of the understanding, which is tied to the senses, one reality *passes* into another. Hegel regards this succession of realities as external illusion. There is only a change of structure within absolute actuality. Everything that will be has already been present. Nor are there actuali*ties*, and hence no transitions between actualities either, but only the self-negation within one absolute unity. What has been real will ineluctably *become* being-in-self; what has been 'in itself', will ineluctably *become* realized. What allegedly is real is totally subject to the action of the all-embracing whole. In this unified movement, the boundaries, that is, the presuppositions of a dualistic account of actuality, are breached, and have thus lost all significance. The difference between the real and the actual, then, is merely a distinction of the understanding. Dialectic sublates all reality into actualtiy.

2.3. SUBSTANTIALITY AND CAUSALITY

Dialectic also *sublates* the difference between causality and substantiality. Things possess but the illusion of substantiality; their essence calls for self-dissolution. *Real* substance, then, is essentially subject to, and integrated into, a process of development.

2.31. 'The Substance'

Hegel uses the term 'substance' primarily in Spinoza's sense. *The* substance is the absolute substance. However, he regards it as being dynamic: The form which comprises the process of absolute necessity in a unity and has sublated every relation to an other is the only true substance.[14]

Because of its all-encompassing form, the substance possesses no accidents which are outside itself: nothing can be added *(accidere)* to what is all-encompassing. The difference between substantiality and accidentality, as Hegel characterizes it, rests on the preliminary distinction between the absolute essence in itself, which *subsists* in absolute actuality, *and* its externalization, which returns to it again. Thus, this difference occurs *within* the all-encompassing substance, namely, as the relationship of the absolute essence to its intro-reflection; but this difference will be sublated into the logical process.

Dialectical-logical essence, as relative substance, possesses the following properties: (a) Since the essence necessarily externalizes itself, the substantial relationship is of equal necessity *dynamic*. The substance is not indifferent to accidentality, since substance is essentially 'actuosity'[15] (b) *Accidentality has an absolute unity of form*; there is no interruption between the externalizing and the dissolving activity of absolute essence.[16] (c) *The distinction between finite substance and its accident is without significance.* The finite accident subsists, not because of the power and activity of finite substance, but in virtue of the totality.

One accident, then, expels another only because its own *subsisting* is this totality of form and content itself in which it and its other equally perish.[17]

(d) In Scholastic terminology, Hegel's distinction between substantiality and accidentality is a *distinctio rationis cum fundamento in re*: The substance causes its accidentality and — because its essence *is* 'reflective movement' *(Scheinen)* — it is inseparably connected with its accidentality.[18] In this way, the analytical distinction between cause, substance and accident is acknowledged, but at the same time their inseparability with respect to the all-inclusive actuality is emphasized.

2.32. *Causal Relationship*

The analysis of causality is analogous to that of possibility and actuality. Dialectical logic sublates formal, real (determinate) and conditional causality into the absolutely acting whole.

The substance, as the totality of *pure* essentialities, acts necessarily, for these essentialities — contradictory in their pure form — strive for the sublation of their abstract mode of being. The substance acts, it is the original matter *(ursprüngliche Sache)* and cause *(Ur-sache)*. This causality of *formal* substance '*is extinguished in its effect*'[19], i.e., it dissipates itself, it is in itself without result. This is due to its formal nature. The content of cause and effect is indeed the same, since, on the one hand, something is a cause only insofar as it externalizes itself as its effect; on the other hand, an *effect* is attributed to a cause only insofar as it has been present in the latter. Yet formal substance contains nothing but *pure* essentialities. In formal causality, therefore, both cause and effect remain without determination. Formal causality is thus nothing other than a mere form of dynamism without any determinate result.

The *determinate*, or *real*, causal relationship obtains between *finite* substances. The sequence 'cause-effect-cause-effect, etc.' forms an infinite series, and will perish because of its bad infinity.[20] Such a causal relationship, then, dissolves into pure determinations; in itself it is without significance. Only its negation is relevant, for it is through its negation that it has an effect on the original substance, evoking in this substance the reaction which consists in taking back the pure determinations. This causality is '*conditioned*' causality, because 'pure being, or essence',[21] as the original substance, is here passive, while finite causality, in its dissolution, *acts* on this substance. Through this sublation, the formal cause is preserved, since the real passes over to its other, the formal. The eternality of the original substance is thus guaranteed. A second consequence of this sublation of determinate causality is that formal substance loses its indeterminateness.

[The action of conditioned causality] is thereby just as much *becoming* as positing and *sublating of the other.*[22]

In its nullification, the real becomes formality, so that the boundary between the two domains is breached. In this way, formal substance is related to, and thus can act on, reality; this evokes in reality a *determinate* reaction. Does this relationship involve a *reciprocal action* between the two substances? Are the two domains of the all-comprising whole opposed to one another as equivalent poles? Since reality can have an influence and a conditioned effect on formal causality only insofar as it negates itself, there are not two equivalent poles opposite to each other, but only the unified movement of pure essentialities.

Reciprocal action is, therefore, only causality itself; the cause not only *has* an effect, but in the effect it stands, *as cause*, in relation to itself.[23]

(aa) 'Reciprocal action' is 'causality itself'. Formal causality is in itself without result; finite causality is in itself only negative and, in its effect, is *'bent back'* into formal causality.[24] Thus, both kinds are in themselves void; their dynamism implies their self-dissolution. Nor is there, in the strict sense, any original substance subsisting in itself; everything is merely causality: one action which posits its presupposition itself. Causality acting in this way has neither an antecedent nor a subsequent element, neither a primary nor a secondary element, neither a conditioning nor a conditioned element; everything is one. The two moments of the circular form condition each other mutually: Formal causality does not give rise to real causality without receiving its determinateness from this very causality; real causality does not determine formal causality without dissolving itself and receiving existence from formal causality.

(bb) What is the meaning of 'the cause not only *has* an effect'? While every finite cause has its effect, it *is* not its effect. According to Hegel, the *'true'* cause is to *be* its own effect, for if this effect *existed* outside the cause, then it would also *act* outside and independent of the cause. An effect acting outside its cause should not in any case be ascribed to this cause. Consequently, a cause has an effect only when this effect exists *within* it. Such relationship is only possible in a causality circling within itself. Only the circular form *is* and acts. None of its elements has an independent effect.

(cc) 'In the effect, the cause stands in relation to itself'. Spinoza had stipulated that the absolute must be the *cause of itself (causa sui)*. Hegel considers this stipulation correct,[25] but its elaboration in Spinoza's system as unsatisfactory. This definition of the absolute can only be justified in terms of the cycle theory, in which 'the cause posits, becomes, is, its other and acts in this other upon itself.'

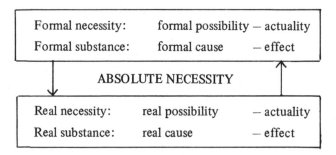

2.33. *The Sublation of Metaphysics*

It has become clear that the schema of the circular movement explained above governs Hegel's ontology. The account of the circle of absolute necessity is to be regarded as the most important. In this account, a certain correctness is attributed to previous metaphysics of the understanding, which reached its climax in Spinoza's system. The absolute is a substance, but not a being-in-self *(In-sich-Sein)* which stands opposite its accidentality. In this form, the absolute substance would be neither absolutely necessary, nor self-subsisting, nor cause.

Hegel's refutation of Spinoza is a *sublation* in the narrow sense of the term. Substance distinguished and separated from its accidentality exists only as a moment and, because of the return-into-self, continues to subsist *forever* as a moment of the whole circle. In the yonder world it is neither absolutely necessary nor self-subsisting nor absolute cause; this is why it has to *vanish* into this world, and this world into that beyond. The union of the two spheres both negates and preserves Spinoza's distinction between the substance and its externalizations.

For Spinoza, thought is a *modus* distinguished from the absolute substance; for Hegel, thought and self-consciousness is to form the nature of the absolute.[26] In a sense, this requirement is fulfilled by the *sublation*. It follows from the analysis of necessity that the whole is a process involving universal determinations which turns within itself and is without any spatial or temporal distinctions. Yet such a process is a process of thought.

There is no object opposite to the all-inclusive form of thought, which thus is a subject that posits its other in absolute freedom — nothing resists it, for there is nothing outside it.[27] In this way, metaphysics of being is sublated into a theory of thought; the ontological categories — necessity, causality substantiality — form the moments of a free process of thought. Yet, for Hegel, 'freedom' means the sublation of natural necessity.[28] This unavoidably raises the question about the relationship between this process of thought and inorganic and organic nature. If this nature remained outside the process of universals, then the process would not be free. From this point of view, Spinoza's metaphysics is not yet sublated, and the identity of being and thought not yet attained. The question raised is answered by the *Doctrine of the Concept.* It teaches about the nature of the subject thinking itself and about how inorganic and organic nature constitute a moment in the all-encompassing process of thought. We cannot agree, therefore, with N. Hartmann's accusation[29] that Hegel has done violence to the dialectical method when passing from the *Doctrine of Essence* to the *Doctrine of the Concept,* for these new problems ensue from the solution of the former. Hegel's dialectic consists precisely in that the object of investigation changes and then sublates itself. Just as the sublation of becoming into the circle *being-nothingness + becoming + being-nothingness* led from becoming to determinate being, to finite being, and established the transition to the inquiry into true infinity, so will metaphysics of being be sublated into the theory of thought which is the *Doctrine of the Concept.* After the demonstration of the *ideality* of the categories of being, the illusory reality of the subject-side-H and the object-side-H is to be analyzed and dialectical-logically sublated.

CHAPTER 3

BEING IS THOUGHT

3.1. THE SUM TOTAL OF ALL REALITIES

3.11. *The Subjective Concept*

The circles of the metaphysics of being have been closed; the doctrine of being has become the theory of thought. Before determining the relationships between inorganic and organic nature and thought, Hegel examines, in the first section of the *Doctrine of the Concept,* the presuppositions of freedom and of the identity between nature and thought. With this identity, he wishes to express that all of nature possesses an ideal mode of being or — which means the same — that it exists as objective being in general, as a moment in the thought of the all-embracing subject.

Can this theory be reconciled with the common view that the individual given in sense experience is inexhaustible? Does this unlimitedness not necessarily imply an insurmountable barrier for thought and cognition in general? Does not the singular individual thus constitute an essential opposition to ideality? It surely can never be exhaustively characterized in any analysis! While such an individual is not appropriate to thought, this incomprehensibility — as Hegel answers — is not due to a deficiency of thought, but to the lack of determinateness and content of the given individual itself. The true and comprehensible individual does not contain any badly infinite multiplicity of universals.[1] The 'bad' in what is objectively given is finite, 'vanishing', and without significance.

If one were to reply that for our knowledge this identity is but an ideal and is not objectively given, Hegel would agree with the first assertion and reject the second. If one assumes the *possibility* of adequate knowledge, one must also accept its presuppositions. The identity between the individual and the universal must be granted objectivity, for it is an objective presupposition for the possibility of understanding reality.[2] To be sure, this identity is not evident from immediately given actuality; but it must be present in objective being.

This identity also has consequences concerning *the particular.* If the universal = the individual, then also the universal = the particular = the individual, since the particular = a composition of universalities. In absolute being, there is thus a moment in which the individual = the particular = the universal. This identity constitutes the subjective concept, the absolute 'I', the presupposition of all *conceivable* actuality in general.

The finite 'I' develops at the cost of its environment; the absolute 'I', by contrast, can only draw upon itself, as there is nothing opposite to it. Therefore, it is the task of science to derive reality from this concept.[3] One could ask whether Hegel demanded this of science for purely theological reasons. This suspicion is not entirely unfounded, for he explicitly calls the subjective concept 'God' and, in the context of the problem of derivation, he deals with the ontological proof. However, if one considers only the theological aspect of these problems, he overlooks their philosophical significance. Hegel is dealing with the objective conditions of our knowledge. The endeavor of any scientific research presupposes the possibility that reality can be summed up in an ideal synthesis. This synthesis, the absolute 'I', not only must exist in the objective whole, but *given reality* must also have been 'deduced' from it; *otherwise the synthesis aspired by the sciences is without significance for the world of experience from the very beginning,* since the two would be unrelated. Dialectical logic critically determines the relationship between the asymptotic synthesis of all scientific knowledge and given reality. As regards the problems involved in this deduction, Hegel comes to terms with the metaphysical and the Kantian views of the sum total of all essentialities.

3.12. *The Metaphysical Concept*

3.121. *The Identity in the Metaphysics of the Understanding*

Anselm of Canterbury, Descartes, and Spinoza worked out a concept that from the outset included within itself all essentialities of things existing in the past, present, or future.[4] Kant calls it the 'sum total *(Inbegriff)* of all realities'. Yet being is a reality; consequently — as the metaphysicians of the understanding believe — the existence of this sum total must be postulated.

Hegel regards this argument as being correct, but he stresses at the same time that its scope is limited. The 'sum total' surely implies 'being', but only abstract, indeterminate, empty being. Thus, by no means does the 'sum total of all realities' mean supreme perfection. In the *Doctrine of the Concept,* then, the same problems as those in the beginning of the *Logic* return — although on a more concrete level — namely, the analysis of indeterminate formal ideality, and the analysis of its resulting dynamic.

Being merely as such, or even *determinate being*, is such a meager and restricted determination, that the difficulty of finding it in the concept may well be the result of not having considered what *being* or *determinate being* itself is.[5]

In his examination of the ontological proof, Hegel repeateadly stresses that *being* is 'meager' and 'restricted'; he also calls it 'the abstraction of the relation-to-self'.[6] These expressions illustrate the extent to which he accepts the so-called ontological proof. The 'being' of the sum total is abstract, ideal, and entirely different from that of given reality. On the one hand, this difference expresses the surmounting of the real limitedness of ideal being, but on the other hand, it points to the negativity, and the power of positing, of ideality. This is why Hegel accepts the being of the conceptual sum total − as did metaphysics − but not its perfection. By accepting the reality of the absolute subject and, at the same time, insisting on its negativity, Hegel inseparably unites being and positing. This means, in the language of imagination, that God's being is identical with this activity of creating:

... this still abstract reality completes itself in objectivity.[7]

Of necessity, ideality asserts itself.

3.122. *The Critical Non-Identity*

When I imagine an amount of money, it does not mean that it exists: just as little does the sum total of all realities exist when I think it. According to Hegel, Kant's objection to the ontological proof involves the same misunderstanding as the metaphysical proof itself: the being of finite things is put on one level with that of ideality.

Now though it is of course true that concept is different from being, there is still a greater difference between God and the hundred thalers and other finite things. It is the definition *of finite things* that in them concept and being differ, that concept and reality, soul and body, are perishable, whence they are perishable and mortal; the abstract definition of God, on the other hand, is precisely that his concept and his being are *unseparated* and *inseparable.*[8]

Hegel's requirement that the subjective concept and its formal-ideal being be inseparable is not an isolated thesis; it finds its justification in negative dialectic, which stipulates the irrefrangible persistence of universal determinations, in contrast to the inner fragility of their finite, real combinations. The universal is separable from its real being, and *in*separable from its own, ideal being. The same properties are attributed to the subjective concept, the universal in general.

Even though one democracy is bad and transitory, one cannot call the ideal of democracy bad and transitory. In the same sense, one cannot *imagine* any determinate realities which would not be as transitory as 100 thalers; but their ideals persist, and return on ever higher levels.

3.123. *Dialectical Identity and Non-Identity*

Hegel, from the outset, rejects any separation within being, but he by no means rejects differences of being themselves; for precisely this reason, he comes to postulate the twofold contradictions. Accordingly, the subjective concept is identical with being in general, i.e., the abstract moment of being, and non-identical with being in general, i.e., *being* as that which is *(Sein als Seiendem)*. It is the *same unitary* being which is present, and not present, in the subjective concept.[9]

The contradiction of this identity and non-identity, then, rests on a postulated monism as regards being. The *'one being'* is the sum total, and also not the sum total; this is why it *becomes* what it has not been, namely, objectivity. At the same time, it loses what it has been, namely, pure ideality, so that this second state is contradictory in the reverse sense, and it will perish and generate the first state again. In this way, absolute, unitary being turns within itself, because it can find its adequate and exhaustive content neither in ideality nor in reality.

God is not *a* concept, but *the* concept; this is the absolute reality which is ideality. God is all of reality, and hence that of being, that is, being is contained in the concept. This is correct; as has been said above, being is this immediate identity, and hence a moment of the concept. But concept as subjectivity differs from being, and it is precisely the sublation of this difference which is at issue.

Of the subjective concept, the ontological proof shows that it is not what one commonly understands by a concept, something opposite to what is objective – (it *ought* not to be infected with being). – This means that the concept negates its determinateness of being subjective, that this determinateness is negated, or rather, that the concept is this dialectic of itself.[10]

(aa) The absolute subject is *the* concept, i.e., the concept of all concepts, which exists even independently of the thought of any individual man. (bb) The text shows how Hegel 'manipulates' being in the double way we have explained, in order to obtain the contradiction. (aaa) The subjective concept is absolute reality, ideality, being in the form of the immediate – i.e., without mediation taking place in a circular form – identity. (bbb) The concept of all concepts is equally opposed to being; its wealth of content does not prevent it from being pure ideality and subjectivity. In no case can *objective* being be attributed to it. Because there is only one being, (aaa) and (bbb) are contradictory in opposite senses. (cc) Pure identity and non-identity form the starting-point for the dialectical movement of the subjective concept. This concept negates itself, because its subjectivity is contradictory, and it thus sublates the difference between itself and objective being; the content of the subjective concept passes over into its 'other', the objective concept.

3.13. 'The Derivation of the Real'

Because of its inner contradictoriness, the subjective, formal concept externalizes and realizes itself.

The *derivation* of the real from it if we want to call it derivation, consists in the first place essentially in this, that the concept in its formal abstraction reveals itself as incomplete and through its own immanent dialectic passes over into reality in such a way that it generates reality out of itself, but does not fall back again onto a ready-made reality that is found opposite to it, nor take refuge in something which has shown itself to be the unessential element of appearance because, having looked around for something better, it has still failed to find it.

Its externality is manifested in the *fixed being* of its *determinations*, each of which appears independently as an isolated, qualitative something which is only externally related to its other. But the *identity* of the concept which is precisely the *inner* or *subjective* essence of these determinations, sets them in dialectical movement, through which their isolation vanishes and with it the separation of the concept from the object, and there emerges as their truth the *totality* which is *the objective concept.* [11]

(aa) The last part of the first quotation refers to Kant's dialectic which, while taking the universal determinations to be the *essential*, and the individual aspect the *unessential,* element of phenomena, did not assume a concept in-and-for-itself and exclusively recognized the given phenomena as the only reality of the concept. (bb) Given reality is 'derived' from the formal concept, i.e., it presupposes this concept. 'Derivation', 'realization', 'externalization', etc., are not to be confused with the ordinary concept of creation. The latter is a free act, the former are positings *of natural necessity* which have their presuppositions in what is objectively given. (cc) In the physical world, the unity of the content of the subjective concept seems to be completely split, fallen asunder, and lost. (dd) However, the *identity* of the concept 'acts' in externality, in the physical mode of being, and arouses a second dialectical movement which is opposite to the first. While at first the non-identity split the identity of the formal concept, it now is the identity which turns against the separation. The formal, abstract being of the universal determinations constitutes the inner essence of the physical world, the original identity emerges again and dissolves the isolated and independently existing being into the totality of the objective concept.

The relationship between the subjective and the objective concepts by far transcends human experience; analogous relationships, however, are to be found in human experience. The being of ideals in human self-consciousness is merely formal. The opposition between the perfection of these ideals and their formal mode of being becomes more paradoxical as the ideals assume 'more concrete' forms and as they are given more thorough consideration.

148   DIALECTICAL METAPHYSICS

Hegel's 'absolute' contradiction,[12] which is the source of all activity, is nothing other than that paradoxical relationship in *logical* form. Ideals compel man to act; in their realization, they generate the unified form of the totality of their elements which prior to the activity have existed outside, and independently of, one another.

Man realizes his ends, i.e., what first was merely ideal is made to lose its one-sidedness, and is thus made to be. The concept is eternally this activity of positing being as identical with itself.[13]

Just as man can enjoy his realized ideals and can enter into a relationship with them, so will the subjective and objective concept create a unity which Hegel calls the 'idea of life'.

3.2. THE IDEA OF LIFE

3.21. *External Purposiveness*

Only the uneducated, primitive consciousness thinks that the split being of the physical world is true being; any scientific education, on the other hand, leads to the conviction that every object is subject to an all-encompassing lawfulness. The mechanical and chemical processes unite physical nature into one total movement from which no single body can escape. This nature — apparently self-sufficient — seems to exist completely in itself.

The processes of life, however, break through the blind lawfulness of mechanical and chemical nature moving within itself, they act upon it and utilize it. Does the physical world, then, exist by virtue of, and for, living beings? Such an assumption is no doubt absurd, for the existence of the sun, moon, and the universe is easily conceivable without the action of individual living beings. From this point of view, the inorganic world seems to be the original. A vulgar theory of evolution, according to which life has originated from non-living nature, is regarded by Hegel as a childish and primitive assumption. Living beings manifest clearly their exceptional position with respect to physical nature, and it is precluded that the higher level in nature is caused by the lower.

In short, for Hegel the problem of purposiveness consists in this, that *on the one hand* organic nature does not exist by virtue of, and for, individual living beings, since they are finite, and that *on the other hand* living beings do not exist by virtue of, and for, inorganic nature, since it is for them a mere means of preserving their life. The concept of an external purposiveness, i.e., the view that the relation between ends and means is merely an external one, is incapable of solving this problem. According to this view, living beings and inorganic nature exist as autonomous magnitudes independent of one another. Historically, this view leads to the assumption of a third autonomous magnitude, the extramundane understanding which sees to it that inorganic and organic nature are in harmony with each other. The absurdity of this assumption is evident: it is unworthy of the absolute wisdom to order inorganic nature for the sake of preserving certain species of animals which later disappear again, to create mice so that cats have something to eat, etc. Moreover, it has been scientifically proven that the extinction of certain species was due to mundane lawfulness.

The more the teleological principle was linked with the concept of an extramundane intelligence and to that extent was favored by piety, the more it seemed to depart from the true investigation of nature, which aims at knowledge of the properties of nature not as extraneous, but as *immanent determinatenesses*, and recognizes only such knowledge as valid *comprehension.* [14]

For the dialectician, the solution in terms of external purposiveness is untenable. The extramundane wisdom can only be finite, since the material world exists opposite to it and independent of it. The latter is limited by its dependence on the former.

3.22. Internal Purposiveness

(a) Abstracting from the dependence of living beings on their environment, one obtains the concept of a totality closed in itself:

Regarded in one aspect, the organism is infinite since it is a c i r c l e o f p u r e r e t u r n - i n t o - s e l f; but it is at the same time in a state of tension relative to external inorganic nature, and has needs. Here the means come from the outside. [15]

There is 'internal purposiveness' in a subject which achieves its self-preservation through means present within itself. An animal, for instance, stays alive by means of the harmonious interaction of its organs. From this point of view, animal life is an eternal process in virtue of the sublation of any dependence on outside factors. Since, however, the action of its organs is insufficient, and nutrients have to be taken from the environment, the life of an animal is infinite only 'in one aspect'.

(b) Inorganic nature cannot exist by virtue of, and for, individual life, since the latter is dependent on it. However, the problem is solved if inorganic and organic nature form one single life, because then life and its means no longer exist separately from one another.

Now the basic proceeding is from this finite vitality to absolute, universal purposiveness, which means that this world is a *cosmos*, a system in which everything is essentially related to everything else, and nothing is isolated: a system ordered in itself, where everything has its place, influences the whole, subsists by virtue of the whole and is equally active, effective, in generating the whole. The main point then is that one proceeds from finite purposes to the one universal vitality, the one purpose which subdivides itself into particular purposes, and that this particularization is such that the particular purposes are in harmony with, and in mutual essential relation to, one another. ... As life is essentially something which is living, or subjective, so is this universal life something subjective, a soul, the *nous*. Thus, universal life contains the soul, the determination of the one *nous* which plans, governs, and organizes everything. This is how far the ontological proof has gone in its determination.[16]

In the assumption of the *cosmical* life, the true relationship of *unity* and *difference* between inorganic and organic nature is acknowledged.

3.23. *The Speculative Death*

The teleological consideration has not yet found its conclusion in the assumption of the absolute life. The absolute is still to be recognized and acknowledged as spirit. This is why the dialectic turns against the perfection of absolute life.

The idea of life involves two distinct parts: externality and *nous*. The former consists of the externalized content of the absolute subject, content which tends to fall asunder into completely conceptless multiplicity. This externality, or this body, is deprived of its independence by the universal soul, and is sublated into the *one* life of the cosmos. While this life is imperishable, it is still changeable because of the duality of externality and *nous,* and it is by no means dialectical-logically necessary.

Finitude in this sphere has the determination, for the sake of the immediacy of the idea, that soul and body are *separable*; this constitutes the mortality of the living being. It is, however, only insofar as the living being is dead that these two sides of the idea are distinct components.[17]

The idea of life comprises in its *unity* two *distinct* elements. Yet every unity amidst distinctness produces a contradictory state of affairs which must be consequently resolved. This death of cosmical life has been expressed by Christianity in terms of images: The son (universal soul) dies and returns to the father (subjective concept). Their unity is the spirit. The death of life thus produces the spirit.[18]

Analogously, the 'speculative Good Friday' takes place in the life of every scientist in*spired* by the subject matter of his analysis. He detaches himself from the particularity of his own private interests and overcomes the limitation of his ken of experience once he has gained true insight into the action of the universal in his world of experience.

3.3. TELEOLOGY

3.31. *Absolute Spirit*

The death of cosmical life repels its soul, *consciousness,* back to the original *self,* the subjective concept. This return-into-self underlies *absolute self-con-sciousness,* whose 'movement' consists in the separation from itself, on the one hand, and the reunification with itself, on the other. Self-consciousness presupposes self-duplication, namely, the possibility of regarding oneself as an object; it is precisely through that double movement that this self-duplication is achieved.[19]

The unity of absolute self-consciousness does not yet mean that every type of dualism is overcome. The external world, commonly regarded as the concrete world, seems to be far removed from that *self-consciousness.* Does not externality stand in opposition to absolute consciousness, and is it not, therefore, independent of it? In the *Logic,* this question is answered in the chapter on the idea of the true and the good. The speculation presented there does not in any essential way differ from our analysis of negative dialectic. The only difference is that, in the latter, it is man who elevates himself from the self-conscious state to that of reason, while in the former, the absolute does so. Just as man acquires the insight into universal rationality in history, so does this transition occur in the logical movement of the absolute spirit. In it, unconscious positing, becoming self-conscious, and becoming rational are united in a dialectical form which sublates and preserves life. From this point of view, everything that makes its appearance in history has been present in the dialectical-logical essence. History is nothing other than the temporal explication of the logical.

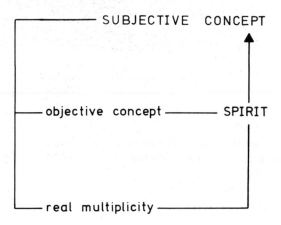

3.32. *Absolute and Finite Spirit: Freedom*

The absolute subject externalizes itself and attains its freedom when the illusory independence of its externalized content, externalized into multiplicity and into the absolute essence, is sublated. An analogous process takes place in human spirit which divests non-living nature of its independence by means of nutrition and technology, although human spirit does not itself posit non-living nature. It acquires its freedom through knowledge, which eliminates the accidental from what is given, brings out the universal structures, and grasps the possibilities of accomplishing a novel realization by means of ideals. In this way, spiritual activity links the object to the subject, and overcomes their opposition. The sublation elevates the subject to unlimited freedom.

To what extent, however, does the restricted sublation of the subject-object opposition on a human level necessarily correspond to its dialectical-logical form? Critical philosophy circumvents this difficulty: For Kant, man attains his freedom through duty, the content of which remains inaccessible to reason. Hegel, by contrast, considers it irrational to chase after the realization of an undetermined and questionable content.[20] The good in-and-for-itself, which elevates man above natural necessity and enables him to be free, must be determinate and knowable at least in its ideal ('logical') structure. This eternal form is the absolute spirit as logical idea.

The true form [of teleological considerations – *A.S.*] is this: There are finite spirits. But the finite has no truth; the truth of the finite spirit is the absolute spirit. The finite is not true being; it is in itself the dialectic of sublating itself, negating itself, and its negation is the affirmation as the infinite, the universal in-and-for-itself.[21]

(aa) The 'true' spirit is the absolute; in the human individual, there is present but a limited, contradictory form of spirituality. (bb) The old metaphysics started from experience: There are finite things and rational, finite beings; *this is why* there ought to be – to explain their existence – an absolute reason too. Hegel's 'experience' is fundamentally different: Because being *cannot* be ascribed to finite spirits, there is an absolute spirit. The negativity of finite reason guarantees the freedom of absolute reason. While the process of human knowledge partly overcomes the subject-object opposition by resolving what is given into pure determinations; while the human individual attempts to realize in his own way the good known to him; his freedom can never influence absolute freedom, because it is finite like its subject, and cannot escape the negative dialectic of the finite. This is why the human individual cannot offer resistance to what is historically necessary. Here, as in every dialectical analysis, the subject of determinations *passes* from the finite to the absolute individual. It is for this reason that the human conquest of the object is that of the absolute, that human freedom is that of the *logos*, not because the latter restricts the former,[22] but because the former is lowered and raised to a *moment*. Man's supreme good is his freedom, which is the freedom of the infinite. Freedom can master history only by knowing what is rational and by committing itself to carry it out. Only human spirit which rises to the absolute point of view is able to develop an epoch-making activity.

3.33. *All of Hegel's Dialectic Is Teleological*

The absolute good asserts itself as absolute truth, in its self-realization, attains supreme agreement. Ontological truth is not a status, but a pulsating dynamic of ideals. An abiding state of agreement between reality and ideality is impossible, for positive and satisfactory structures can result neither from dissolution nor from realization. *The all-embracing whole is thus the process in which unity and separation sublate each other. The process of human activity complies with this law.*

(a) Separation and reconciling reunification is the *logos* of all negativity. All realizing activities are given their unity and their immanent end through return-into-self and reunification of the content that has fallen asunder with the subjective concept.

(b) The separation and unity between the *logos* and the forms of space and time demand that, in addition to the logical, there also be a spatial and temporal externalization of the subjective concept.[23]

(c) This would be non-sensical without the self-contemplation of the absolute in the cognition of finite spirit. No matter what man is doing or working on, he necessarily strives for knowledge; every form of knowledge is abstract and reproduces the original universal. In this way, man — whether he wants to or not — co-operates in the circular process of self-glorification of the absolute spirit. The dialectic provides him with insight into this situation, and enables him to unite his knowledge, the scattered images of the subjective concept, into a synthesis and to obtain an adequate representation of the original source of all actuality. Since he exists but by virtue of the absolute spirit, it is this spirit which in man returns to itself, and in this way reconciles its spatial and temporal mode of being with itself. Yet, on the other hand, finite spirit overcomes the unconscious and the *blind* necessity by attaining insight into, and self-identification with, the absolute rational with the help of dialectic. In the most concrete circular movement of self-cognition all others are absorbed and *sublated*. The most abstract is that of absolute being, which negates itself and thus passes over into becoming. Becoming, however, vanishes again; yet at the same time, it continues to subsist, since it eternally flows back into the original source by which it is established anew. Becoming as sublated in this cyclical process, which has grown subsistent, is *determinate being*, which later, in the logical process, appears as the reality of the circle of true infinity. This second rotational form differs from multiplicity by its unity (being-for-self). But multiplicity is not exempted from sublating movement either. Through its linkage with being-for-self in the circular form, it has become the determinateness of unity, quality. Hegel's doctrine of transcendentals, the first book of the *Logic*, concludes with the demonstration that the circle of quantity must necessarily merge with that of quality into the 'true' measure relationship – again a circle. The essential characteristics of the reflecting movement in the transcendentals reveal themselves in the world of things and phenomena, and make it 'fall to the ground' into its ideal primordial source. The world, as regards its essential content, cannot exist in separation from the sum total of all realities. The world is the body and objectivity of the latter. In the process of the *Logic*, the world has doubled. This world, being a logical moment of the idea, and the transitory world are foreign and opposite to each other. The reconciliation is accomplished by the spirit. In human knowledge, the logical appears anew in its specific shape. In this way, all being, all movement, and all activity is determined by the absolute subject and is focussed on its self-contemplation and self-liberation.

The goal of the spirit, when we use the term in this way, is to comprehend itself so that it is no longer concealed from itself. And the way thereto is its development; and the series of developments are the stages of its development.[24]

The spirit aims at contemplating itself as concretely in its historical externalization as it 'logically' cognizes itself.

SUMMARY

We have analyzed the following theses in our exposition:

I. Hegel's dialectic is the method by which only a certain kind of idealism can be demonstrated.

1.   Negative dialectic shows the transitoriness and nullity of reality.

1.1. (a) Hegel's method aims at providing an insight into the all-comprehensive essence *(Wesen)*.

(b) The problem of dialectic is closely linked to the problem of universals; the absolute alone is truly concrete and permanent.

(c) The dialectic is thus directed against what is apparently concrete.

1.2. (a) Things are merely momentary and accidental concretions of idealities.

(b) It would indeed be absurd to believe that the universal is tied to a definite and limited reality.

(c) The task of demonstrating this absurdity is accomplished by 'negative dialectic'.

1.3. (a) Negative dialectic demonstrates the necessary dissolution of idealities which have momentarily become concrete in real things.

(b) This theory of 'dissolution' presupposes the ideal reality of pure ideals.

(c) In a quite definite sense, Hegel can be called an extreme realist: For him the formal is present in things. However, there are no universalities existing in themselves; they concresce in the process of 'sublation'.

2.   Ideal dialectic investigates the ground of being of given reality.

2.1. Hegel is one of the greatest philosophers of history. He conceived the *Logic* in order to elucidate reality and the development of philosophy.[1] By means of his system he attempted to solve and 'sublate' the problems of both German and Christian philosophy and those of Greek philosophy.[2]

2.11. For an understanding of Hegel's dialectic it is important to note that philosophers before Aristotle had already acquired a limited insight into the principle of non-contradiction, which — at least in the judgment of contemporary interpreters — they used differently from Aristotle, namely, to demonstrate the transitoriness of reality and the permanence of ideality.

2.12. (a) 'Nothingness' for Hegel issues from the resolution of a contradictory state of affairs. He distinguishes it from (aa) the Skeptical-Critical 'nothing' which expresses the futility of a contradictory argument; (bb) the Sophist 'nothing' which expresses the vanity of our knowledge and by way of inference means unbounded freedom for the individual; and finally, (cc) Eleatic 'nothing' which also appears in several Platonic dialogues, and which means the nullity of reality as well as the permanence of ideality, but does not provide a starting-point for the positive explanation of reality.

(b) Like the Eleatic dialectic, Hegel's dialectic establishes nullity, the inevitable annihilation and the necessary transition to the opposite pole. In contrast to the Eleatic method, Hegel's does not confine itself to the negativity of what is objectively given, but also attempts to establish nullity and necessity of externalization in the realm of pure ideals. In this way, every one of Hegel's considerations, following the law of the negation of negation, returns to the starting-point.

2.13. The circle of being is an example of the cyclical nature of his considerations.

2.14. The dynamic, all-pervading totality of ideal being, which posits its reality within itself and immediately dissolves it again, is logical reason.

2.2. Hegel compares the all-encompassing subject with the object of Kant's and Fichte's epistemology. Hegel took over many elements of his theory of creative ideality from these German philosophers and incorporated them into a new context.

2.3. Double negation is the principle law of Hegel's dialectic methodology: The first negation is formed by the unity of identity and non-identity, and demands the realization, externalization and objectivization of the pure ideals; the second is formed by the unity of identity and distinctness of reality, the world of things and phenomena and objectivity.

3. The material object of Hegel's philosophy is the universal, its formal object the contradiction; the goal to be attained by this philosophy is supposed to be identical with that of history.

3.1. Dialectical reflection starts with either pure ideality or realized ideals.

3.2. Contradiction is an ontological law.

3.21. The view that Hegel's system is at variance with formal logic is based on an untenable confusion of two meanings of 'principle'.

(a) Hegel's principle of contradiction and that of formal logic are essentially *different* from one another: (aa) For Hegel, ideal being is equal to being *insofar* as it is equal to non-being, i.e., is ideal; and the things are independent *insofar* as they are dependent in the same respect. (bb) According to the principle of non-contradiction of formal logic, it is not permissible to ascribe two opposite predicates — i.e., one implying the *negation* of the other — to the same subject in the same respect *(-.p - p; p/ -p)*.

(b) Still, the Hegelian contradiction does *not contradict* logical freedom from contradiction, for — to speak in Hegelian terms — there is no identity which encompasses the two of them, i.e., they do not belong to the same realm. (aa) Dialectical contradiction is an *ontological* principle, that of *formal logic* is a rule of the understanding. (bb) Dialectical logic is not opposed to formal logic any more than a demonstration that something is absurd is itself absurd. (cc) The formal-logical principle leads to externally fixed, 'permanent' and formal 'truths', whereas Hegel's principle is the ontic ground of movement.

(c) In the demonstration of the absurdity and nullity — the contradiction — of reality, Hegel follows the rules of correct knowledge, the principle of non-contradiction.

3.22. (a) The contradiction that determinately is *(daseiende Widerspruch)* indicates the inadequacies of *pure* as well as of *realized* ideals. The absurdities are sublated into the circular form of self-contemplation.

(b) Something is 'sublated' when it is eternalized through return into the primordial origin and received into a circular form.

(c) The whole is without contradiction, movement, or relation, and is 'true'; this dialectical-logical truth does not hold for any reality.

3.3. *Logos* externalizes iself in order to reflect itself adequately in mankind which exists within *logos*. This finite self-contemplation — in contrast to logical-ideal self-contemplation — is subject to development.

II.   Dialectic is in conformity with metaphysics, and is opposed to it. Dialectic is metaphysical since it shows that given reality transcends itself so as to reappear in a new form. But dialectic is the opposite of the method by means of which transphysical being — one severed from the physical world — is established.

1.   Dialectical logic is a metaphysics, a doctrine about 'logical' ideality which posits reality, and in which reality exists. Whereas the *Logic* investigates this ideality in and for itself, it is the task of other sciences to analyze its external — i.e. spatial and temporal — forms.

2.   By means of the concept of self-movement, dialectic overcomes the opposition between ideality and reality, which previous metaphysics have regarded as two self-subsistent poles acting independently of one another.

III.   With the help of dialectic, a new doctrine of being is established. The proofs by which the metaphysics of the understanding established the existence of a transcendent being were correct from a formal-logical point of view; however, rationalists overlooked the contradiction inherent in the content of their proofs. Kant, who discovered these antinomies, nonetheless assumed a contradictory position: he reduced the absolute of metaphysics of the understanding to limited, finite reality. Neither the metaphysical separation nor the Critical unity can be 'true', i.e., be in accordance with the content of opposite determinations. Hegel's concept of truth includes the circular form, in which unity and separation constitute one moment. He demonstrates the presence of this form in various relationships, e.g.,

(1)   between the infinite and the finite,
(2)   between the necessary and the accidental,
       (a) formal and real actuality-possibility,
       (b) substance and its accidents (attributes and modi),
       (c) formal and real causality,
(3)   between the universal and the individual.

All reality, according to Hegel's dialectic, is teleological: The new ideal which is demanded by the negativity of reality will be realized. Outside itself, the reality of the ideal is without any significance, so that the universal sublating this reality is that which is in-and-for-itself.

Hegel's position with respect to the principle of realization and individuation is of fundamental importance. If, following him, one assumes the reality of the infinite, the ideal, and the abstract in what is objectively given, then the dialectical procedure will automatically follow: then the infinite in existing objects is at the same time finite, the unlimited universal in the world of experience is at the same time individual, and the abstract in objective reality is at the same time concrete; in each case, dialectical contradiction becomes inevitable.

All of reality is thus nothing other than the activity of the absolute ideal: the realizing of ideals and the dissolving of their realizations, because reality remains inadequate as compared with true ideality. Man in his practical life conforms to this 'logic'. On the one hand, he realizes his ideals, on the other, he contemplates, analyzes and enjoys the realization. His freedom and enjoyment conform to the ideals forced upon him by the spirit of the time. He overcomes these ideals by pointing out the limits, limitation and absurdity inherent in their reality, in order to prepare the ground for the externalization of new idealities. It is then clear that this theory of self-movement remains unintelligible without its extreme realist presuppositions: For Hegel, solely what is ideal lives and moves.

We hope to have rendered Hegel's system more accessible with this summary of its most important theses. Without doubt, insight into this system is significant for the development of philosophy, for the unquestionably greatest philosopher of modern times and his wide-spread influence can be overcome and 'sublated' only when one has become completely familiar with his thought.

HEGEL'S DIALECTIC AND CONTEMPORARY ISSUES

1. ANALYTIC AND DIALECTIC

Our philosophical-historical study, 'Hegel's Dialectic', has been accepted as a dissertation by the Philosophical Faculty of the University of Fribourg. The motive for this inquiry was not a striving for academic honors, but the desire to gain insight into contemporary dialectical thought. Western thought has in various ways – depending on the concrete situation of our society – come to terms with Hegel's dialectic. This is why the analysis of Hegel's philosophy should not remain an enjoyment of a purely museum-like nature, but should contribute to an understanding of present trends of thought and debates.

To achieve this goal, we have attempted to elucidate Hegel's dialectic by means of the analytical method.[1] This attempt is neither aimed at supplying a synthesis of the two methods – for analytic and dialectic cannot be combined without conflict[2] – nor at imposing a restriction on dialectic or analytic. As we have shown, Hegel appreciated analytic thought – and his authority is still esteemed in contemporary dialectic. His criticism concerns only totalitarian analytic, which excludes dialectical reflection.

Yet it is precisely problems of this kind which lie at the roots of the 'positivism controversy' which has been going on in Germany and in Amsterdam. Habermas – like Hegel – criticizes the analytical method only insofar as it excludes reflection.[3] The positivist fights against the dialectician only insofar as the latter, with the totalitarian militant slogan 'Down with value-free research', undermines analytical thought as an indispensable tool of non-philosophical, and even of philosophical, sciences.[4] The controversy harbors a danger because the total loss of one of the methods at issue would mean a loss in scientific quality. Suppression of the dialectic endangers the understanding of ourselves *(Selbstverständnis)* within technological and scientific progress. But it is just as much a danger for the dialectic itself when critical analytic suffers an impairment. 'Scientific' ideologies easily become dogmatic, abstract and repressive, and ineluctably call forth a positivistic criticism of ideology which demands the separation of research and value.[5] It makes sense to demand reflection of the scientist, but the reflective positive scientist should be aware of the double necessity, and the equally double methodology. Critical reflexion would be lost, if it were identified with positive knowledge. This is why the positivism controversy cannot end with an exclusive either-or; history would *immediately* take up the totalitarian result and — in Marx's word — 'drum dialectic into it', because it would contradict the starting-point of the controversy, emancipation.

Marcuse's authority bears some responsibility for the blind passion with which the positivism controversy is conducted in certain circles; while he has restored dialectic to honor, he has not shed any light on the relationship of analytic and dialectic. The *One-Dimensional Man* champions a second dimension in which emancipation finds its realization. Man, however, is not a dualistic being 'squatting outside the world'; the split characterizes the the bondage of the *'unhappy* consciousness'.[6] True philosophical and scientific self-understanding[7] can only be hoped for from a *self-conscious* and *enlightened* transition of the boundaries, where in each case the unity of the scientific endeavor is relinquished only momentarily. This presupposes that the boundaries have been cognized and recognized.

By equating 'analytic' with 'logic of domination', and 'dialectic' with 'logic of protest', Marcuse has posed the question about the truly emancipatory method in a stimulating way, but has also made it possible to solve it in a one-sided fashion.[8] The 'logic of ought', however, loses its subversive power precisely when it completely dispenses with the 'logic of being'.[9] It is only by means of a strict analysis of being that the contradiction with ideality, and the evolutionary possibility of actuality can be shown.

In view of the historical situation in which he restored dialectic, which had fallen into oblivion, Marcuse's one-sidedness becomes understandable. But this situation must be overcome, for it leads to an equally one-sided reaction. In this respect, Habermas' dialectical design is more promising inasmuch as he, on the one hand, appreciates analytical positivism and even acknowledges the merits of Dewey's pragmatic test of values, and, on the other hand, crosses the positivistic-analytical barrier by demanding the reorientation toward values that issues from self-understanding.[10] This does not mean that all friction between the methodologies has been dissolved, for the tension between being, ought, and what is technologically feasible remains; it means at the same time that technological research is saved from its value blindness, and Marcuseanism from its *'indeterminate* negation of what is' which soon grows fruitless.[11]

Our inquiry, which focussed on the relationship of dialectic and analytic in Hegel's system, in no way claims to solve the controversy over positivism, but it does — we believe — furnish an indispensable footnote. Hegel's method is primarily designed for the 'sublation' of traditional *analytic,* hence it is strongly tied to tradition and not cut to fit contemporary problems. Elements of this method, however, are still taken as *the* dialectical model. This is why the positivism controversy cannot be carried on as if Hegel had not existed at all. That which remains undiscussed, influences us unawares. The fact that representatives of positivism cannot discover anything in dialectic but the heritage of Hegelian theology clearly shows the need for a clarification of where Hegel's dialectic differs from and where it agrees with contemporary dialectics.[12]

2. THE SUBLATION OF HEGEL'S DIALECTIC

The laws of double negation and sublation, designed by Hegel for interpreting the historical process, can also be applied to the historical moment constituted by his system, and, for instance, to the history of Marxism.

2.1. *First Reversion*

The Hegelian methodological law of double negation demands that the two faces, the limitedness *and* the rationality, of each reality, each phenomenon, and each social institution or function be brought out. The insight into the limitedness leads to a call for renewed justification, evolution, or revolution; it undermines any totalitarian claim and, for the rational man who cannot submit to any absolutism, it becomes a weapon for criticizing structures which have come into opposition and contradiction with their ideals, and have thus become oppressive. It calls for the realization of a new ideal which promises a *higher* freedom.

But dialectic also has a *'rational'* side to it. Not only is the negativity of every institution and every historical system of thought pointed out, but so is their historical necessity. Everything that was ever actual, was once rational. This rational aspect is the positive element that must be preserved in the sublation. Speaking of rationality and necessity, however, easily gives the impression of a fully convinced vindication or justification. The dialectical method, then, is the venture of pairing criticism with limited approval, and of defying the attacks from 'left' and 'right'. Yet it will sublate these extremist tendencies and bring about the necessary break-through in social thought and practice.

Hegel's philosophy is just *one* such break-through — although it may be one of the greatest. It was the first design of the methodology for the *immanent* developmental analysis of history, and the attempt to save mankind from chasing after ideas which have become meaningless and abstract, i.e., no longer historically adequate. It *sublated* the mystical tendency. But the liberation was at the same time a preservation. It rejected only the mysticism in traditional transcendence, but did not go beyond this sublation of tradition, emphasizing only the abstract possibility of immanently transcending freedom, whereas it has turned out in industrial society that the domain of biological needs cannot be sublated and transcended without conflicts.[13] This problem calls for the 'reversion', namely, the concentration on the *material preconditions* for immanent transcendence, so as to make the latter possible at all. The problem of the proletariat requires a more concrete, more sophisticated, and more complex model of freedom.

For an adequate assessment of the historical significance of the 'reversion' by Marx it should be noted that Hegel's *sublation* of tradition was regarded as its pure *recognition* in many circles of politically committed and conservative intellectuals. The *Right*-Hegelian simplification provoked a radicalization of the left-wing ideas of 'reversion'. Hegel himself was not entirely without responsibility for this radicalization: In his lectures on right and religion he would often 'flirt' with traditional ideas, and all too frequently he was concerned with emphasizing historical analogies to his *logos*, and the rationality of its effect. Insight into existing injustice engenders aggressive reaction when confronted with the 'rational' justification of institutional reality. This is why it is easy to find passionate rejection of Hegel's dialectic in Marx and Engels. Actually, however, they were the first to try to sublate it, and to assail only the interpretation of dialectic as an extreme idealism and as an unconditional transcending, because this interpretation seeks the justification and fulfillment of what is given in an essentially different realm. With the theory of the decisive effect of the base on the superstructure, Marx and Engels hoped to have de-theologized dialectic once and for all.

Yet this does not mean that they abandoned the method of double negation. In precise accordance with its schema, Marx applied the *negative dialectic* to the structure of capitalist society. For him, capitalist society is the *identity* which finds its *unity* in the striving for wealth by industrialization. But it inevitably produces the *distinctness* of proletariat and bourgeoisie, which grows into an *opposition,* and develops into a *contradiction* with its starting-point, namely, the complete impoverishment of the majority of this society, and this just as inevitably furthers the revolution.[14]

Likewise, Marx's preclusion of the dialectic that transcends unconditionally does not mean the rejection of the positive-ideal, or first, negation. His historical-materialist analysis appreciated the *ideal* of the bourgeoisie, recognized the *necessity of its realization,* and regarded the capitalist society as a *rational actuality* inasmuch as it included, and developed, the preconditions for a genuine Communist liberation of man. In accordance with this, Lenin — very passionately, in his struggle with the *narodniki* — defended the necessity of capitalism.

2.2. *Second Reversion*

The Russian Revolution as such did nothing to change the backwardness of the 'base'. This is why Lenin concentrated on technological, economic and bureaucratic development, and Stalin carried it out with iron discipline. Deborin's endeavor to develop critical-dialectical thought through the publication of Lenin's *Philosophical Notebooks* and the translation of Hegel's works, was suppressed by Stalin with the justification that theory must not be separated from the *practical* struggle for the victory of socialism — which he identified with technological progress.[15] As a consequence, dialectic lost its critical and evolutionary significance.

Characteristically, 'dialectic' for Stalin meant only discussion or class struggle.[16] Because of its technological and economic backwardness, Soviet Russia could not afford any critical intro-reflection.[17] The people had to be called upon to co-operate in the development of those fields without criticism. The ideological realm of Communist freedom had to be postponed to an indefinite future. Whereas Marx saw the promise of freedom in the development of the base, Soviet Russia in Stalin's era sacrificed freedom to the infrastructure. It was only after the Stalin era that the publication of the *Philosophical Notebooks* gained in importance, and at the present time all of Hegel's determinations of reflection are under discussion.

Meljuxin, Ukraincev and Vorob'ev, for instance, attempt to show in detail that *unity* is the primary element of the material structure of being, and *difference* the secondary and additional element.[18] El'meev and Kazakov, on the other hand, regard *difference* as the most fundamental element of the contradictory structure of things and phenomena, because it is precisely difference and struggle which are progressive.[19] In this context, there are diverging opinions about the extent to which 'difference' and 'struggle' should be equated.[20] Kozlovskij regards this discussion as abstract, and demands — as does Rozental', too — that it should follow from concrete analysis alone whether difference, distinctness, or identity is primary.[21] This most promising demand for concreteness is made good by Kozlovskij himself and his colleagues in 'a natural stance': Determinately existing contradictions are only to be found outside Soviet society; since 'the Great October' there can be no more antagonism! This makes it understandable why, for many a Soviet philosopher, the relationship between contradiction and progress becomes blurred, or, why he sees even in development a contradiction (sic!).[22] Because of the identification of sociology and historical materialism, every field of social research is subject to this totalitarian undialectical dialectic. This shows how slowly true de-Stalinization is asserting itself.

2.3. *Third Reversion*

Positivist de-ideologization of the sciences, striving for allegedly value-free progress without critical reflection on the values involved in existing trends, performed in the West what pragmatic Stalinism accomplished in the Soviet Union. This positivist ideology — a trend which excludes ideology is itself an ideology — made possible a saltatory development of the technological side of the 'base'. According to the traditional analysis in historical materialism, Communism as the realm in which all alienation will have been sublated should thus be possible; but the class which has to carry out this revolution is missing, because the proletariat is content with wage increase, the possibility of renting an apartment and owning a car, and — to the extent that these wishes are fulfilled — is not interested in a more fundamental change of society. The Western proletarian voluntarily renounces criticism and, just as voluntarily, concentrates on technological development; Stalin achieved this goal only by wielding an iron fist.

In view of the development of highly industrialized society the traditional Marxist criticism of Feuerbach has grown 'stale'. 'Happiness', 'freedom', 'democratization', and 'humanitarianism' have again become political categories,[23] because technology by no means guarantees the liberation of the concrete individual man; it rather carries him along as an uncritical collaborator, and harbors merely an *abstract*, '*potential* basis' for the sublation of alienation.[24]

While the socialism of the turn of the century was concerned with social justice — meaning 'material' justice, for all practical purposes — present criticism sees in this concern precisely one of the fetters tying man to the base.[25] Marcuse proceeds from the *Dialectic of Enlightenment* of Adorno and Horkheimer, and 'encircles' technocracy in order not to stall its development, on the one hand, and so as to develop an awareness of the realm of freedom, on the other.[26]

By protesting against the reduction of the superstructure and of man in general to quantitative development through his theory of desublimation;

by criticizing traditional idealism through his thesis of repressive sublimation; and by looking upon true sublimation — which is not a mere reflection, but also a criticism, of technological and economic aspirations — as a solution to the problem of 'negative dialectic' posed by Adorno and Freud, and to the discontent with civilization, Marcuse attempts to *sublate* Hegel, Marx, the Stalinist-pragmatist tendencies of Marxism, and the pessimism of Adorno and Freud. His ideal of human freedom is by far more complex and more concrete than that of Hegel and Marx, because the cycle of history of ideas has since experienced several break-throughs.

2.4. *Fourth Reversion*

It is generally known that socialist student movements detest the originators of Social Criticism and turn to the classical 'authorities' of Lenin and Mao. This tendency is an anachronism merely by allegation and can be explained in terms of the history of philosophy. *L'histoire se repète:* Traditional Marxist criticism of Hegel and Feuerbach is reappearing in a new shape. *Philosophical-sociological* criticism of society is supposed to lead to a changing of the world, and not merely to a new *interpretation of the world.* According to Marx: "The coincidence of the changing of circumstances and of human activity can be conceived and rationally understood only as *revolutionizing practice.*"[27] Yet Lenin and Mao designed the tactics and strategies for the realization of social liberation. Western Leninism and Maoism, therefore, are to be understood as tendencies which aim at converting the theoretical emancipation into practice; but they are anachronisms to the extent that they harbor Stalinist tendencies; the *masses* can no longer be *mobilized* to build the preconditions for true liberation, for the preconditions as preconditions are supposed to be already given. What is at issue is the emancipation of the real individual. The contradiction of this starting-point would be anachronistic.

Among the official representatives of Social Criticism, it is Jürgen Habermas who comes closest to the evolutionary striving for practical and structural change. Whereas Marcuse's ideal of sublimation is pragmatic and idealistic, because he opposes it to technological development — in which he can only discover techno*cracy* and loss of subjectivity — and thus leaves a domain reserved for technology,[28] Habermas strives for the dialectical unity of enlightened willing and self-conscious capability.[29]

His theory is the attempt of a new sublation. By means of his dialectical pairing of knowledge and interest, he tries to overcome bondage to the object, which is expressed in Hegelian and Soviet ontology as well as in empiricist-analytic and even Marcusean pragmatism. The human subject does not find its freedom in the identification with an absolute, self-transcending spirit, but in overcoming objectivism with the help of 'knowledge-guiding interests' which are recognized and interpreted as such interests: In the power of self-reflection, knowledge and interest are one.[30]

Thus, the history of dialectic is the struggle of knowledge for freedom. Dialectic should not be confused with 'belief' in view of the sensational *Spiegel* interview with Horkheimer,[31] or on the basis of the fanaticism of some groups, for — as history has shown — it is the knowledge which *knowingly* attempts to surpass itself.

CONCERNING NOTES AND ABBREVIATIONS

As a general principle, in quotations, our emphases are s p a c e d, those of the authors quoted are in *italics*.

Hegels sämtliche Werke — edited by Georg Lasson and Johannes Hoffmeister and incorporated into the *'Philosophische Bibliothek' (PhB* in what follows) published by Felix-Meiner-Verlag (Hamburg) — are the main sources for our study. While this edition is currently the most critical (a new edition has been promised by the same publishing company), it is not the most complete. This is·why we were forced to refer to the edition of 1832 and thereafter in a few cases.

In our notes, we use the following abbreviations.

Berl. Schr.	*Berliner Schriften 1818-1832* (PhB, Vol. 240: 1st edition, ed. by. J. Hoffmeister), 1956.
Bew.	*Vorlesungen über die Beweise vom Dasein Gottes* (PhB, Vol. 64: reprinting of the 1st edition, ed. by G. Lasson, 1930), 1966.
Differenz	*Differenz des Fichte'schen und Schelling'schen Systems der Philosophie* (PhB, Vol. 62 a: unaltered reprint of the 1st edition, ed. by G. Lasson, 1928), 1962.
Enz.	*Enzyklopädie der philosophischen Wissenschaften 1830* (PhB, Vol. 33: 6th edition, newly ed. by F. Nicolin and O. Pöggeler), 1959.
Gesch. I	*Einleitung in die Geschichte der Philosophie* (PhB, Vol. 166: 3rd edition, ed. by F. Nicolin), 1959.
Gesch. II	*Georg Wilhelm Friedrich Hegel's Vorlesungen über die Geschichte der Philosophie* (Vol. XIII of the 1st edition, ed. by Dr. C. L. Michelet), Part One (2nd impression), Berlin 1840.
Gesch. III	*idem*, Part Two (2nd impression), Berlin 1842.
Gesch. IV	*idem*, Part Three (2nd impression), Berlin 1844.
Gl. u. W.	*Glauben und Wissen* (PhB, Vol. 62b: unaltered reprint of the 1st edition, ed. by G. Lasson, 1928), 1962.
Jen. Log.	*Jenenser Logik, Metaphysik und Naturphilosophie* (PhB, Vol. 58: unaltered reprint of the 1st edition, ed. by G. Lasson, 1923), 1967.
Log. I	*Wissenschaft der Logik, erster Teil*, (PhB, Vol. 56: unaltered reprint of the 2nd edition, ed. by G. Lasson, 1934), 1963.
Log. II	*Wissenschaft der Logik, zweiter Teil* (PhB, Vol. 57: unaltered reprint of the 2nd edition, ed. by G. Lasson, 1934), 1963.
Phän.	*Phänomenologie des Geistes* (PhB., Vol. 144: 6th edition, ed. by J. Hoffmeister), 1952.
Realphil.	*Jenaer Realphilosophie* (PhB, Vol. 67: unaltered reprint of the 1st edition, ed. by J. Hoffmeister, 1931), 1967.
Recht	*Grundlinien der Philosophie des Rechts* (PhB, Vol. 124 a: unaltered reprint of the 4th edition, ed. by J. Hoffmeister), 1962.

Rel. I-I   Vorlesungen über die Philosophie der Religion, Vol. I, First Half: *Begriff der Religion* (PhB, Vol. 59: reprint of the 1st edition, ed. by. G. Lasson, 1925), 1966.

Rel. I-II   *idem*, Vol. I, Second Half: *Die bestimmte Religion* (PhB, Vol. 60: reprint of the 1st edition, ed. by G. Lasson, 1927), 1966.

Rel. II-I   *idem*, Vol. II, First Half: *Die bestimmte Religion* (Chapter 2) (PhB, Vol. 61: reprint of the 1st edition, ed. by G. Lasson, 1927), 1966.

Rel. II-II   *idem*, Vol. II, Second Half: *Die absolute Religion* (PhB, Vol. 63: reprint of the 1st edition, ed. by G. Lasson, 1929), 1966.

In the notes, references to secondary literature are given by the name of the author and page numbers alone if only one publication of the author has been considered. If several publications of the same author are mentioned, they are referred to by Roman numerals or other abbreviations as specified in the Bibliography.

NOTES

INTRODUCTION

[1] *Enz.* §15. Cf. *ibid.* §17; *Log.* I 56; *Log.* II 500, 503f.

[2] *Jen. Log.* 140ff., 154f., 161ff., 168, 171, 175, 178, 181, 185; *Realphil.* 19, 29.

[3] Cf. E. von Hartmann 119.

[4] Marx 19.

[5] Sartre 101: "Si l'on se refuse a voir le mouvement dialectique originel dans l'individu et dans son entreprise de produire sa vie, de s'objectiver, il faudra renoncer à la dialectique ou en faire la loi immanents de l'Histoire."

[6] Lossky 70ff.

[7] Feuerbach I 222f.: "Yet the secret of *speculative philosophy* [is] *theology, speculative theology* which differs from ordinary theology in that it transfers the divine being which the latter, for fear and folly, removed into yonder world, into this world, i.e., it renders the divine being *present, determinate, real.*" Cf. also Feuerbach II 426.

[8] Lenin 321f.

[9] Lenin 90, 172f., 197.

[10] Lenin 182f., 250, 275.

[11] Cf. Wetter I; and II 70, 116, 118, 130.

[12] Cf. Bocheński I, and II 86-99, also IV 19-26.

[13] Gropp's (151) accusation is directed against E. P. Sitkovskij in particular.

[14] Efirov 26ff. – Equally characteristic of the Hegel interpretation in East-European philosophy are the publications by Gulian and Ovsjannikov. Gulian writes (II 725): "As has been noted, we discovered in the various parts of Hegel's works a fickle relationship between these two aspects, a contradiction between method and system." Ovsjannikov notes (284): "Hegel's philosophy, as is clear from the entire preceding exposition, suffers from an internal contradiction. It includes in one unity opposing and, as it were, mutually exclusive aspects – a revolutionary method and a conservative system."

[15] Cf. A. Hartmann.

[16] Weisse II 36ff.; cf. also I 143ff.

[17] I. H. Fichte I 308: "Not *contradiction,* but opposition that is infinitely overcome, the seeking and finding which *complement* each other, *love,* is the inner pulse of the

world." − I. H. Fichte II 29: Hegel's view of the contradiction as determinately being "is his error, from which all the other errors can just as consistently be deduced in detail".

[18] Trendelenburg III 7; Haring 100.

[19] Trendelenburg III 12ff.; cf. also I 125.

[20] Überweg 204, 218.

[21] E. von Hartmann 41.

[22] Cf. Part I, Section 3.21, First Interpretation (C).

[23] Cf. Michelet (Preface, p. viii).

[24] Cf. Haring's (98f.) criticism of Liebmann.

[25] Haring 139. One could object to Haring that it is incorrect to represent dialectical-logical movement, movement of pure thought, by figures of circles. The same objection could be raised against our presentation, against Hegel's expression 'circle' which appeals to the imagination, against drawings in mathematics and against mathematical-logical symbols. This objection can partly be invalidated by the advice that our figures be correctly interpreted: the elements of the dialectical movement which are dissociated in the figures must not be taken as spatially and temporally separate.

[26] Albrecht 15ff. − A severe criticism of Coreth's interpretation is to be found in Kruithof 290f. − N. Hartmann attempts to interpret and criticize Hegel using a notion of dialectic which is altogether unrelated to metaphysics and idealism (cf. our Part III, Section 2.33); according to Albrecht (9), Hegel's method is inseparably conjoined with idealism, must rely on it as an 'essential presupposition', and loses all meaning when severed from it. According to *our* interpretation, Hegel's method presupposes extreme realism (in the sense explained in Part I, Chapter 1), and has idealism (the theory according to which the absolute is formed by a process of universals, in which there is no room for spatial and temporal separation) for its goal.

[27] Haring 138.

[28] Phalén 170.

[29] Kroner 312; Kruithof 37.

[30] Kruithof 25: "Many books on Hegel ... in Belgian and Dutch libraries are not cut open."

[31] Mure II (Introd., p. viii).

[32] Kruithof 296.

[33] Cf. Part I, Section 3.21, First Interpretation (B), (c).

[34] Cf. Kruithof 19ff., 43f.

[35] Hyppolite (II 234ff.) and Garaudy (I 200ff.) criticize the dualist interpretation of A. Kojève. They themselves (Hyppolite I 386; Garaudy I 213), however, fall into dualism when they claim, like dialectical materialists (cf. note 14), that there is an opposition between method and system.

[36] Cf. Epilogue, note 13.

PART I, CHAPTER 1

[1] Coreth 20, 35.

[2] *Log.* I 35.

[3] *Log.* I 23, 35.

[4] N. Hartmann II 5.

[5] N. Hartmann I 375.

[6] *Log.* II 484.

[7] *Gesch.* III 192; *Jubiläumsausgabe*, Vol. 18, p. 128: "The other species, what is thought in the soul itself, is that where the soul proceeds from an hypothesis or presupposition to a principle which is above hypotheses, and makes its way *(methodon)*

not by means of images, as in the former cases, but through ideas *(eidesi)* themselves."
Cf., e.g., *Log.* I 35: 'scientific progress' *(wissenschaftlicher Fortgang); Log.* II 490.

8 *Log.* I 35.

9 *Log.* I 29; *Log.* II 490; *Enz.* §164, note; *Gesch.* I 30, 97, 111.

10 Cf. *Log.* I 15f.

11 *Gl u. W.* 92f.

12 *Log.* I 14.

13 *Enz.* §§ 19-25.

14 *Log. I* 40f.

15 *Log.* I 32.

16 *Log.* I 24f.

17 *Log.* I 25; *Log.* II 440. Cf. *Gl. u. W.* 1.

18 *Enz.* §20, note.

19 *Enz.* §§8, 12, 24.

20 Feuerbach III 341 ff.; cf. Part III, Section 3.11.

21 In the *Phenomenology* (*Phän.* 73) the subject experiences the nullity of its objects.
In the *Logic (Log.* I 15f), Hegel summarizes this thesis substantiated in detail in the
Phenomenology: "But if the truth of the matter is what we have already stated and also
is generally admitted, namely that the *nature,* the peculiar *essence,* that which is
genuinely *permanent* and *substantial* in the diversity and contingency of appearance
and fleeting manifestation, is the *concept* of the thing, the *immanent universal,* as
every human individual, though being infinitely unique, has in himself what is prior
(das Prius) to all his pecularities: to be man, as has each individual animal the *prius* of
being an animal: then it would be impossible to say what – if this foundation were
removed from the individual, no matter how richly endowed it might be with other
predicates, although this foundation can be called a predicate like the others – what
such an individual could still be."

22 *Log.* II 159.

23 *Phän.* 89-103, esp. 98 and 100.

24 *Phän.* 100.

25 *Phän.* 102-125, esp. 112.

26 N. Hartmann I 329.

27 *Phän. 138; Log.* II 480.

28 *Recht* (Preface, pp. xix-xx).

29 *Enz.* § 564, note.

30 Cf. this Part, Section 2.33.

31 *Enz.* §164, note.

32 N. Hartmann I 283.

33 *Log.* I 63, *Log.* II 354.

34 *Gesch.* III 289.

35 *Gesch.* III 184.

36 Manser 617-667.

37 *Phän.* 192; *Log.* I 66f.

38 *Phän.* 81.

39 *Phän.* 82.

40 Section 3.221 of this Part explains the relationship of being-nothingness-becoming.

41 On the infinite, cf. Part III, Chapter 1.

42 *Jen. Log.* 8

43 *Log.* I 104 ff.

44 *Log.* I 115, 231 ff.

45 *Phän.* 90.

46 *Log.* II 61.

PART I, CHAPTER 2

1 Sichirollo 18-34.
2 *Metaph.* A, 6, 987 b 32; M, 4, 1078 b 25. – Diels 128 (lines 25f.).
3 Hegel calls both Zeno (*Gesch.* II 284) and Plato (*Log.* II 491) 'originator' of the dialectic.
4 Diels 121 (line 12).
5 Diels 120 (lines 1-34).
6 It is commonly believed that the reference is to the Pythagoreans; cf. Raedemaeker 175.
7 Diels 114.
8 Diels 133ff.
9 While E. von Hartmann (2) and Raedemaeker (121) consider this report as unreliable – according to them, the principle had not yet been sufficiently worked out at the time – they contradict themselves when they claim at the same time that the contemporaries of Heraclitus, Parmenides and Zeno based their theories on the same principle (E. von Hartmann, 1; Raedemaeker 155). It should also be noted that Parmenides' accusation about the "fools which holdt that being and not-being are the same" is directed at Heraclitus (Diels 117, line 18). Plato's statements (*Soph.* 242 D) are similar to those of Aristotle.
10 Diels 70 (line 19).
11 This expression is stressed by Hegel (*Gesch.* II 312); Heraclitus also speaks of the *'logos'* (Diels 161, lines 30f.).
12 Raedemaeker 124 f., 146f.
13 Diels 314 (line 24).
14 Diels 320 (line 26), 312 (line 24).
15 Raedemaeker 239.
16 Cf. Reinhardt 242.
17 The book by Schmitz-Moormann is devoted to this topic. – Concerning the Platonic dialectic in general, cf. Marten, and Gundert.
18 *Republic* 511 B
19 *Republic* 532A.
20 *Republic* 525 A. – E. Chambry (Platon, *Oeuvres Compl.,* vol. 7, p.1) renders "Alla mentoi, efè, touto g'echei ouch hekista hè peri auto opsis ..." by "Cette propriété, la vue de l'unité l'a certes au plus haut point ... ." Similarly, W. Wiegand (Platon, *Werke* II, Berlin).
21 *Parmenides* 127 E.
22 E. von Hartmann 4ff.; Sichirollo 81, note.
23 Hoffmann 64; Prauss 93-98, esp. 94f.; Gundert 297, 332, 389, 400ff., 407.
24 *Parmenides* 135 C, D.
25 Cf. Bocheński III 53, 59; E. von Hartmann 8ff.
26 *K.r.V.* A 63f.
27 *K.r.V.* B (p. xxx): "Therefore I had to abolish *knowledge* to make room for *belief,* ...". – Cf. *K.r.V.* A 824-831. – K. Dürr has, in his article, referred to the Socratic-Aristotelian sense in which Kant uses the term 'dialectic'. – Concerning the ambiguity of the Kantian term 'dialectic', cf. Heintel.
28 *Log.* II 493.
29 *Log.* I 31.
30 *Gesch.* II 473.
31 *Enz.* §60, note.
32 The Skeptic sees merely nothingness, and does not discover in it the positive determinateness of its being the result of a dissolution (*Phän.* 68).

[33] *Gesch.* III 24f.

[34] *Gesch.* II 260.

[35] *Gesch.* II 286.

[36] *Gesch.* II 299.

[37] *Gesch.* III 198.

[38] *Gesch.* III 207.

[39] *Timaeus* 47 B, C.

[40] *Log.* I 35ff.

[41] *Log.* II 489. In this context (*Log.* II 491) Hegel expressly notes the Platonism in his methodology.

[42] Log. II 495f.

[43] *Log.* II 497ff.

[44] *Log.* K 66f., 93.

[45] N. Hartmann II 12.

[46] Trendelenburg III 23 f.; Erdei 12, 142.

[47] Nink 100f.

[48] *Enz.* §20, note.

[49] *Log.* I 68.

[50] *Gesch.* II 301.

[51] *Log.* I 69.

[52] *Log.* I 31.

[53] *Phän.* 31

[54] Cf. Section 2.12 (B), (b).

[55] *Log.* II 58-63; *Enz.* §120ff.

[56] *Log.* II 159f.

[57] Cf. Schmitz-Moormann.

[58] *Log.* I 145.

[59] The importance of these philosophers for an understanding of Hegel's philosophy has been stressed by Kroner and N. Hartmann (I).

[60] *Log.* I 32; *Log.* II 10; *Phän.* 181.

[61] *Log.* I 24ff.; *Log.* I 29ff.; *Log.* II 231ff.

[62] *Log.* I 29.

[63] *Log.* I 25. This objection of Hegel holds for any epistemology which assumes that objective reality exists outside the subject, and that this reality amounts to more than a mere combination of formal determinations. At the end of his book, Maier points out the inadequacy of Hegel's criticism of Kant: What Kant has in mind is not at all an epistemological immanence.

[64] *Log.* II 408f.

[65] *Rel.* II-I 20.

[66] *Enz.* §60, note.

[67] *K.r.V.* A 583-631.

[68] *K.r.V.* A 426-461.

[69] *K.r.V.* A 345f.

[70] On the Kantian *'as if': K.r.V.* A 672ff., A 861, A 685f., A 700. On error and illusion: *K.r.V.* A 295ff. On transcendental illusion: *K.r.V.* A 298ff., A 517ff.

[71] On the positive meaning which the thing-in-itself received in Kant's dialectic, cf. Kroner, Vol. 1, p. 125: "While the cause of sensation is a concept borrowed from the treatment of being in the metaphysics of the understanding where the problematic object has no more than a negative, limiting and limit-preserving significance, it is in the idea where the positive aspect which the thing-in-itself acquires in Kant's philosophy is first revealed. Yet it is only in Kant's successors, starting with Maimon, that this aspect has been exposed in its full significance: The thing-in-itself becomes a task,

inasmuch as the understanding encounters in the matter of intuition an infinity of possible determinations, an infinite *determinability*. This infinite determinability which permits the understanding to enlarge its sphere step by step, and to expand it into the realm of what is given (wherein, basically, lies the essence of experience) ... introduces into the concept of experience the p r a c t i c a l   e l e m e n t." – Since Kant, thinking is identical with creating one's object.

[72] *K.r.V.* A 477

[73] *K.r.V.* A 833.

[74] *Log.* I 38.

[75] *Glu.W.* 1; cf. also *Glu.W.* 2 and 14.

[76] *Log.* II 220ff., 225, 493ff.; *Phän.*, Preface, *passim*, esp. 23; *Enz.* § § 28ff., 33.

[77] *Gesch.* I 30ff., 96ff., 113ff., 145ff., 300.

[78] *Log.* II 485: All content has its truth only by virtue of the method.

[79] On Fichte's dialectic, cf. Kroner and Radermacher..

[80] Like Kant before him, J. G. Fichte (61) ascribes to contradiction a positive significance, if only on the subjective level: "Provided that this alien proposition also is systematically founded in consciousness in the way described above, the system to which the proposition belongs – because of the merely formal contradiction in its determinate being – would also have to contradict the entire first system materially *(materialiter)*, and must be based on a principle exactly opposite to the first principle; so that if the first principle were, e.g., I am I, the second would have to be: I am not I. From this contradiction one ought not, and cannot, flatly infer the impossibility of such a second principle." – The idea of circular movement can also be found in Fichte (61, 92).

[81] *Differenz* 76f.

[82] *Differenz* 79: "As the synthesis, the transition becomes an antinomy: but reflection, which means separating absolutely, cannot permit a synthesis of the finite and the infinite, of the determinate and the indeterminate, and it is reflection which legislates here. It has the right to assert a solely formal unity, because the dichotomy into infinite and finite, which is its work, has been granted and adopted; reason, however, synthesizes them in the antinomy, thus nullifying them. While an opposition of an ideal nature *(ideelle Entgegensetzung)* is the work of reflection which totally abstracts from the absolute identity, a real opposition is the work of reason which identifies the opposites not only in the form of knowledge, but also in the form of being, i.e., it also identifies identity with non-identity. And it is real opposition alone in which both subject and object are posited as subject-object, both existing in the absolute, in both the absolute, hence reality in both." – Cf. also *Log.* II 61.

[83] *Phän.* 31; *Log.* I 7.

[84] *Log.* II 58, 469.

[85] *Phän.* 23; *Log.* II 61; *Gl.u.W.* 123.

[86] *Log.* I 35.

[87] *Log.* II 9ff. – Cf. Garaudy I 333.

[88] *Log.* II 202, 15.

[89] *Log.* II 58f.

[90] *Log.* I 92. Originating and perishing, as moments of *becoming*, have been left out of consideration above in order to facilitate the first encounter with the cycle theory. However, consideration of *both* these moments is requisite for comprehending the essence of the dialectical movement.

[91] *Log.* II 33; cf. Section 3.221.

[92] *Log.* II 35.

[93] *Log.* II 40. Hegel often writes the article *'Ein'* with a capital ("... in Einer Identität

verschiedene ...") in order to emphasize that we are dealing with one subsisting unity.
[94] *Log.* II 48f.
[95] *Log.* I 35f.
[96] *Log.* II 60; cf. also *Log.* II 72.
[97] Cf. Chapter 1 of this Part.
[98] *Phän.* 20f.

PART I, CHAPTER 3

[1] *Log.* I 11; *Phän.* 28.
[2] *Phän.* 25.
[3] N. Hartmann I 310-15, 321, 371ff., 384 ff.; Nink 104.
[4] *Gesch.* I 142.
[5] *Log.* II 486. – 'Law of thought' is here not taken in the sense of 'rule of formal logic', but in that of 'epistemological law'; for the justification, see Sections 3.2235 and 3.2236.
[6] Vera 69ff.; Stommel 16, 22; Brunswig 84; Ogiermann 42; Garaudy II 32ff.
[7] Phalén 169, 123, 166; Coreth 42, 54.
[8] Guzzoni 101.
[9] Sesemann, (aa) = 32, (bb) = 41, (cc) = 59.
[10] N. Hartmann, (aa) = I 394, 398 and II 17, (bb) = I 398, (cc) = 401.
[11] Gregoire III 96; Coreth 37f.
[12] Schmitt 13. – Lakebrink, too (130f. and 150ff.), emphasizes the difference between the analytical and the dialectical points of view.
[13] Aebi 5; Trendelenburg II 14f.; Überweg 204; Borelius 28.
[14] Berman" 89; E. von Hartmann, (aa) = 38, (bb) = 39, (cc) = 44, (dd) = 41, (ee) = 46, (ff) = 52.
[15] Nink 105; Devizzi 472; Pelloux 103; Fischer I 498; Kroner II 326; Maggiore 30; Sfard 30.
[16] Albrecht 52; Lasson, Introduction to the *Logic (Hegels sämtliche Werke*, Vol. 3, Leipzig 1932, p. lxii); Stace 94.
[17] Mure II 139ff.
[18] Bullinger 17, 25; Michelet 14, 31f.; Rosenkranz I 300ff.; Il'in: Iljin 133-141; Chiereghin II 61,63. The positions of Cunningham (40ff.) and Clay (12ff.) remain obscure; they probably have to be counted among this group.
[19] Chiereghin III 61: "...mai essere data né detta ..."
[20] *Ibid.:* "La riduzione del contraddittorio a contrario."
[21] McTaggart 8; Glockner 133, 124; Maier 80f.; Gregoire, (aa) = I 47 and II 57, (bb) = III 68, (cc) = II 69-63, (dd) = I 50, II 58 and III 70, (ee) = II 56, (ff) = III 117 and II 56. – A discussion similar to the one presented here can be found in Soviet literature. However, this discussion is not to be regarded as an interpretation of Hegel, for what is at issue is the dialectical-materialist contradiction; on this point, cf. Lobkowicz. – On the relationship of Soviet metaphysics of knowledge to Hegel, cf. Ballestrem.
[22] McTaggart 8: "Imperfection and contradiction are really, according to Hegel, due only to our manner of contemplating the object."
[23] Grégoire III 117: "Ce qui est logiquement contradictoire, n'est pas." II 56: "Toute chose a l'état 'abstrait', c'est-à-dire à l'état d'isolement, *serait logiquement contradictoire,* impossible."
[24] Cf. First Interpretation (C).

[25] *Log.* II 60. Cf. *Phän.* 100.
[26] Borelius 29f.
[27] Aebi 2.
[28] *Log.* II 61.
[29] *Jen. Log.* 132-143; *Log.* II 23-62, esp. 58 – Cf. Chapter 2 of this Part.
[30] *Enz.* §115, note; *Log.* II 58.
[31] *Log.* II 61.
[32] *Log.* II 59.
[33] *Log.* II 409.
[34] *Log.* II 58.
[35] *Log.* I 94.
[36] Cf. First Interpretation (B).
[37] *Log.* I 95.
[38] *Log.* I 143.
[39] *Log.* I 31.
[40] *Enz.* §214, note.
[41] *Enz.* §193, note; cf. also *Rel.* II-II 85f., where the double form of the logical idea is explicitly dealt with.
[42] E. Weil 262f.
[43] *Phän.* 39,29
[44] *Jen. Log.* 136.
[45] *Enz.* §24, note; *Log.* I 32. This separating activity in the subject-side and the object-side of absolute reason has been discussed in detail in Section 2.23, and we saw in Section 32221 how Hegel attributes it to a universal reason.
[46] *Rel.* II-II 58.
[47] To justify our use of the quoted text, it should be noted that, although it is taken from the *Lectures on the Philosophy of Religion*, it is not taken from the students' notes, but rather from Hegel's manuscripts themselves. Besides, the assertions in question were already implicitly present in the text of the *Encyclopedia* which was quoted in Section 3.2221.
[48] *Log.* II 490f.
[49] *Enz.* §26.
[50] *Enz.* §16, note and §62, note; Borelius 27.
[51] E. von Hartmann 42.
[52] *Gesch.* III 365f.
[53] Cf. *Enz.* §24, note, §§116ff., §§181ff.
[54] *Gesch.* III 368.
[55] *Gesch.* III 367: "But here again we come across the drawback in the whole Aristotelian manner – as also in all subsequent logic – and indeed in its highest degree: that in thought and in the movement of thought as such, the individual moments fall asunder; there is a host of kinds of judgments and conclusions, each of which is deemed to hold independently *(für sich)*, and is supposed to have truth in and for itself, as such. ... in this isolation they have, however, no truth; it rather is their totality alone which is the truth of thought, because this totality is at once subjective and objective." – Cf. also *Log.* I 46.
[56] Bocheński-Menne 38; cf. also Bocheński V 13.
[57] Phalén 171.
[58] *Phän.* 34.
[59] N. Hartmann I 255; Kroner II 217.
[60] Cf. N. Hartmann 321.
[61] *Enz.* §214, note: "... not separate in time, nor indeed in any other way ..."

Log. II 411: "The idea is, therefore, in spite of this objectivity utterly *simple* and *immaterial*, for the externality exists only as determined by the concept and as taken up into its negative unity; insofar as it exists as indifferent externality it is not merely at the mercy of mechanism in general, but exists only as the transitory and the untrue."

[62] *Gesch.* I 140: "We thus have to distinguish the natural concrete from the concrete of thought."

[63] According to Lenin (321f.), for instance, the assumption of an absolute is at variance with a theory of development.

[64] Several times, Hegel compares the unfolding of the idea to the career of a man (e.g., *Gesch.* I 104, 140f.; *Phän.* 22) or the development of a plant (*Gesch.* I 102).

[65] Cf. *Gesch.* I 108, 123, 148, 242, 247.

[66] *Gesch.* I 117ff.

[67] *Gesch.* I 36: "Nature *is* as *it is*; and its changes are thus only *repetitions*, its movement is merely cyclical.

[68] *Rel.* I-II 49.

[69] *Gesch.* I 124: "History of philosophy considers only *one* philosophy, only *one* action, which is, however, subdivided into various stages." *Gesch.* I 126: "The various philosophies have not only contradicted, but refuted, one another."

[70] Kroner II 381: "Insofar as it is alive, topical and timely, each philosophy has the double peculiarity of being dependent on the time and still timeless, absolute. ... In the preface to philosophy, Hegel draws attention to the connection of his philosophy and the point in time in which it is appearing." (The reference is to *Phän.* 10.)

[71] The most fundamental principle of the Hegelian interpretation of history is: "The beginning stages of the spirit are poorer, the later are richer" (*Gesch.* I 141).

[72] *Enz.* §564, note: "The old conception of Nemesis ... was confronted by *Plato* and *Aristotle* with the doctrine that God is not *envious.*"

[73] *Log.* 505f.

PART II, CHAPTER 1

[1] Cf. the analysis by Zimmermann.

[2] *Met.* I A c 1 982 a 1-3.

[3] *Met.* I A c 1 983 a 8-9.

[4] *Met.* VI E c 1 1026 a 13-16.

[5] Cf. Heidegger 17; Owens 229; Moser 11; Zimmermann 101-108.

[6] *Metaph.*, Proem; Moser 13ff.

[7] *De Trin.* 5, 1, c: "... quia scientia de necessariis est ... Omne quod necessarium inquantum huiusmodi est immobile."

[8] Eisler 128; Martin 203.

[9] Wolff, C., *Philosophia Rationalis*, Frankfurt-Leipzig 1728, III, §99.

[10] Descartes, R., *Principia philosophiae,* Amsterdam 1657, p. 7.

[11] *Log.* I 35. Cf. *Phän.* 35f. Cf. Martin 205.

[12] *K.r.V.* A 337, note.

[13] *Metaphysik* 19. Cf. Eisler 129f.

[14] *Anfangsgründe* 17.

[15] *Berl. Schr.* 743ff.

[16] *Bew.* 91: "... for I identify logic with metaphysics ..."

[17] *Bew.* 85f.

[18] *Log.* I 46f.

[19] *Log.* I 32f.

[20] *Log.* I 10, 16, 18f.

[21] Interpreters have evaluated this identification in diverse ways. N. Hartmann regards it as compromising dialectic; Kroner (II 302f.), by contrast, as a revolution in the history of philosophy: "Hegel breaks with the view, sanctioned and fixed by a tradition of two thousand years, which alleges that logic is a science which can be taken out of the organism of philosophy ... and be treated separately. With his innovation, he returns to Plato, for whom dialectic was a member of the whole of science."

[22] N. Hartmann III 17.

[23] *Log.* I 16.

[24] *Log.* I 31; *Log.* II 356.

[25] *Log.* I 46. It should be noted that the content of imaginative representations *(Vorstellungen)* – including religious ones like 'God' – are thing-like and therefore subject to the same criticism as the world of things.

[26] *Bew.* 2; *Rel.* I-I 7f. The relevance of formal logic for the study of religions has only recently be pointed out (Bocheński VI).

[27] Bruaire 29; J. Hoffmeister (*Hegels Werke*, Vol. XIX, Leipzig 1932, p. 115); G. Lasson (in *Rel.* II-II, p. viii); Garaudy I 428; Kojève 538f.; Kruithof 76; Grégoire III 210. – Grégoire's position is shared by Ballestrem. We cannot deal with this question in detail since we would have to take up too many questions which lie outside the realm of metaphysics of being (e.g., that of the relationship of faith and knowledge).

[28] On the modern conception of formal logic, cf. Bocheński III, *passim*, esp. p. 326ff.

[29] Cf. *Enz.* §§24, 42, 119 note, 162.

[30] Cf. Part I, Chapter 3, notes 44ff.

[31] *Log.* I 33.

PART II, CHAPTER 2

[1] *Log.* I 109; *Enz.* §§26ff.; *Rel.*. II-II 87.

[2] *Log.* I 25; cf. also *Log.* I 12, 31.

[3] Cf. *Gesch.* IV.

[4] Hegel's discussions of medieval philosophy are almost exclusively based on secondary sources.

[5] *Phän.* 163

[6] *Enz.* §27.

[7] *Log.* II 408. Cf. also our Part III, Chapter 1.

[8] *Enz.* §60, note; *Log.* II 434f.

[9] *Glu.W.* 92f.

[10] *Enz.* §28: "superior to the later Critical philosophizing."

[11] *Enz.* §§49f.

[12] *Log.* I 4; Rel. I-I 208.

[13] *Enz* §36, note

[14] *Phän.* 23. Cf. also *Rel.* II-I 23, note.

[15] *Enz.* §30.

[16] *Phän.* 35f.

[17] *Enz.* §32.

[18] *K.r.V.* (Preface B, p. xxxv); *K.r.V.* A 430; *K.r.V.* A 763f.

[19] *Log.* I 109.

[20] *Log.* I 10.

[21] *Rel.* I-II 43.

[22] *Enz.* §36.

[23] *Log.* I 128.

[24] On the impossibility of a dualistic interpretation of Hegel as regards the relationship of the logical idea to nature, cf. Kruithof 271ff.
[25] *Log.* II 357.
[26] *Log.* II 355.
[27] *Bew.* 1.
[28] *Bew.* 85f.

PART II, CHAPTER 3

[1] *Log.* I 100; *Log.* II 164.
[2] *Log.* I 66f.
[3] Mure II 119, note.
[4] Stommel 17.
[5] *Bew.* 139; *Rel.* I-II 45.
[6] *Rel.* I-I 212f., 146; *Rel.* I-II 54f.; esp., *Bew.* 156.
[7] *Rel.* I-II 46ff.
[8] *Log.* II 498.
[9] *Bew.* 78, 135.
[10] *Log.* II 166.
[11] *Rel.* I-II 52; *Bew.* 129.
[12] *Bew.* 129; *Enz.* §50.

PART III, CHAPTER 1

[1] *Bew.* 1. – In Domke and Ogiermann, who have dealt with the topics of this Part, the unity of the dialectical method remains obscure.
[2] *Log.* I 117: Finite things *"are,* but the truth of this being is their *end."*
[3] *Rel.* I-II 44.
[4] *Bew.* 139; *Rel.* I-II 45.
[5] *Log.* I 143.
[5] *Lre.* I-II 46ff.
[6] *Rel.* I-I 212.
[8] *Log.* I 131.
[9] *Log.* I 118.
[10] *Rel.* I-I 133; *Log.* I 138.
[11] *Log.* I 128; *Rel.* I-I 138f.; *Bew.* 115f.
[12] *Log.* I 140f.
[13] *Log.* I 133; *Log.* I 117; *Bew.* 110.
[14] *Bew.* 110; Rel. I-I 133.
[15] *Enz.* §24, second note *(Sämtliche Werke* 1832 and foll., Vol. 6, 1834, p. 52).
[16] *Log.* II 409f.
[17] Garaudy I 323.
[18] *Log.* I 140ff.
[19] *Phän.* 34.
[20] *Log.* I 140.
[21] *Log.* I 145.
[22] *Log.* I 138.

PART III, CHAPTER 2

[1] *Bew.* 88.
[2] *Bew.* 126.

[3] *Rel.* II-I, 24.
[4] *Bew.* 92.
[5] *Bew.* 92; *Rel.* II-I 26.
[6] Cf. Part I, Section 3.21, 3rd Interpretation (C).
[7] *Bew.* 141.
[8] *Rel.* II-I 24.
[9] *Bew.* 94; *Log.* II 181.
[10] *Log.* II 156.
[11] *Log.* II 173.
[12] *Log.* II 180.
[13] *Log.* II 178, 181.
[14] *Log.* II 185; cf. Part II, Chapter 3.
[15] *Log.* II 186.
[16] *Log.* II 187.
[17] *Log.* II 188.
[18] *Log.* II 188f.
[19] *Log.* II 191.
[20] *Log.* II 196ff.
[21] *Log.* II 199.
[22] *Log.* II 202.
[23] *Log.* II 203.
[24] *Log.* II 202.
[25] *Log.* II 165.
[26] *Log.* I 337; *Log.* II 164ff.
[27] *Log.* II 183; *Log.* II 203f.
[28] Cf. *Enz.* §502, note.
[29] N. Hartmann I 462; cf. Part II, Section 1.224.

PART III, CHAPTER 3

[1] *Log.* II 270, 311, 317ff., 338.
[2] *Log.* II 222.
[3] *Log.* II 225.
[4] *Rel.* I-I 219; *Enz.* §76, note.
[5] *Log.* II 355.
[6] *Rel.* I-I 221.
[7] *Log.* II 354.
[8] *Log.* I 75.
[9] *Rel.* I-II 43; *Log.* II 354f.
[10] *Rel.* II-II 42f.
[11] *Log.* II 230, 236.
[12] *Log.* II 61.
[13] *Bew.* 175f.; *Rel.* I-I 220f.
[14] *Log.* II 385. The example of the cat-mouse relationship can be found again in Engels.
[15] *Bew.* 165.
[16] *Rel.* I-I 216f.
[17] *Enz.* §216.
[18] *Enz.* §187; *Log.* II 429.
[19] Cf. *Log.* II 437ff.; *Phän.* 138f.
[20] *Phän.* 189f.: "... what *ought* to be, in fact, *is* too; and what merely *ought* to be and *is* not, has not truth."

21 *Rel.* I-I 218.
22 To some interpreters, this theory has become an impediment. N. Hartmann (I 369), for instance: "... [the absolute] has its self-consciousness merely in us." Garaudy (I 427), on the other hand: "It would be incorrect to infer from his precluding any transcendence of God that Hegel reduces God to man..."
23 *Rel.* II-II 85f.
24 *Gesch.* I 111.

SUMMARY

1 *Gesch.* I 32ff.
2 Bratuschek, Chiereghin, K. Dürr, Glockner, Haring, E. von Hartmann, N. Hartmann, Kroner, Maier, Michelet, Mure, Pensa, Stenzel have pointed out in detail in their works that, in addition to German philosophers, the Greek philosophers had a decisive influence on Hegel.

EPILOGUE

1 For the most part, we owe our knowledge of the analytical method to Prof. Dr. Dr. J. M. Bocheński. Unfortunately, we cannot enter into a discussion of the difference between the analytical and the positivist method.
2 This is why H. Heimann's striving for *"synthesis* of the critical-dialectical and the positivist conceptions of science" cannot be regarded as an unproblematic solution of the positivism controversy ('Wissenschaftskonzeption, Pluralismuskritik und politische Praxis der neuen Linken', *Aus Politik und Zeitgeschichte,* suppl. to the weekly *Das Parlament,* Beilage 14, 1970, p. 17). The Soviet synthesis of science and dialectic, for instance, is not a very happy one, because it compels even the natural scientist to discover contradictions; cf., e.g., V. P. Čertkov, *Jadro dialektiki,* Moscow 1963, pp. 8-10; V. P. Čerktov, 'O vzaimosvjazi zakonov dialektiki', *VF* 1 (1959). 46-55; V. E. Kozlovskij, *Razvitie V. I. Leninym marksistskogo učenija o protivorečijax,* Moscow 1966; M. M. Rozental', *Lenin i dialektika,* Moscow 1963, pp. 73-96; L. V. Smirnov, 'Obščie zakonomernosti dviženija i ix projavlenija v častnyx formax dviženija', *Vestnik LGU* 17 (1961).p. 80; M. F. Vorob'ev, 'Vorposy sovremennogo glavnyx zakonov materialističeskoj dialektiki', *Nekotorye voprosy dialektičeskogo materializma,* Leningrad 1962, p. 8.
3 "To deny reflection *is* positivism" (J. Habermas, *Erkenntnis und Interesse,* Frankfurt a. M. 1968, p. 9).
4 In this respect, Habermas agrees with the positivists. Cf. *Der Positivismusstreit in der deutschen Soziologie,* Neuwied/Berlin 1969, p. 235. In part, then, the 'positivism controversy' is a misunderstanding. When we visited the *Wirtschaftshochschule* in Mannheim on January 13, 1970, Prof. H. Albert assured us that "Habermas and myself have rather misunderstood than fought one another."
5 Cf. J. Habermas, *Technik und Wissenschaft als 'Ideologie',* Frankfurt a. M. 1969, p. 130.
6 The purely theoretical refutations of Marcuseanism, e.g., by A. MacIntyre (*Herbert Marcuse: Orientatie op morgen,* Den Haag 1970) and L. Colletti *(Monthly Review,* Ital. ed., May/June 1968) evidence great acumen, but they render the phenomenon 'Marcuse' unintelligible.
7 How public opinion is to become integrated with this self-understanding has been worked out by Habermas (*op. cit.,* pp. 120-145).
8 *One-Dimensional Man,* London 1969, pp. 105f., 120f.

[9] Cf. *ibid.*, pp. 112, 136.

[10] *Op. cit.*, pp. 126, 130.

[11] *Antworten auf Herbert Marcuse*, Frankfurt a. M. 1968, p. 13.

[12] We have been unable to understand why K. Gödel's proof, in which formal thought becomes dialectical itself and demonstrates the contradiction of the totality, was not mentioned in the positivism controversy.

[13] *Interpretations* of Hegel that are overburdened with criticism do not shed any light on the emancipatory *and* the *tradition-bound significance* of Hegel's dialectic, for it is only within the immanent context of the system that the methodological statements acquire their meaning, and only in the historical context that the historically necessary sublation of tradition, which was performed by Hegel, becomes evident. Therefore, it is only through concretizing sublation that Hegel's dialectic can be assessed, criticized, and overcome in an up-to-date manner.

[14] *Die Frühschriften*, (ed. by S. Landshut), Stuttgart 1953, vol. 1, pp. 278f., 376.

[15] J. Stalin, *Voprosy Leninizma*, Moscow 1947, p. 275.

[16] *Geschichte der kommunistischen Partei der Sowjetunion (Bolschewiki)*, Moscow 1939, p. 127.

[17] Cf. 'Socialisme en Kapitalisme' *(Kursus Maatschappelijke en politieke Orientatie*, Wittmarsum-Culemborg 1970, Chapter 5), where we clarified the various meanings of 'socialism' in terms of the developments of capitalism.

[18] S. Meljuxin, *O dialektike razvitija neorganičeskoi prirody*, Moscow 1960.

[19] V. Ja. El'meev, A. P. Kazakov, 'K voprosu ob osebennostjax dejstvija zakona edinstva i bor'by protivopoložnostej v uslovijax socializma', *Vestnik LGU* 17 (1961), p. 64.

[20] Vorob'ev, *op. cit.*, p. 99; Meljuxin, *op. cit.*, p. 118.

[21] Kozlovskij, *op. cit.*, pp. 52, 81; Rozental', *op. cit.*, p. 118.

[22] Cf. B. S. Ukraincev, A. S. Koval'čuk, V. P. Čertkov, *Dialektika pererastanija socializma v kommunizm*, Moscow 1963, p. 101.

[23] *One-Dimensional Man*, p. 19; H. Jäckel, 'Über das Glück als politische Kategorie', *Aus Politik und Zeitgeschichte*, suppl. to the weekly *Das Parlament*, Beilage 22, 1970.

[24] *Ibid.*, p. 21; cf. also his 'Re-examination of the Concept of Revolution', *New Left Review* (1969), p. 34: "There is in Marx a strain that may be called a rationalistic, even positivistic prejudice, namely, this belief in the inexorable necessity of the transition to a 'higher stage of human development', and in the final success of this transition. Although Marx was very aware of the possibility of failure, defeat, or betrayal, the alternative *'socialism or barbarism'* was not an integral part of his concept of revolution. It must become such part."

[25] *One-Dimensional Man*, p. 44.

[26] *Ibid.*, p. 20. Marcuse consciously reversed the pragmatic interpretation of Marxism; cf. *ibid.*, p. 21: "... the political trend may be r e v e r s e d ...". Cf. also *ibid.*, p. 60.

[27] 3rd Thesis on Feuerbach; cf. Habermas, *Technik und Wissenschaft als 'Ideologie'*, p. 138.

[28] *Ibid.*, p. 58.

[29] *Ibid.*, p. 135.

[30] *Ibid.*, pp. 129f.

[31] *Der Spiegel* 24, No. 1/2 (January 1970), pp. 76-84.

BIBLIOGRAPHY

Aebi, M., 'Hegel als Logiker' (unpublished manuscript). The author was kind enough to make a copy of her 7-page paper available to me.

Albrecht, W., *Hegels Gottesbeweis, eine Studie zur 'Wissenschaft der Logik'*, Berlin 1958.

Ballestrem, K. G., *Die sowjetische Erkenntnismetaphysik und ihr Verhältnis zu Hegel*, Dordrecht 1968.

Berman'', Ja. A., 'O dialektike', *Očerki po filosofii marksizma*, St. Petersburg 1908, pp. 72-106.

Beyer, W. R., *Hegel-Bilder, Kritik der Hegel-Deutungen*, East Berlin 1967.

Bocheński, J. M., 'Kommunistische Ideologie I, II', *Informationen zur politischen Bildung*, 106 and 107, 1964. (= I)

Bocheński, *Der sowjet-russische dialektische Materialismus (Diamat)*, Berne-Munich 1962. (= II)

Bocheński, *Formale Logik*, Freiburg-Munich 1962. (=III)

Bocheński, *The Dogmatic Principles of Soviet Philosophy [as of 1958]*, Dordrecht 1963. (= IV)

Bocheński, *Die zeitgenössischen Denkmethoden*, Berne-Munich 1965. (= V)

Bocheński, *The Logic of Religion*, New York 1965. (= VI)

Bocheński, J. M. and Menne, A., *Grundriss der Logistik*, Paderborn 1962.

Borelius, B. B., *Ueber den Satz des Widerspruchs und die Bedeutung der Negation*, Leipzig 1881.

Bratuschek, E., 'Wie Hegel Plato auslegt und beurtheilt', *Philos. Monatshefte* 7 (1871-1872), pp. 433-463.

Bruaire, C., *Logique et religion chrétienne dans la philosophie de Hegel*, Paris 1964.

Brunswig, A., *Hegel*, Munich 1922.

Buhr, M., *der Übergang von Fichte zu Hegel*, East Berlin 1965.

Bullinger, A., *Hegels Lehre vom Widerspruch, Missverständnissen gegenüber verteidigt*, Dillingen 1884.

Chiereghin, F., *L'influenza dello spinozismo nella formazione della filosofia hegeliana*, Padua 1961. (= I)

Chiereghin, *L'unità del sapere in Hegel*, Padua 1963. (= II)

Chiereghin, *Hegel e la metafisica classica*, Padua 1966. (= III)

Clay, J., *De Dialektik en de leer van de tegenstrijdigheid bij Hegel en Bolland*, Bloemendaal 1919.

Coreth, E., *Das dialektische Sein in Hegels Logik*, Vienna 1952.

Croce, B., *Ciò che è vivo e ciò che è morto della filosofia di Hegel*, Bari 1906.

Cunningham, G. W., *Thought and Reality in Hegel's System*, London-Bombay-Calcutta 1910.

Devizzi, A., 'Il significato del principio di contradizzione nella logica Hegeliana', *Rivista di filosofia neoscolastica XXXI* (1939), pp. 463-473.

Diels, H., *Die Fragmente der Vorsokratiker I*, Berlin 1906.

Domke, K., *Das Problem der metaphysischen Gottesbeweise in der Philosophie Hegels*, Leipzig 1940.

Dürr, A., *Zum Problem der Hegelschen Dialektik und ihrer Formen,* Berlin 1938.
Dürr, K., 'Die Entwicklung der Dialektik von Plato bis Hegel', *Dialectica* 1 (1947), pp. 45-62.
Éfirov, S. A., *Ot Gegelja k ... Džennaro,* Moscow 1960.
Eisler, R., 'Metaphysik', *Wörterbuch der philosophischen Begriffe,* Vol. 2, Berlin 1929, pp. 126-139.
Erdei, L., *Der Anfang der Erkenntnis, Budapest 1964.*
Feuerbach, L., 'Vorläufige Thesen zur Reform der Philosophie', *Sämtl. Werke,* ed. by W. Bolin und Fr. Jodl, Vol. 2, Stuttgart 1904, pp. 222-244. (= I)
Feuerbach, 'Zur neueren Philosophie und ihrer Geschichte', *Sämtl. Werke,* Vol. 4., Stuttgart 1910, pp. 299-448. (= II)
Feuerbach, *Vorlesungen über das Wesen der Religion (Sämtl. Werke,* Vol. 8), Leipzig 1851. (= III)
Fichte, I. H., *Grundzüge zum System der Philosophie,* 3 vols., Heidelberg 1833, 1836, 1846.
Fichte, J. G., 'Über den Begriff der Wissenschaftlehre oder der sogenannten Philosophie', *Johann Gottlieb Fichte's sämtliche Werke,* ed. by I. H. Fichte, First Part; *Zur theoretischen Philosophie,* Vol. 1, Leipzig 1925, pp. 27-534.
Fischer, K., *Hegels Leben, Werke und Lehre,* 2 vols. Heidelberg 1901.
Garaudy, R., *Gott ist tot* (transl. from the French), East Berlin 1965. (= I)
Garaudy, *Pour connaître la pensée de Hegel,* Paris 1966. (= II)
Gentile, G., *La riforma della dialettica hegeliana,* Messina 1913.
Glockner, H., *Beiträge zum Verständnis und zur Kritik Hegels sowie zur Umgestaltung seiner Geisteswelt (Hegelstudien,* Suppl. 2), Bonn 1965.
Grégoire, F., 'Hegel et l'universelle contradiction', *Revue philosophique de Louvain* 44 (1946), pp. 36-73. (= I)
Grégoire, *Aux sources de la pensée de Marx, Hegel, Feuerbach,* Louvain-Paris 1947. (= II)
Grégoire, *Etudes hégéliennes,* Louvain 1958. (= III)
Gropp, R. O., 'K voprosu marksistskoj dialektičeskoj logike kak sisteme kategorij', *Voprosy filosifii* 1 (1959), pp. 149-157.
Gulian, K. I., *Metod i sistema Gegelja,* Vol. I, II, Moscow 1962, 1963.
Gundert, H., 'Dialog und Dialektik', *Studium Generale,* Vol. 21, Fasc. 4 and 5 (1968), pp. 295-449.
Günther, G., *Grundzüge einer neuen Theorie des Denkens in Hegels Logik,* Leipzig, 1933.
Guzzoni, U., *Werden zu sich, eine Untersuchung zu Hegels 'Wissenschaft der Logik',* Freiburg-Munich 1963.
Haring, G. H. (= Michelet-Haring).
Hartmann, A., *Der Spätidealismus und die Hegelsche Dialektik,* Berlin 1937.
Hartmann, E. von, *Über die dialektische Methode; historisch-kritische Untersuchungen,* Berlin 1868.
Hartmann, N., *Die Philosophie des deutschen Idealismus,* second edition, Berlin 1960. (= I)
Hartmann, N., 'Hegel und das Problem der Realdialektik', *Blätter für Deutsche Philosophie,* Vol. IX (1935/36), No. 1, pp. 1-27 (= II)
Hartmann, N., *Zur Grundlegung der Ontologie,* Meisenheim on Glan 1948. (= III)
Haym, R., *Hegel und seine Zeit,* Berlin 1857.
Heidegger, M., *Kant und das Problem der Metaphysik,* Frankfort-on-M. 1951.
Heimann, B., *System und Methode in Hegels Philosophie,* Leipzig 1927.
Heintel, P., 'Die Dialektik bei Kant', *Studium Generale,* Vol. 21, Fasc. 5 (1968), pp. 450-470.
Hoffmann, E., *Drei Schriften zur griechischen Philosophie,* Heidelberg 1964.

Hyppolite, J., *Genèse et structure de la phénoménologie de l'esprit de Hegel*, Paris 1946. (= I)

Hyppolite, *Logique et existence; Essai sur la logique de Hegel*, Paris 1953. (=II)

Iljin, I., *Die Philosophie Hegels als kontemplative Gotteslehre*, Bern 1946.

Kant, I., *Kritik der reinen Vernunft*, Leipzig 1966. *(K.r.V.)*

Kant, 'Welches sind die wirklichen Fortschritte, die die Metaphysik seit Leibnizens und Wolffs Zeiten in Deutschland gemacht hat?', *Werke*, Vol. III, ed. by W. Weischedel, Wiesbaden 1958, pp. 587ff. (= *Metaphysik*)

Kant, 'Metaphysische Anfangsgründe der Naturwissenschaft', *Werke*, Vol. V, ed. by W. Weischedel, Wiesbaden 1957, pp. 11ff. (= *Anfangsgründe*)

Kanthack, K., 'Das Wesen der Dialektik im Lichte Martin Heideggers', *Studium Generale*, Vol. 21, Fasc. 6 (1968), pp. 538-554.

Kojève, A., *Introduction à la lecture de Hegel; Leçons sur 'La phénoménologie de l'esprit' professées de 1933-1939 à l'Ecole des Hautes-Etudes*, collected and published by R. Queneau, Paris 1947.

Kroner, R., *Von Kant bis Hegel*, 2 vols, Tübingen 1921, 1924.

Kruithof, J., *Het Uitgangspunt van Hegel's Ontologie*, Bruges 1959.

Lakebrink, B., *Hegels dialektische Ontologie und die thomistische Analektik*, Cologne 1959.

Laske, O.-E., *Über die Dialektik Platos und des frühen Hegel*, Frankfort-on-M. 1966.

Lenin, V. I., *Filosofskie tetradi*, fifth edition, Moscow 1963.

Lobkowicz, N., *Das Widerspruchsprinzip in der neueren sowjetischen Philosophie*, Dordrecht 1959.

Lossky, N., 'Hegel als Intuitivist', *Blätter für Deutsche Philosophie*, Vol. IX (1935/36), No. 1, pp. 62-74.

Maggiore, G., *Hegel*, Milano 1924.

Maier, J., *On Hegel's Critique of Kant*, New York 1939.

Manser, G. M., *Das Wesen des Thomismus*, Freiburg i.Ü. 1935.

Marcuse, H., *Hegels Ontologie und die Grundlegung einer Theorie der Geschichtlichkeit*, Frankfort-on-M. 1932.

Marten, R., *Der Logos der Dialektik; Eine Theorie zu Platons Sophistes*, Berlin 1965.

Martin, G., *Leibniz, Logik und Metaphysik*, Berlin 1967.

Marx, K. and Engels, F., *Die deutsche Ideologie*, East Berlin 1959.

McTaggart, J., *Studies in the Hegelian Dialectic*, Cambridge 1896.

Meulen, J. van der, *Heidegger und Hegel oder Widerstreit und Widerspruch*, Meisenheim-on-Glan 1953.

Michelet, C. L. and Haring, G. H., *Historisch-kritische Darstellung der dialektischen Methode Hegels nebst dem gutachtlichen Berichte über die der Philosophischen Gesellschaft zu Berlin eingereichten Bewerbungsschriften und einer Geschichte dieser Preisbewerbung*, Leipzig 1888.

Moog, W., *Hegel und die hegelsche Schule*, Munich 1930.

Moser, S., *Metaphysik einst und jetzt*, Berlin 1958.

Mure, G. R. G., *A Study of the Logic of Hegel*, Oxford 1950. (= I)

Mure, *An Introduction to Hegel* (first edition 1940), Oxford 1948. (= II)

Negri, E. de, *Interpretazione di Hegel*, Florence 1943.

Nink, C., *Kommentar zu Hegels Phänomenologie des Geistes*, Regensburg 1948.

Ogiermann, H. A., *Hegels Gottesbeweise*, Rome 1948.

Ovsjannikov, M. F., *Filosofija Gegelja*, Moscow 1959.

Owens, J., *The Doctrine of Being in the Aristotelian Metaphysics*, Toronto 1963.

Pelloux, L., *La Logica di Hegel*, Milano 1938.

Pensa, M., 'Le Logos hégélien', *Dialectica* 1 (1947), pp. 277-287, 347-353; 2 (1948), pp. 47-62.

Phalén, A., *Das Erkenntnisproblem in Hegels Philosophie, die Erkenntniskritik als Metaphysik,* Upsalla 1912.

Prauss, G., *Platon und der logische Eleatismus,* Berlin 1966.

Radermacher, H., 'Fichte und das Problem der Dialektik', *Studium Generale,* Vol. 21, Fasc. 6 (1968), pp. 475-502.

Raedemaeker, F. de, *De Philosophie der Voorsokratici,* Antwerp-Amsterdam 1953.

Reinhardt, K., *Parmenides und die Geschichte der griechischen Philosophie,* Frankfort-on-M. 1959.

Rosenkranz, K., *Wissenschaft der logischen Idee,* 2 vols., Königsberg, 1858-59 (= I and II).

Rosenkranz, *Apologie Hegels gegen Dr. R. Haym,* Berlin 1858. (= III)

Sartre, J.-P., *Critique de la raison dialectique,* Vol. 1, Paris 1960.

Schmitt, E. H., *Michelet und das Geheimnis der Hegelschen Dialektik,* Frankfort-on-M. 1888.

Schulz, W., 'Hegel und das Problem der Aufhebung der Metaphysik', *Martin Heidegger zum siebzigsten Geburtstag,* ed. by N. Günther, Pfullingen 1959, pp. 67-92.

Sesemann, W., 'Zum Problem der Dialektik', *Blätter für Deutsche Philosophie,* Vol. IX, (1935/36), No. 1, pp. 28-61.

Sfard, D., *Du rôle de l'idée de contradiction chez Hegel,* Nancy 1931.

Sichirollo, L., *Dialegesthai-Dialektik; Von Homer bis Aristoteles (Mit einem Anhang: Hegel und die Antike,* pp. 171-204), Hildesheim 1966.

Schmitz-Moormann, K., *Die Ideenlehre Platons im Lichte des Sonnengleichnisses des sechsten Buches des Staates,* Münster/Westf. 1959.

Specht, E. K., *Der Analogiebegriff bei Kant und Hegel,* Cologne 1952.

Stace, W. T., *The Philosophy of Hegel,* Dover 1955.

Staudenmaier, Fr. A., *Darstellung und Kritik des Hegelschen Systems,* Mainz 1844.

Stenzel, J., 'Hegels Auffassung der griechischen Philosophie', *Kleine Schriften zur griechischen Philosophie,* Darmstadt 1956.

Stommel, C., *Die Differenz Kants und Hegels in bezug auf die Erklärung der Antinomien,* Halle 1876.

Sancti Thomae de Aquino expositio super librum Boethii de Trinitate, recensuit B. Decker, Leyden, 1955. *(de Trin.)*

Sanctus Thomas, *In Metaphysicam Aristotelis commentaria,* Taurini 1915. *(Metaph.)*

Trendelenburg, A., *Logische Untersuchungen,* 2 vols. Leipzig 1870. (= I and II)

Trendelenburg, *Die logische Frage in Hegels System,* Leipzig 1843. (= III)

Tricot, J.: Aristote, *La Metaphysique,* New edition entirely rewritten with comments by J. Tricot, Paris 1962.

Ulrici, H., *Über Prinzip und Methode der hegelschen Philosophie,* Halle 1841.

Überweg, F., *System der Logik und Geschichte der logischen Lehre,* Bonn 1868.

Vera, A., *Introduction à la Philosophie de Hegel,* Paris-London 1855.

Wahl, J., *Le malheur de la conscience dans la philosophie de Hegel,* Paris 1911.

Wall, K., *Relation in Hegel,* Fribourg 1963.

Weil, E., 'Hegel', *Les philosophes célèbres,* Paris 1956.

Weisse, C. H., *Über den gegenwartigen Standpunct der philosophischen Wissenschaft in besonderer Beziehung auf das System Hegels,* Leipzig 1829. (= I)

Weisse, *Ueber das Verhältnis des Publikums zur Philosophie in dem Zeitpuncte von Hegel's Abscheiden,* Leipzig 1832. (= II)

Wetter, G. A., *Die Umkehrung Hegels,* Cologne 1963. (= I)

Wetter, *Sowjet-Ideologie heute (Dialektischer Materialismus I),* Frankfort-on-M. 1963. (= II)

Zimmerman, A., *Ontologie oder Metaphysik?* Leyden-Cologne 1965.

INDEX OF NAMES

(Numbers in parentheses refer to our Notes)

SOVIETICA

Publications and Monographs of the Institute
of East-European Studies, University of Fribourg, Switzerland

1. BOCHEŃSKI, J. M. and BLAKELEY, TH. J. (eds.): *Bibliographie der sowjetischen Philosophie.* I: *Die 'Voprosy filosofii' 1947–1956.* 1959, VIII + 75 pp.
2. BOCHEŃSKI, J. M. and BLAKELEY, TH. J. (eds.): *Bibliographie der sowjetischen Philosophie.* II: *Bücher 1947–1956; Bücher und Aufsätze 1957–1958; Namenverzeichnis 1947–1958.* 1959, VIII + 109 pp.
3. BOCHEŃSKI, J. M.: *Die dogmatischen Grundlagen der sowjetischen Philosophie (Stand 1958). Zusammenfassung der 'Osnovy Marksistskoj Filosofii' mit Register.* 1959, XII + 84 pp.
4. LOBKOWICZ, NICOLAS (ed.): *Das Widerspruchsprinzip in der neueren sowjetischen Philosophie.* 1960, VI + 89 pp.
5. MÜLLER-MARKUS, SIEGFRIED: *Einstein und die Sowjetphilosophie. Krisis einer Lehre.* I: *Die Grundlagen. Die spezielle Relativitätstheorie.* 1960. (Out of print.)
6. BLAKELEY, TH. J.: *Soviet Scholasticism.* 1961, XIII + 176 pp.
7. BOCHEŃSKI, J. M. and BLAKELEY, TH. J. (eds.): *Studies in Soviet Thought,* I. 1961, IX + 141 pp.
8. LOBKOWICZ, NICOLAS: *Marxismus-Leninismus in der ČSR. Die tschechoslowakische Philosophie seit 1945.* 1962, XVI + 268 pp.
9. BOCHEŃSKI, J. M. and BLAKELEY, TH. J. (eds.): *Bibliographie der sowjetischen Philosophie.* III: *Bücher und Aufsätze 1959–1960.* 1962, X + 73 pp.
10. BOCHEŃSKI, J. M. and BLAKELEY, TH. J. (eds.): *Bibliographie der sowjetischen Philosophie.* IV: *Ergänzungen 1947–1960.* 1963, XII + 158 pp.
11. FLEISCHER, HELMUT: *Kleines Textbuch der kommunistischen Ideologie. Auszüge aus dem Lehrbuch 'Osnovy marksizma-leninizma, mit Register.* 1963, XIII + 116 pp.
12. JORDAN, ZBIGNIEW A.: *Philosophy and Ideology. The Development of Philosophy and Marxism-Leninism in Poland since the Second World War.* 1963, XII + 600 pp.
13. VRTAČIČ, LUDVIK: *Einführung in den jugoslawischen Marxismus-Leninismus. Organisation. Bibliographie.* 1963, X + 208 pp.
14. BOCHEŃSKI, J. M.: *The Dogmatic Principles of Soviet Philosophy (as of 1958). Synopsis of the 'Osnovy Marksistskoj Filosofii' with complete index.* 1963, XII + 78 pp.
15. BIRKUJOV, B. V.: *Two Soviet Studies on Frege.* Translated from the Russian and edited by Ignacio Angelelli, 1964, XXII + 101 pp.
16. BLAKELEY, TH. J.: *Soviet Theory of Knowledge.* 1964, VII + 203 pp.
17. BOCHEŃSKI, J. M. and BLAKELEY, TH. J. (eds.): *Bibliographie der sowjetischen Philosophie.* V: *Register 1947–1960.* 1964, VI + 143 pp.
18. BLAKELEY, THOMAS J.: *Soviet Philosophy. A General Introduction to Contemporary Soviet Thought.* 1964, VI + 81 pp.

19. BALLESTREM, KARL G.: *Russian Philosophical Terminology* (in Russian, English, German, and French). 1964, VIII + 116 pp.
20. FLEISCHER, HELMUT: *Short Handbook of Communist Ideology. Synopsis of the 'Osnovy marksizma-leninizma' with complete index.* 1965, XIII + 97 pp.
21. PLANTY-BONJOUR, G.: *Les catégories du matérialisme dialectique. L'ontologie soviétique contemporaine.* 1965, VI + 206 pp.
22. MÜLLER-MARKUS, SIEGFRIED: *Einstein und die Sowjetphilosophie. Krisis einer Lehre.* II: *Die allgemeine Relativitätstheorie.* 1966, X + 509 pp.
23. LASZLO, ERVIN: *The Communist Ideology in Hungary. Handbook for Basic Research.* 1966, VIII + 351 pp.
24. PLANTY-BONJOUR.: *The Categories of Dialectical Materialism. Contemporary Soviet Ontology.* 1967, VI + 182 pp.
25. LASZLO, ERVIN: *Philosophy in the Soviet Union. A Survey of the Mid-Sixties.* 1967, VIII + 208 pp.
26. RAPP, FRIEDRICH: *Gesetz und Determination in der Sowjetphilosopie. Zur Gesetzeskonzeption des dialektischen Materialismus unter besonderer Berücksichtigung der Diskussion über dynamische and statische Gesetzmässigkeit in der zeitgenössischen Sowjetphilosophie.* 1968, XI + 474 pp.
27. BALLESTREM, KARL G.: *Die sowjetische Erkenntnismetaphysik und ihr Verhältnis zu Hegel.* 1968, IX + 189 pp.
28. BOCHEŃSKI, J. M. and BLAKELEY, TH. J. (eds.): *Bibliographie der sowjetischen Philosophie.* VI: *Bücher und Aufsätze 1961–1963.* 1968, XI + 195 pp.
29. BOCHEŃSKI, J. M. and BLAKELEY, TH. J. (eds.): *Bibliographie der sowjetischen Philosophie.* VII: *Bücher und Aufsätze 1964–1966. Register.* 1968, X + 311 pp.
30. PAYNE, T. R.: *S. L. Rubinštejn and the Philosophical Foundations of Soviet Psychology.* 1968, X + 184 pp.
31. KIRSCHENMANN, PETER PAUL: *Information and Reflection. On Some Problems of Cybernetics and How Contemporary Dialectical Materialism Copes with Them.* 1970, XV + 225 pp.
32. O'Rourke, James J.: *The Problem of Freedom in Marxist Thought.* 1974, XII + 231 pp.

E.

1